MW01252024

To Lead the Way

A Fantasy Journey into Leadership Development

D. B. Clark

Writers Club Press

San Jose New York Lincoln Shanghai

To Lead the Way
A Fantasy Journey into Leadership Development

Published by Writers Club Press
an imprint of iUniverse.com, Inc.

For information address:
iUniverse.com, Inc.
620 North 48th Street
Suite 201
Lincoln, NE 68504-3467
www.iuniverse.com

ISBN: 0-595-09762-6

Printed in the United States of America

My appreciation and continued respect for George Emerson and Marie Nock who were my colleagues and co developers during the many years we have conducted our leadership training workshops and course.

Contents

To Lead the Way

The Way to Lead

Introduction

Suppose you had a job to do that you couldn't do effectively by yourself, a job that would require a number of people working together, how would you go about getting that job done? This is of course a rather common problem. Everyday you are faced with the necessity of directing, instructing, and motivating others to get something done. The job might be as simple as working with a friend to put up an awkward sign, or showing a group of children how to play a game, or as complex as directing the government. Many of these tasks involve working with people who might not care about the task, and therefore need motivating. But even if motivated, these people might have ideas of their own on how to accomplish the task, and conflict is inevitable. Someone has to manage the conflict, coordinate the effort, and motivate the workers. In other words, somebody has to lead the way.

This book is concerned with this broad concept of **leadership**: *the talent, skill and practice of influencing or enabling others to do whatever is necessary to accomplish the common goal of a group.* This book is intended to enable you to understand the concept of leadership style and to use this concept to better understand your own style of leadership. Unlike other books on leadership, however, it is not just a theoretical discussion or a set of guidelines—though it is both of these. Rather, it is a book that takes a specific theory of leadership style and tries to bring the theory to life. The rationale for the book is this, if this theory of leadership is a reflection of how people really lead then a novel in which people lead according to the theory would seem real. Thus, in the novel, the characters' leadership behavior carefully follows a specific theory of leadership style, and then, for those who wish to learn more about the theory and their own styles of leadership, the novel is used to illustrate the theory in a textual section following the novel.

Thus the book hopes to make an entertaining experience of learning by making that which is to be learned a form of entertainment. Part of the entertainment should be trying to guess, while reading the novel, what style of leadership is being illustrated. Like a good mystery, it will all be revealed in the end—when you read the text. So as not to spoil your entertainment, I will say little more. May this book lead you to a better understanding of leadership and how you lead.

1

WHO LEADS WHO
FOLLOWS WHERE

As they set forth on their holiday adventure, it seemed right to Front that Wons should lead the way out of Sebasa and through the foothills of Mount Stareye. He glanced up the narrow, rocky trail to where the head and shoulders of his tall, slender friend rose above the three others who followed. Wons' height certainly commanded attention, but it had been Wons' enthusiasm and his deep, confident voice that had convinced Front and the others that the adventure of scaling and delving into the mysteries of Mount Stareye would be worth the effort.

Those initial doubts seemed even more out of place now, as he followed Wons and the others on this clear morning and as he allowed himself to experience the pleasure of their rhythmic step-by-step assent up the gradually inclining trail.

Front let his eyes slide downward from the lead form of Wons to the sturdy broad shoulders of Nash, who was next in line. He hadn't known the fellow for long, but Nash's rough openness made him easy to know, and to like. Then came Wonina. Front slowly caressed her slender curves with his eyes. Wonina, fluid and sensuous when she moved, and always gentle, always friendly, but unfortunately, Front reminded himself, always incline to treat him like her brother.

As the trail ahead twisted sharply, Wonina turned and discovered his eyes. She smiled and chuckled to herself, apparently amused at Front's attention to her backside. Front quickly dropped his eyes to Fyva, who climbed just ahead of him. Fyva was slender and curvaceous, but not so smoothly rounded as Wonina, and tall, almost as tall as Front. She was, some thought, even more beautiful than Wonina, but so serious that, for Front, her beauty was sometimes harder to see. That seriousness, however, was vital to the group. They could always depend on Fyva to insist that every aspect of their plan and preparation be completed.

He let his sight glide up the winding pathway to take in all four of his companions. He felt their matched strides moving as one with his own, and he realized that his doubts were now behind him. He was where he wanted to be, with his four friends, climbing the hill from Sebasa, setting out on their unusual but long awaited holiday.

At the next bend in the trail, however, Front paused to look out over the rooftops of the small town he had just left. The flat red clay shingled roofs were now feeling the first touch of the morning sun. Front gazed beyond the town to where he could just sight the edge of the Commons, where a flotilla of small, shallow-bottomed fishing boats were moored to the wooden wharf extending from the Commons or strung out northward along the beach of the now becalmed blue green Bay of Sebasa. To the south, beyond the bay, the sun had arisen enough to illuminate the gray mist shrouded meeting of the Great Swamp and the dark green ocean. A tug of doubt returned as Front remembered he would not be fishing that day, skimming his fragile, broad sailed craft across the shallow bay to the edge of the distance swamp.

He pulled his eyes away from that familiar sight. Although he enjoyed his lonely work, he had also looked forward to these hot, now calm, now turbulent days of late summer, when the fishing was poor and his well-deserved holiday could begin.

"Are you with us, Front?"

Wonina's teasing voice seemed far away, and Front realized he had lingered longer with his view of Sebasa than he had intended. He hurriedly caught up with the group and fell again into the rhythmic pace of the climb. He heard Wons humming to himself and, and then the tune was joined by Wonina's gentle soprano. Uncharacteristically, Front joined those two in their song, and soon all five were singing. As the cadence of their song increased, so did their pace, and as Front's feet moved faster, his heart floated lighter and higher. Finally he drew in a great breath and let go of his concerns. He as on holiday, and he very well deserved it.

His moment of release made him even more one with his companions. As he shared their light-hearted melody, he knew they were experiencing the same much needed release. For Wons, it was release from his studies for the Stewartship. For Nash it was an opportunity to be away from his responsibility for the family goatherd, now turned over to the care of his many younger brothers. As the late summer heat slowed down the pace of life in Sebasa, so the marketplace slowed its activities, and Wonina was not needed in the family shop, and she would not be needed in their orchard until fall. Fyva's family trading business was likewise at a standstill. Until fishing picked up again with cooler weather, the trade boats and caravans from the north would not be back to carry away the dried and salted fish that was be mainstay of Fyva's father's business. The five of them were free, and now in their early adulthood, they were old enough to use their annual holiday for this great adventure, one last departure from duty before the full responsibilities of adulthood finally settled upon them.

With Wons' encouragement and insistence, this was to be their grand adventure, their last chance to do what most stayed unimaginative Sebasans would never do. Indeed, the sturdy, hard-working folk of Sebasa seldom had time for any activity that smacked of frivolity, particularly such obviously pointless frivolity as a trip up the steep and treacherous side of Mount Stareye. But Wons had convince the small band that atop that distance peak there would be wonders worthy of their efforts, even worth the mild ridicule they had received from their parents and their other friends.

Even before Wons' encouragement, sometimes from out at sea on those rare days when the mountaintop cleared, Front's curiosity had been aroused by what appeared to be a domed building perched on the very tip of that lofty peak. Therefore, Front was ready to listen when Wons began to relate at length, but somewhat vaguely, the description given to him by his great-uncle who had supposedly made the climb to the top of Mount Stareye fifty years earlier. That occasionally glimpsed structure was, Wons insisted, a temple, vacated long ago by the Angle Beings. Front was amused again as he pondered Wons' fascination with the Angle Beings. Front wondered how Wons could explain to his uncle, the Chaplain of Sebasa, his almost religious interest in those mythical beings. As he thought further, however, Front was sure that Wons could find a way to explain, since Wons seemed able to explain almost anything. But, with the Chaplain, he could hardly use his favorite evidence, his constant reference to the words of Emanuel. Front also wondered about that strange book Wons' adventurous great-uncle had brought into their lives. *Words of Emanuel, Leader of the Ship*, a strange title for a strange book, full of verse and sayings that seemed to mean nothing or everything and seemed to tell a tale that was always just beyond understanding. Wons, however, was convinced and convincing to others that he knew the meaning behind those words.

It was one of those apparent meanings that had convinced the most doubting of their party, Nash, to leave his goats to his brothers' care:

"When the people fear and confront one another,
I bring forth the greatest weapon in my arsenal.
We must climb the mountain of our own mistrust.
There is power enough in truth
To arm us against the enemy within."

Front recalled the day Wons had read those words and how eagerly Nash had responded. "Does that mean the Angle Beings had an arsenal, had weapons we could use against those...those Outhans?"

"It seems to imply that, doesn't it?" Wons nodded slowly.

"Then, if we find such weapons," Nash had continued, "we won't be so helpless if the Outhans come."

Outhans! Even now, the very word caused Front's steps to falter. The warmth and brightness of the day seemed suddenly dimmed. He glanced behind at Sebasa, thinking of his mother and sister alone in the town and his father gone these past several months. Front shook his head from side to side, as if to cast out those painful thoughts. He breathed deeply, and again was able to hear the cheerful sounds of his companions. He was on holiday, and he would not allow those unbidden thoughts to oppress his mind. He was thankful for the quickening pace of the other four, as he had to hurry to catch up.

They soon reached the top of the rise that overlooked Sebasa. The slope of the path lessened, and they headed into an orchard of oil-fruit trees. Wonina skipped ahead and threw herself down at the foot of one of those spreading trees.

"Wheee," she sighed as she put her arms around the base of the tree and pressed her cheek to its bark. "Well, I'm home. You people go on without me, the shade of this tree is holiday enough for me."

The others laughed while Nash pulled her to her feet and hugged her roughly.

"You can make love to your trees down here, but on the mountain they'll only be me to shade you," Nash said with mock menace.

Wonina shoved Nash away with what seemed to Front to be an unusual amount of vigor, but Nash was obviously not put off. He returned to give her a sharp pat on her bottom before she coquettishly scurried out of reach.

"Come on, children," Fyva admonished. "We have work to do while we're here."

Wons took over. "Nash, you and Front look for sturdy, straight branches to cut for our walking staffs. Girls, begin gathering some of the fruit."

But Nash was already reaching up into the nearest tree to pick ripe darkening clusters of fruit.

"No, Nash," insisted Wonina. "Just take the falls."

"Oh, don't worry, Mother Orchard," chided Nash. "These are not your father's trees."

"We agreed," Fyva reminded him, "to take only the partially dried fruit. It weighs less and lasts longer."

As all knew, their plan was to try to live off the land as much as possible on their journey. They certainly had ample supplies for their four or five-day trip, but the challenge was to use those supplies as little as possible. Like the others, Front's pack contain tightly leaf wrapped packages of ground, dried fruit and fish flakes mixed with honey, hollow swamp reeds filled with fermented fish pudding, cakes of hard goat cheese, and a supply of even harder biscuits. These trail supplies would last far longer than they expected to be on the trail, and although all carried water flasks at their sides, water would also be no problem. The arid country surrounding Sebasa was a strange contrast between almost rocky barrenness and fast-moving water. Front carried in his mind a vivid picture of his land, seen from his small boat off the coast of Sebasa. The undulating slopes of the hills rising beyond the town was streaked with hundreds of flashing silver threads as small streams cascaded down the slopes of the mountain. The land and the air were dry; the moisture traveling across the Great Swamp, which spread from the south and north of the coastal range, was borne up the slopes of those Upback Mountains. All that east windblown moisture was lost on the tops of the usually cloud-covered peaks. But there was enough water coming down the west side of the mountains to fill all of those many cascading streams. In spite of the dryness of the air and the soil, the thrifty Sebasans were able to use this ample water to irrigate their orchards and fields. It was controlled moisture in a pleasantly dry land and a very livable homeland for the Sebasans.

The knife that Front used to follow Wons' orders was his most prized possession. Metal deposits were not found locally. The Sebasans had to trade with the far northern towns for their metal tools. Fortunately, red clay was plentiful, so clay took the place of metal whenever possible. Front used his knife to cut three straight branches from the tough, stringy oil-fruit trees. The two staffs of middle length would be for himself and Fyva, and the slightly shorter one for Wonina. He shaved the bark away from the handgrips. It pleased him to leave an even smaller bark grip for Wonina's smaller hand, and to put even more effort into smoothing the grip with a rough stone.

He looked up from his work to spy Wonina sitting next to Nash, as Nash was also carving on one of the two long branches he had cut. Wonina was apportioning the fruit she had gathered. They were laughing and whispering as they worked, and Front suddenly felt his apartness from them. He was reminded that he was in fact something of an outsider in their small band. He was perhaps the youngest; he was not sure whether he was a month or two older or younger than Wonina. He only knew that they were both eighteen. Fyva and Nash were nineteen, and Wons was twenty. Wons, Fyva, and Wonina were town folk, while he and Nash were considered more rustic, and therefore outsiders. But Nash and Wonina were either promised or promised-to-be-promised; at least he knew they always attended festivals and gatherings together. Fyva and Wons were members of two of the wealthiest families in town. Fyva's father was a leading merchant, and Wons was a son of the Town Steward, leader of the town officers. Front's father had been just another fisherman, and now Front, since his father's disappearance, was just another much less experienced fisherman and sole support for his mother and his younger sister. His mother maintained a small stall in the marketplace and sold fish and the fermented fish pudding she prepared from leftover fish scraps. Since Front was away from town so often, he had little time to partake in the life of his age-mates. Still, Wons had accepted him, perhaps flattered by

Front's active interest in most of the many things that interested the studious Wons.

Front had even spent three weekends reading and struggling to make sense of the *Words of Emanuel.* Wons, of course, would not let this precious volume out of the house, so Front had spent those hours sitting by the small library in a corner of the Steward's office. That was another and thoroughly fascinating world for Front. Although he had little time to delve into those ancient volumes, he felt their presence and the other worlds they held. He often pondered those wondrous titles, as he sat in his small boat near the edge of the Great Swamp, and speculated on what those titles might mean. More fascinating, he also wondered what those precious volumes could reveal about the confusing and contradictory history of the Sebasans. Where had the Sebasans come from and how had they arrived in the land? What little Front knew of that history, he suspected, was more myth than fact. The Chaplin preached that the Sebasans were created by God, a being who was of spirit or perhaps mind and not of body. God was first from the heavens. Then, upon creating this world, He resided within it. The Sebasans were brought to Earth by the angels of God, beings that were both mental and physical, and being physical could transport physical beings such as man.

Most of the working people of Sebasa seemed to give at least lip service to their religion. After all, the Chaplin's god was a benevolent god, who taught kindness to others and proper behavior for children. Front suspected, however, that even the common people toyed with the new ideas that some of the young intellectuals discussed, that the Heavenly angels and the mythological Angle Beings were the same, and that the "God" who brought the Sebasans to Earth was something other than spiritual.

Front had also begun to consider that there might be more history than theology to the myths of angels and Angle Beings, but he continued to wonder about Wons' fascination with the Angle Beings and the seeming reverence he evidenced when he spoke of them.

Now, however, as he sat watching under his eyelids as Nash and Wonina jostled and kidded one another, he was more fascinated, and somewhat painfully fascinated by the history of those two very physical beings. What did their easy intimacy indicate regarding their very short history and their longer future together? More important, what did Wonina's and Nash's history mean to *Front's* future. Although Wonina's family, with their orchards and vegetable farm and their town market stall, were certainly above Front in wealth, they were not about him in station. He could, in his lonely imaginings, picture himself becoming more involved with that warm person. Certainly her smiles were encouraging, although it did seem that she preferred to think of him as a brotherly friend, and sometimes even a younger friend at that. Moreover, he didn't want to intrude upon her obviously closer friendship with Nash.

Wons rose, and taking the staff Nash had finished for him he motions grandly down the now broader pathway through the trees. Front fought down his feelings of separation and joined his companions, walking abreast with them, as they continued their journey. Wons, obviously feeling expansive, reached out his long arms as though trying to hug all four of his friends at once, and recited grandly.

"'Whether the sun shows, whether the gale blows, whether the ice flows, if the people go together, there's always fair weather.'" With mock, pomposity, he concluded, "*Emanuel*, Chapter Three, Verse Six."

The others laughed and jostled him about.

"And what would Emmanuel say about our trip to Stareye?" asked Fyva.

Wons paused only briefly, and then, pointing his staff to the distant mountain, he recited again.

"Keep your eye fixed starward, and you'll go where you're bound, if your mind sees the future and your feet seize the ground."

Front chuckled, pleased at catching be different meanings in the words "sees" and "seize."

Fyva looked puzzled. "I don't recall reading that in Emanuel."

Wons grin, "I guess I paraphrased it a bit. But certainly you see that Emanuel intends that we climb Mount Stareye, to rediscover the secrets of the Angle Beings, to bathe ourselves in the brisk waters of that mountain of ancient wisdom."

"And to find their arsenal so we can blast those bastard Outhans," Nash broke in harshly.

Wons took his eyes away from the mountain to stare at Nash's anger contorted face. Then quietly he intoned,

"'And Emanuel smote the Mutanos with his greatness weapon, and they could not stand before the might of his words.'"

Nash harsh expression turned to puzzlement. "What does smote mean?" he asked.

"Well...I'm not quite sure. Sounds like something smoking and something strong, so I suspect your weapon must be one that causes fire and has a great deal of force."

Nash looked satisfied. "Yes, fire and force, that's what we damn well need."

Raising her eyebrow, Fyva corrected Wons, "I think it just means hit. And furthermore, I don't recall anything about weapons in your book, Wons. I understand Emanuel to be talking about truth when he talks about dealing with the Mutanos."

Nash look concerned, and Front could tell the stout young man was turning to Wons for reassurance.

"We'll see soon enough, Nash. The words of Emanuel aren't always clear, but it's clear to me that there's something to be discovered on Mount Stareye. You've had a clear view of it, Nash, when up here with your herd. You know there's something up there that's not just a part of the mountain. The peak's too flat. Then there's that dome-like structure."

"You can't be sure," worried Nash. "The mist is usually so thick, and it's a long way off...."

Wons interrupted the hesitating Nash. "Front, you've seen it. Tell him what you told me."

Front paused before speaking. He was of mixed minds. He looked first at Fyva, identifying with her cautiousness, and then he glanced at Nash. He also felt his new friend's concern and the anger he knew to be underlying that concern.

"I don't always know what to think, Wons. When you see Mount Stareye at just the right time on one of those rare, calm and clear days, and when the boat isn't bobbing up and down, it does seem as though there's a structure there, perhaps even a temple, like you say. But I don't know what the words mean either. Certainly Emanuel did something to the Mutanos when they did whatever they did to threaten him and the people."

Wons looked exasperated. Shaking his head he started to speak again.

Wonina broke in. "Oh, who cares about the Angle Beings, or Emanuel's weapons and all that nonsense! We're on holiday." She grabbed Wons' hand, and clutching Nash's arm, she scampered ahead with them, pulling the reluctant males until they could no longer resist her insistent gaiety. Soon they were all five bounding along on the now level pathway, their doubts no longer so important.

By midmorning they left the orchard country and began moving up a rocky slope, not so steep as that pathway leading out of Sebasa, but nevertheless more taxing than the level road through the orchards. This was the beginning of high goat country, the upland pastures for the many goat herds that supplied milk, cheese, and meat for the Sebasa. Front could see ample evidence of the goats' presence. In addition to the droppings alongside and even in the pathway, the smell of goat was in the air. In the distance he spotted several small herds tended by their herdsmen.

As the companions ascended even higher up the slope, the breeze freshened, and Front's nostrils drew in the familiar smells of sea and swamp. The salt tang in the air tugged at his feelings and revived his uneasiness as he looked back toward the now hidden Sebasa. Was it right for him to leave his mother and his sister at a time when threatening rumors about the Outhans were becoming so commonplace? He looked quickly ahead, searching for the sight of Mount Stareye, hoping to grasp with his eyes that distant peak to pull him from his worried uncertainty. But the mountain was also somewhere beyond the slope of Goatherder's Hill.

He was heartened somewhat and diverted by the spring that had sudden come into Nash's step. This was Nash's country; the goat herder was familiar with these pastures, having spent half his life climbing over the dry boulders of these sparsely turfed hills.

Nash seemed to sense Front's need and smiled. "Come on, Sea Legs," he kidded. "Last one up the hill is a goat turd."

Front was thankful for this diversion, and he bounded off after Nash."

"Wait for me," shouted Wonina, and she followed with surprising speed.

Allowing her to pass him, Front admired the grace and strength in Wonina's slender, rounded but obviously sturdy body. He wanted both to stay near her and to dash ahead to catch up with Nash. But, reluctantly, he pulled past Wonina, and with his more agile body he was soon overtaking Nash. When he reached the top of the small knoll, however, Nash turned to await him. Then, he grabbed Front in a great hug. Tumbling to the ground together, they rolled down the other side of the hill. Wonina soon joined them, flinging herself bodily on top of them, laughing and hugging them both, and, it seemed to Front, with equal affection. Wons and Fyva then overtook them and, smiling indulgently, passed them by to continue to the next rise.

The flailing three, now somewhat subdued, followed after their more reserved companions. Front, however, didn't mind the gentle rebuke. He felt too much relieved, after having exerted himself. The struggle for breath and the slight pain in his side were preferable to his former feelings of doubt and concern. He also held onto the memory of warmth and wetness from Wonina's perspiring cheeks that briefly had pressed against his.

They lunched on another knoll further up the hill, still out of sight of both the sea and the mountain. Their lunch consisted of tangy fish pudding, strong goat cheese, and the freshest of the oil-fruit they had gathered. Nash plucked some lemon grass, which they chewed to freshman their breath after their pungent meal. They lounged against the warm boulders, enjoying the sun, now that the higher elevation was instilling a crispness in the air.

Front felt the sun induced lassitude seeping into him, and was almost reluctant to follow the conversation that Fyva started with Wons.

"Tell me again exactly what your uncle said he found on top of Mount Stareye."

"Well, to tell the truth, he didn't say too exactly. After all, he was rather old, and I was only ten years old when he died."

Front noticed that Nash was again becoming restless.

Wons spoke more firmly. "He told me that he'd been traveling along the west slope of the mountain chains, returning from a buying trip to some of the towns in the North. He had traveled up the coast by trader boat, but had decided to journey overland on the return to Sebasa. In one of the towns along the way, a town that had a particularly good view of Mount Stareye, he talked to an old man, a sort of priest, who believed in the Angle Beings and claimed that the top of Mount Stareye was one of their main temples, a temple from which they communicated to their home in the heavens."

"You talk like the Angle Beings were gods," admonished Wonina.

Front was not sure whether her admonition was serious or in jest.

"Oh, no," assured Wons. "I don't know what they were, but I don't believe they were gods—maybe more like ancient heroes or something. Anyway, they must have known more and had more power than we do or they couldn't have built a temple on top of Mount Stareye."

"It remains to be seen if there is such a *temple*," Fyva corrected.

Nash squirming and started to speak, but Wons continued forcefully. "The temple is the people, and the people are the temple, and I will lead the people in the worship of their work."

"I'm not sure what that has to do with anything," Fyva laughed, "but get on with your story."

"Well, this old man said that he would give my uncle an ancient and valuable volume if my uncle would climb to the top of Mount Stareye to worship...uh, that is, to examine or discover what there was at the top. Anyway, that ancient volume was the *Words of Emanuel, Leader of the Ship* that you've all seen in my father's office. So my uncle took the book and climbed Mount Stareye.

"And all by himself!" Wons hastily added, "You'll see. It's not that steep a climb when you get up there."

Nash's did not seem to be assured, but he said nothing further.

"But what did he find there?" asked Fyva.

"I told you before, a great dome on top of a stone temple filled with all sorts of strange things."

"But you've never said what those strange things were."

"Well, as I said, my uncle was old, and I was quite young, but I can remember feeling that they were wonderful things—things that I had to see for myself."

Somehow Front recalled, when the group had talked about journeying to Mount Stareye, that Wons had been more convincing. Perhaps it was the words he had read from the volume, and without the presence of that volume, Wons was losing some of his authority.

"You'll see," he said someone weakly as he pulled himself to his feet. "You'll all see when we get there."

Front glanced up at the already tall Wons now standing and towering above his four seated friends. After a moment of looking down on them, Wons' voice again deepened.

"Oh, come ye of little faith. I will lead ye to the mountains and to wisdom."

Wonina laughed. "Come, fellow goats. Let us follow our brave goat herder. In fact, let's get ahead of him so we'll be downwind. Sometimes he lets out such bad wind he smells worse than we do."

Wons seemed about to say more, but when the others laughed, he merely smiled and bowed Wonina ahead of him.

By late afternoon they had reached the top of Goathearder's Hill. The sky had finally cleared, and from the top of the hill, Front could finally see in one sweep all the elements of his world. To the south, just before the rocky land suddenly ended and the marshes began, the town of Sebasa shone like a white and red flower in the late afternoon sun. On the far edge of the town, seen clearly from this height as an apparently perfect circle, lay that strange platform-like rock known as the Commons—rock so hard that although it would have been an ideal location for the town itself, foundations could never be dug into its surface. The sharp walls of that platform, nevertheless, made an ideal wharf for the many fishing boats of the town, and the circular platform was a perfect site for the annual planting and harvest festivals. Extending west of the Commons and the small Harbor was Sebasa Bay, curving to the southwest and merging into the becalmed sea grass flats that were the beginnings of the Great Swamp. The foothills of the mountain range that began with Mount Stareye disappeared beneath that endless swamp.

As he turned to his right, Front's eyes followed the gradual rise of those hills to the north. One knoll led to another, each reaching higher, becoming almost mountains themselves, until directly behind them stood forth the highest, Mount Stareye. It was as he had remembered on those clear days. Now, closer to the mountain than he had ever been, the peak did indeed seem to be absolutely flat, as if a giant hand had crushed the top of the mountain and placed there a rounded ball to attract and hold the rays of the descending sun.

All eyes were now on that distant object. Front heard Wons' voice hiss as he suddenly expelled his breath. It seemed he then heard Wons utter a prayer like whisper, but he couldn't make out the words.

With effort, Front tore himself away from the enchantment of that distant brightness. As he turned, he sensed Wonina turning with him, and out of the corner of his eye he saw Nash, who seemed to be wavering between Sebasa and the mountain.

Front stood now with his back to Mount Stareye. Out in the distance beyond Sebasa, beyond the bay, far into the ocean itself, Front could see the turbulence of the deep sea. A bank of dark clouds covered horizon to

horizon. A storm was brewing, and beyond that storm, beyond that darkness, was it as the rumors whispered? Were the Outhans coming?

Front tore his eyes away from the blackness to gaze longingly on the
peaceful town of Sebasa. He imagined he could see the small house where
his mother and his sister were waiting. His mother would be preparing
their evening meal, and his sister would be sewing and perhaps thinking
of her brother, her brother now far from her. Would she also be thinking
of their father? Slowly Front raised his eyes to stare again at the distance
storm. Had his father indeed disappear into that perpetual bank of blackness? Had those churning waves engulfed the man who had loved him and
taught him all he knew? Was that churning darkness to engulf all of what
he saw before him? Was Sebasa to follow into the night?

2

WE WORK UP, THE WORDS
COME DOWN

The team began traveling down the backside of Goatherders' Hill, leaving the view of Sebasa behind, but Front's mood of foreboding remained with him. The black mood wasn't lifted until just before sundown when he and Nash were able to down a rabbit and a small ground bird with their slings. The girls had been gathering groundnuts, garlic, and wild parsley along the way, so that by the time they reached the wooded valley at the base of the hill, they had most of the makings for their evening meal.

Streams tumbling down the mountain collected in a shallow marshy valley. Unlike in Sebasa, the air here was damp, and as the sun disappeared, an unpleasant coolness set in. Front and the others soon put on the sea-serpent jackets they had strapped to their backpacks. With the small cooking fire Nash had kindled, and their jackets buttons, it was soon much cozier.

"Thank God for sea-serpents." Wonina was huddling close to Nash. "And thank God for fisherman to bring them in," she smiled at Front.

Front felt a little uncomfortable, partially from the undeserved praise and partially out of envy for the way Wonina snuggled up to Nash.

"I agree, but I'm not one of those fisherman," he explained. "It takes a bigger boat than mine to bring in a sea-serpent. I don't usually go as far out as the reefs where they feed. I'm still learning my trade."

"But haven't you caught at least one?" insisted Wonina.

"Oh, sure. Occasionally I'll net one when they come in near the marshes for their spring mating."

As he spoke he realized he was stroking the arm of his jacket, feeling the smooth, slick surface that was broken by the familiar course, hard knobs. It was this combination of slickness and stone-like protrusions that gave the material a waterproof, almost airtight surface, and great durability."

"In spite of their appearance, sea-serpents aren't really vicious. They're primarily bottom feeders, you know, and their teeth are flat and almost dull, mostly for crunching shells or coral or...."

"Or fishermen's heads?" Nash suggested.

"Oh, come on, the biggest serpent I ever saw was only about eight feet long and no more than eight or nine inches around."

"My father told me about a giant one," Wonina insisted, "a real monster that was covered with jewel-like protrusions and was big enough to swallow people."

"Boy," said Nash, "how'd you like to see one like that oozing out of the fog?" He nudged Wonina and pointed into the darkening mists gathering beyond the campfire.

Wonina started, then laughed at herself. But she dug her elbow into Nash's ribs nonetheless.

Front laughed also. "That's only a legend, or at least it happened so long ago that it might as well be a legend. My father told me that some time ago a fisherman did find the head of some kind of large creature. The body was almost completely decayed, but it did seem to have jewel like or brightly colored spots or lumps on it. The fishermen speculate that perhaps it was a member of a fresh-water species of serpent, one that only lives deep in the swamps. But we'll probably never know. The marshes are so impenetrable it's not worthwhile for fisherman to go further in than where the sea meets the swamp. Besides, the fishing is so good right there, who needs to go any place else?"

"Well, nevertheless," Wonina insisted again, "thank God for little sea serpents and big fishing boats that gather them."

Fyva changed the subject. "And speaking as a fisherman, Front, what do you think of the size of those boat-bark trees in this valley?"

Front turn to Fyva. He was more surprised at her interest in his opinion than in her apparent knowledge of the material from which the fisherman created their small boats.

"It must be because of the moisture collected in this marsh area," he suggested. "Boat-bark trees grow primarily along the edge of the streams on the hillside, but they seldom get this big near Sebasa. "He glanced up at the tall trees whose spreading branches were becoming lost in the mist descending from the mountains. Although there was little breeze, he noticed that the trees seemed to be moving and creaking as they moved. The group quietened and listened along with Front.

Nash suddenly broke the stillness, "And speaking of sounds out of the darkness and sea-monsters, what do the fishermen have to say about the Outhans?"

Front turned to encounter a demanding look on Nash's face. He knew the reason for that demand, but he was reluctant to speak. He realized that, as a fisherman, he really had more information than most of the other town folk, but the Outhans were a painful subject for him.

Fyva rescued him. "Perhaps we can talk about that later, Nash. Right now my stomach wants to have a talk with the rabbit you caught."

"Yes, yes," agreed Wonina, who began turning again the small wooden spit that speared the roasting rabbit and bird. "Let's eat now, we'll talk later. The food's almost ready."

The meal was warming, and now as the darkness thickened and the mist continued to descend, the fire reflecting off the mist seemed to brighten their small enclosed hollow, and Front feel more secure and willing to talk.

"Okay, let's talk about the Outhans," he volunteered.

"Yeah," barked Nash, with as much anger as eagerness.

Wons, who had said very little all evening, seemed to lean back away from the group.

"You don't really want to talk about this, do you Front?" asked Wonina. She turned to Wons. "I'd rather hear about the Angle Beings and Mount Stareye."

"And I think it's time we stopped avoiding the obvious and started talking about what might happen back in Sebasa!" demanded Nash.

Wonina sat up more stiffly and moved perceptible away from Nash.

Front smiled appreciatively at her. "No, Wonina, I don't really want to talk about it. But you all know the rumors. My father probably was the first fisherman to encounter the Outhans and...well, I guess they killed him."

"No, Front, "Wonina tried to hush him. "You don't have to say any more."

"Quiet, woman!" Growled Nash.

Fyva intervened. "Perhaps we could talk about the Outhans in general, Front, and not about what could have happened to your father. Then later, Wonina, we could talk more of the Angle Beings."

"Fyva, Wonina," Front said steadily, "I've more or less accepted the fact that my father's probably dead." His calmness seemed to still them. "It's been five months now. Other fishermen said they saw him enter the black fog bank beyond the reef, where the North current and the deeper ocean begins, and...Well, he didn't come out again." Pausing only briefly, Front hurried on. "In the next several days, three other fishermen also were lost the same way. Soon after that, Bosom and Deck, in their two-man skiff, veered off from the fog bank just in time to keep from colliding with one of the Outhans deep bottom boats. It was probably only because they were so much faster than that deep ocean vessel, they were able to avoid being taken by those creatures."

"Creatures is right," sneered Nash. "Some kind of foul, slimy, creatures."

"Oh come on, Nash," Fyva showed her impatience "They're just as human as you and I."

"Human, hell! Those squat, dark slimes aren't human. They all look alike, like some kind of insects."

"They look alike," insisted Fyva, "because they wear uniforms, and they all wear beards, but that doesn't mean they're inhuman."

"The hell you say! What about their emblem, that proves they worship bugs!"

"Emblem?"

"Yeah, on the sides of their ships, a big black flying roach or something. You tell her, Front!"

"I guess it could be seen as a bug, or a bird...The fishermen say the Outhans have painted on the bow of their ships a black, squarish creature with wings, carrying in its mouth a squirming, brightly colored ferocious looking worm."

"What did I tell you!"

"But they do speak our language," continued Front, "or at least a dialect of our language. After Bosom and Deck moved away from them, their captain, or whatever he was, hailed them. It took a while before they realized the Outhans were actually speaking a language they could understand."

"Do they have their own Outhans language?" asked Wonina, someone timidly.

"I get the idea that in fact their language is the same as ours, just spoken differently."

"I understand they're not even call Outhans," said Fyva.

"You're right. We don't know what they're called, or at least what they call themselves. Their chief spokesman, who seemed to be trying to be friendly, kept talking about their oath. They didn't intend us any harm, he said, but they had come to fulfill their oath. They wanted to know more about our country, but Bosom and Deck were probably wise to say very little. It was days before Bosom and Deck began to realize that they were really saying 'oath,' that they had come to fulfill their oath. By this time, everybody was already calling them Outhans, and the name stuck."

"But who are they, Front?" Wonina, was seemingly interested now in spite of her fearfulness.

"No one knows. They must live on the other side of the storm belt that's always churning beyond the North Current. The old fishermen must be right about their being deep ocean beyond the currents, since apparently it took those deep daft vessels to make it through to our coast. Our own small vessels only venture just inside the edge of the storm bank, and only then when an experienced fisherman like my father spots a big oceangoing fish feeding there."

Front reflected briefly on just how good a fisherman his father had been. Sighing once, he returned to his subject. "They're apparently not really very good seaman either, so I suspect they had no great desire to enter that storm themselves, but seemingly their oath drove them to risk the storm. Fishermen who have seen the Outhan boats state that they all seem fairly new, as if they have only recently begun to build their ocean-going boats, maybe primarily to reach our shore."

"Damn right they want to reach our shore," bellowed Nash. "They live in some foul, dark land and they'd like nothing better than to take over Sebasa and all the other lands along this stretch of the coast. Their filthy oath is probably to destroy us all!" His words were now tumbling one over another. "Well, they'd damn better be able to fight when they get here. My family and I don't plan to surrender an inch of our land to those slimy Outhans." As if looking for an object for his anger, Nash then turned on Wons. He shook his fist. "And that's why I'm on this trip. You promised that the Angle Beings had weapons hidden up there on Mount Stareye, and you'd better produce!"

Wons seemed to move even further away from the circle. Wonina put a tentative hand on Nash's arm as if to restrain him, and Fyva stated quietly but quickly, "I don't remember that Wons actually promised anything, Nash. He merely quoted from Emanuel. And besides," she stated more firmly, "we don't even know if the Outhans are coming back. After all, it's been at least six months since they were last sighted."

Nash then turned on her. " Yeah, and it was during that semi annual calm spell in the fog-bank that they came, like late winter…and right now!"

Fyva said nothing to this, and Wonina, pulling even closer to Nash, turned to Wons and asked, "What about the Angle Beings, wouldn't they have known about the Outhans? Doesn't Emanuel say something about them?"

Wons sat forward again and cleared his throat. "The men on the Officers' Council…" His voice was still horse and he cleared his throat again, then spoke more firmly, "The Councilmen speculate that perhaps the Mutanos and the Outhans are the same people. Some time back in our history the Mutanos apparently broke away or were driven away from the rest of us. Why this happened, no one knows."

"If they were driven away," Nash was now somewhat calmer, "that means Emanuel had some kind of weapon."

"Perhaps," continued Wons. "Emanuel always seemed to have a way of enabling the people to do what was right. Perhaps if we would listen to the words of Emanuel we would know how to find that way." He paused, apparently to be sure they were aware that he was now quoting. "Emanuel said, 'The people are the way, and the way is the people. The people must conflict, for conflict is within the people. Conflict is neither good nor bad, but to run from conflict is to run from ourselves. We must confront conflict. We must confront ourselves if we are to find the way'"

"Yeah," said Nash, apparently pleased with the way things were now going. "And if old Emanuel was willing to confront conflict, that means he did have weapons."

"He did talk a lot about meeting an issue head on," agreed Wons, "and that the only time to back down from a conflict was when that conflict might destroy the group. He also seemed to say that to fail to face conflict was just as likely to destroy the group."

Front wasn't sure that he understood the full meaning of what Wons was saying. He wanted to ask what was meant by the word, 'conflict', but on the other hand, he was afraid that to do so might lead to an answer that would not please Nash. He noticed that Fyva also seemed to be uncertain and teetering on asking her own question.

"But what does all this mean, Wons," she finally asked. "It almost seems as though this conflict Emanuel's talking about is always going on within the group. What has all this to do with the Mutanos or Outhans?"

Nash, who seemed now to be siding with Wons, answered the question. "Well, maybe the Mutanos were originally part of the group, and maybe Emanuel used his weapon to drive them out." He turned again to Wons, "But doesn't the book describes how he did it?"

"Not exactly, Nash, but there is one passage that goes like this." Wons rose to his knees and sat on his heels. As he talked, his voice began to take on its deep, oracular tone:

"'The people were in conflict,

And I stood before the people,

And I shared my heart, and I shared my goals, and I shared my plans, and I ask that they share with me.

But the people were in conflict,

And I stood before the people,

And I ask what part of my way they would choose

And what part of their way I must choose.

But the people were in conflict,

And I stood before the people,

And I said I would wait, and I gave of my heart.'"

As Wons continued, his voice became more powerful and ringing, and it seemed to Front that Wons' words rebounded down from the thick, low hanging mist and filled the hollow with their power.

"'But the people were in conflict,

And I stood before the people,

And I raised my voice and shouted down at them.
You must now follow the way or I shall call on the power,
And the way will be done.

"'But the people were in conflict,
And I stood before the people,
And I shared with them my heart, and I shared with them my goals, and I shared with them my plans, and I shared with them my sorrow that they preferred their conflict to the way.

"'And I turned my back own them.
And they followed me.'"

Wons' ringing voice ceased raining down on them, and there was silence in the hollow.

It was a while before a part of Front began to puzzle over Emanuel's words. He began to realize he did not understand their meaning. But another part of him was pleased that something seemed to have happen to change their small group. They had either been convinced or lulled into silent questioning by the words of Emanuel, and Front was thankful for the change in either case. He was glad when the silence continued and no one reopened the Outhan issue.

Later that evening as they prepared to bed down for the night, Front's earlier feeling of separation from the group returned. They laid out their serpent skin, goat fur lined bags in as arrangement that only served to emphasize his apartness. Wons' was in the middle, and on either side of Wons were the two girls. Nash laid his bag close to Wonina's while Front's bag was on the other side of Fyva's, noticeable apart from the group. He was the last to settle back, and he felt a small twinge of envy as he glimpsed Nash casually placing his arm about Wonina's shoulders. Front tried to think of other things, but his mind first went in an unwanted direction, toward the surrounding night and the troubled ocean beyond. At last he found some comfort in contemplating Mount Stareye and the promised adventure of the morrow.

After a hurried breakfast before down, the group started out again. They had hopes of reaching Mount Stareye's peak at sunset, and they knew they had a long hard trek ahead of them. The previous evening's mist was now a fog blanketing their small campsite valley, and there seemed no sure pathways through the woods. They held hands during the thickest of the morning fog. When the mist lifted slightly a while later, and they reverted to their customary single file, with Wons in the lead, though they still remained close together. This was no challenge, since they had now left the trees and began to mount the lower slope of Mount Stareye, and the steeper incline slowed their pace.

When they rose again to where they should have been able to sight the sea and Sebasa over the top of Goatherders' Hill, they were disappointed. The mist was still too thick to allow a view.

After that small disappointment, the remainder of the morning trek was fairly pleasant. The incline was steep but not yet taxing. The way was made even easier when they eventually came upon what was apparently a goat trail, which wound its way up the mountain in the general direction they wished to go.

The goat trail gave out just before they stopped for lunch. Nash, who had been pleased at the usefulness of the trail, remarked perhaps somewhat defensively that after all his goats were not mountain goats.

Wonina kiddingly responded, "But that's why we brought you along, Nash."

Nash seemed to take Wonina's kidding as a compliment. He patted the coil of rope he had strapped to his pack and commented, "And that's why I insisted on packing these ropes on Wons' and my pack. This goat's was at least smart enough to come prepared."

The ropes were indeed needed soon after that. They had just finished a particularly steep stretch, during which Nash had taken the lead from Wons. Nash had waited for the rest of them as they struggled the last few yards to his side. They found themselves standing between two boulders looking down into a narrow but deep gorge.

Wons groaned, his shoulders drooping and a look of helplessness now on his face. "Oh, Lord, my uncle never told me about this."

Nash grinned, but before he could speak, Fyva already had a plan. "If one of you fellows could toss a loop over that jagged boulder just on the other side of the gorge, we could tie it on this end and shinny our way across."

"But someone might fall," gasped Wonina.

"Oh, don't worry," Nash encouraged as he pulled Wonina to him. "We'll use Wons' rope to tie onto you just in case you do fall."

Motioning Front to come forward, Nash handed him the rope.

"Here, seaman, you know more about ropes than I do. Tie a knot and cast it across just like you would on a piling."

Front tested the rope and was satisfied it would indeed hold even more than the weight of any one of their party. He studied the distant rock for any jagged edges that might cut the rope, and only when satisfied with his preparations did he cast a perfect strike onto the indicated boulder.

"Whoopee!" shouted Wonina, having apparently already conquered her concern.

Front tied the rope securely to a similar boulder on their side of the gorge, and being the lightest male, he volunteered to be the first across. When no one disputed his reasons for going first, he tied Wons' rope to his waist and, securing the other end to another boulder, he handed the looped middle of that rope to Nash and Wons. Then he went across the gorge hand over hand, all the while giving himself courage by imagining that the blue streak of water far below him was actually the soft warm water of Sebasa Bay. The others cheered and he sighed deeply when at last he safely reached the other side.

Tossing back the safety rope, he suggested that the next person to cross should be secured to the middle of the safety rope and one end tossed across to him while the other end remained tied to the rock.

Wonina volunteered to go second, scoffing off everyone's surprise by insisting that although she was cautious, she was no coward. She chose to straddle the rope while Front and Nash held her erect with the safety rope.

"Stop pulling me!" she screeched, as Front became too eager to get her across and was dragging her with the safety rope. "I'll do it myself."

She punched him on the arm after she made it across. "So there, you're not the only hero on this mountain." Then she gave him a hug, which was all the more pleasing to him since she seemed so pleased with herself.

The others also made it across safely, after there was a small disagreement between Wons and Nash as to who would be last. Wons wanted to be last, but Nash won out. Nash came across with one end of the safety loop tied about him and with Front and Wons holding the other end. Front then flipped off the crossing line from the far side, and recoiled the ropes.

Wons again led the way up the mountain. He did not lead for long, however. When the path, or what they now took for a path, became even rockier and steeper, Nash moved ahead, scouting to find places where they could walk rather than crawl. Wons followed, then Fyva. Front was pleased that Wonina was now just ahead of him, so he could come to her aid if needed.

That aid was needed more and more frequently. Once, when Front found it necessary to boost her by placing both of his hand on her bottom, she let out a whoop and giggled. Front reddened and wondered just how necessary it had been to grab her in just that way. The fact that she didn't really seem to mind didn't keep him from promising not to be so familiar next time. In fact, as they continued to struggle up the side of the mountain, he thought it best not to press himself on Wonina in any manner. After all, it was clear that she was Nash's girl, and since they obviously needed to work together on this climb, he didn't want to start any dissention in the group by making advances toward another man's woman.

He found his resolve to keep an emotional distance was particularly difficult to follow, however, when, as they paused on a ridge to recover their breath, Wonina flopped down beside him and rested her cheek on his thigh. Front froze, afraid to move his leg, even as he felt a tingling sensations moving up his thigh. He glanced guiltily toward Nash, but Nash who was involved in trying to catch his breath merely grinned back. He seemed neither to notice Front's predicament nor to care. Front glanced down at the tumble of soft brown hair fallen over his thigh, and had to force himself to pull his eyes away.

He arched back against the jagged rocks and searched the mist-filled distance. From all he could see in the vague whiteness before him, Sebasa and the sea might as well be in another world. His own world now contained only four other people and a rocky ledge on the side of a vaguely mysterious mountain. Without thinking, he put his hand on Wonina's shoulder and squeezed gently. Perhaps she also felt the need for greater closeness. She placed her hand over his and patted him reassuringly.

Wons, who had seated himself a little above the group, called down that it was time to go on. But it was Nash who again led the way.

Very soon the incline lessened and they were able to cover a considerable distance. When Front remembered to wonder about the time, he guessed it was now late afternoon, though he could not confirm that guess by the still hidden sun. Still, he had the satisfying feeling of their having made good progress, and he had almost forgotten his disquieting attraction to Wonina. However, when they came to another cluster of jagged boulders on a steeper incline half way up this section, Wonina turned back to him and complained, "Hey, what happened to my boost buddy?"

In sudden confusion he rather awkwardly shoved her over the next boulder.

"Hey, I said boost, not gore."

"Sorry," he muttered, and tried laughing to soothe his obvious embarrassment.

"Oh, don't be a fuddy duddy, it was my pleasure," Wonina winked at him.

The next time he boosted her, he placed his hands firmly on her rear and kept them there until she was safely up. In turn, she pulled him up after her, and it seemed to Front that she held onto his hand longer than necessary.

For a while Front was lost in his own pleasant speculation, but when they again assembled on a rather broad ledge, he had to become aware of a new problem. Even Nash seemed to be intimidated by what now rose before them, and Wons shrank down in a heap. "Oh, my God," he gasped. "There's no way we can climb that!"

The others remained silent, forcing their eyes to travel up an almost perpendicular embankment that faded out of sight into the mist. It occurred to Front that here was another reason the sedentary Sebasans didn't climb Mount Stareye. This cliff would discourage even more risk-willing climbers.

After a time, Fyva seemed to shake herself and look to the right and then to the left. "If we can't go up, we can go sideways," she said firmly. "Let's not just stand still."

This seemed to rouse Nash. "Front, you go to the left, and I'll explore to the right. Let's see what we can find."

Front groped his way along, being careful to check his footing. He wasn't particularly eager to go up the steep incline that stretched before him, but he didn't want a sudden journey in the other direction either. As he felt his way along, he tried to remember what the shape of the cliff had looked like when spied from the sea. Thinking back, he didn't recall having seen such a sharp rise in the cliff. That must mean, as seen from the west, such an angle wouldn't have been obvious. Assuming they were now on the western slope, the north and south slopes of the mountain would be less precipitous.

To his relief, the ledge ahead of him eventually began to broaden. When he looked up, the incline of the cliff had also lessened. He turned and called to those behind him, but there was no answer. His heart jumped and thumped in his chest, and he lurched back across the ledge, but stumbled and barely clung to the side of the cliff. He had to breathe deeply to calm himself before he could think clearly enough to realize that he had rounded a corner, and that his voice was probably lost among the mist and boulders.

When he worked his way carefully back to the others, he was relieved but not surprised that they were still there. Even Nash had already returned, having reached an impasse in the opposite direction.

"This way," Front gestured. "It will be difficult, but at least possible on this side."

When the group finally congregated before the more hopeful incline to which Front had led them, he described what he had recalled seeing from the open sea. "The slopes on either side of the mountain are continuous at about the angle you see above you. I'm just guessing, but it seems to me that the flat peak of Mount Stareye should be just beyond our sight in the mist."

At this news, Wons recovered himself enough to insist on taking the lead. Nash protested, but Wons began raising his voice, and there was a look in his eyes that clearly announced that now be was so near his goal nothing was going to get in his way. Nash gave in, but not before insisting that they make proper use of the two ropes they had brought. He instructed the impatient Wons to tie one end of his rope to his waist and the other end to Fyva's waist. At each stretch of the rope he was to use the rope to help Fyva reach his new position. Nash secured his own rope to Wonina, leaving only Front to climb alone.

Wonina protested. "But if Front slips, there will be no one to hold him back."

Front laughed. "And if I slip, I won't carry anyone else with me."

Still Wonina was not satisfied. She insisted that Front should at least climb alongside her to be within her reach should he start to fall. Both Nash and Front pointed out how futile her efforts would be, that her hands would hardly be free to hold onto him, but she was adamant.

As it turned out, though the climb was hard and longer than Front had predicted, it was without incident. Moreover, their chances of avoiding mishap were greatly improved when three quarters of the way up the cliff the mist began to clear.

The sun's rays were finally reaching them. The chill had also left Front, and he was growing quite warm. He could see Wons overhead, standing on a ledge bathed in golden light and shouting, "We made it! The temple, it's here! It's here!"

"Not so fast, Wons!" Fyva screeched and fairly scrambled up the last stretch as Wons was urging her with the rope.

By time the other three members of the group quickly made it to the top, however, Wons was cursing. In his haste to release himself he had tangled the knot Nash had tied in the rope about his waist.

After pulling himself to his feet, Front first looked to the center of the flat platform-like peak of Mount Stareye. Wons was right, there was indeed a stone structure, topped by what appeared to be a bulbous dome. It was much as he had imagined seeing it from his boat.

With that brief thought, however, he turned toward home. The little breath he had managed to regain was taken away from him. There before him, above the mist and stretching from one end of the world to the other, was the sea—his home beyond his home. To his far left, beyond the slope of Goatherders' Hill, now a mere anthill below him, was the tiny red and white dab of Sebasa. For moments as he tried to take it all in, he was oblivious to all else until he felt Wonina holding onto his arm, and then he sensed that just beyond her Nash was also standing close and staring homeward.

It was a while before he could begin to fit together some of the details of the scene before him. He had never seen his whole world as one, and he wanted to encompass it completely with his arms as well as with his eyes.

"Look at it, will you!" shouted Wons.

Front pulled himself away from the scene below to realize that Wons was gazing at the stone structure behind him rather than at Sebasa and the sea. Then Front also felt the tug of that strange building, and he became aware that Wons and Fyva were already moving in that direction. Still, he pulled his eyes back to gaze at the sea. The line of storm that marked the edge of the North Current beyond which the fishermen of Sebasa never traveled was indeed a sharp, dark line seen from this height. Now, during the late summer calms, that line was further seaward but clearly it continued from horizon to horizon. Front looked again at Sebasa, and from this distance he could see the Commons as a tiny perfect circle. He could just make out colored specks in the bay, which he knew to be the boats of his fellow fishermen.

A few of these specks could be seen further along the bay as they sprinkled out toward the storm-bank or onto the edge of the swamp. And, oh the swamp—the swamp stretched to infinity, southward from Sebasa and northward, east of the coastal mountain range. Or at least it might as well be infinity. The mist that always hovered behind those mountains hid the unknown vastness of the Great Swamp in a blanket of myths that frightened children and sometimes their parents as well.

With one last look at Sebasa, the swamp, the sea, and the storm bank, Front pulled himself away, and found that he also had to pull at Wonina. Nash had already gone ahead and was hurrying to catch up with Wons and Fyva.

Wonina let out a small moan as he half dragged her away from the edge, but soon they were also scampering after their companions. As they approached the strange structure that rose from the middle of the flattened peak of Stareye, Front felt there was something familiar about the color of that stone. Yes, it was like the Commons when you scratched beneath its thin layer of sand. Underneath that sand on the Commons there was this same smooth blue-gray stone.

Wons had already reached what appeared to be a portal into the structure. Wons then paused, and it seemed to Front that he almost dipped one knee. Fyva, who was beside Wons, caught him, apparently assuming that he was about to fall.

Wons shook her off, and then he regained his full height. He spread his arms and shouted, "Look at it! I told you there'd be a temple."

The word "temple" did not quite fit the building Front saw before him. There was nothing ornate and, except for its size, nothing awe inspiring about it, merely a circular stone building, he guessed about seventy feet in diameter, rising about twenty-five feet straight up, and from which bulged a seemingly circular dome. He could see the dome was made from a different kind of material than the base of the structure, more silvery, a fact which Front realized accounted for its glistening in the sun when seen from a distance.

"Let's try the door," Fyva suggested.

Still, Wons hesitated.

"Yeah, come on," Nash agreed as he started toward the door.

Wons broke his trance and pushed ahead of Nash. There seemed to be no handle on the door, so he shoved gently, but without much effect. Bending slightly and putting his full force behind it, Wons shoved again. Instead of opening, the door collapsed suddenly before him.

Wons jumped back as if struck by the sound of the door's crashing to the floor. No one else moved, although they could clearly see nothing beyond the fallen door to stop them from entering.

Again Nash was first to move forward, and again Wons roused himself in time to move ahead of Nash. Slowly the others followed Wons and Nash's lead.

Once inside it was apparent why they had been able to see clearly into what should have been the darker interior of the building. The back part of the dome, which they had not been able to see from the front of the building, was missing, and great pieces of that roof were lying scattered across the floor. The full light of the sky flooded in from above.

As the group spread itself out in a semi-circle just within the door, Wons let out a painful moan. Front could see why. The debris from the partially collapsed roof was almost all there was to see in the building. In the very center of the floor was a square boxlike form, about three-quarters of the height of a man, and there were four doors leading off the main chamber, but beyond that, nothing.

"But there's nothing here!" cried Wons. "No altar, no idols, no books. Nothing. Nothing!" He dropped to his knees. "Nothing, damn it, nothing!"

Wonina moved beside Wons and placed her arm about his shoulder. She pulled his head gently to her, but he shoved her away. When she came back to his side, however, he no longer resisted her commiserating presence.

Fyva and Front moved toward the center box, while Nash began peering cautiously into the side rooms. Fyva carefully examined the square block, and she first called Front's attention to the hexagonal knobs jutting from the edges of the box. "I think those bolt the box together, but we don't have a tool to turn them. Notice the many smaller holes on the sides of the box. I bet something used to stick into those holes, but I can't imagine way. Now look at this plate affixed to the side of the block.

Front glanced at the plate, but could make little of it.

"This one I'm going to think about," she announced.

As Fyva studied the plate more carefully, Front joined Nash in his search of the four rooms. The doors were missing on the first two rooms they entered, and both rooms were empty. The third room had the door partially ajar, but it was also empty. They had to force their way into the fourth room, but unlike the large entry door, the smaller door at least remained on its hinges. Beyond the closed door there were no surprises; the final room was also empty.

When they returned to the main chamber, Wons had pulled himself to his feet and he had seemingly recovered his composure. "There is obviously nothing here," he sighed. "Time to go back."

"Hey, wait a minute," protested Fyva. "We've barely begun to explore this place."

"Explore? What's to explore?" Wons blurted out. "An empty room with a hole in the roof. " He turned away, a look of disgust on his face. "This couldn't have been an Angle Being's building anyway. It's much too simple."

"Angle Being or not," argued Fyva, "it certainly wasn't made by anyone from Sebasa, or anywhere else on the coast; we could never work this kind of stone. And this block in the middle of the floor, it's metal. I've never seen metal that hard. And there's a plaque on its side. I think it's a map."

"A map to where and for what?" Wons' tone had now changed from disgust to bitterness. "There's nothing here I want and nothing here that would lead me any place I want to go." He turned and stalked toward the door.

"There's still time before sunset," complained Fyva, "plenty of time to make it down the cliff. We haven't looked at the back of the building or the rest of the peak the building's sitting on. Please, Wons, we'll come away in plenty of time to make it down the first cliff."

Nash had hurried to intercept Wons, and it appeared that Wons might even try to bowl him over, but instead he hesitated and turned back to Fyva.

"Oh, go ahead and explore all you damn well please. You won't find anything." With that, he sulked to the side of the building and plopped down against the wall.

The other four made another circuit of the inside of the building, examining more carefully the interior of each of the four rooms, but as Wons had predicted, it was soon apparent there was indeed nothing to discover. They even tapped the walls, hoping to find secret compartments or the hollow sound of a passageway within those walls, but the stone merely resounded with an unpromising denseness. There were drill-holes in the walls where things might have been attached at some time in the past, but of what these things might have been there were no clues.

When they returned to the main chamber, Wons again came to his feet and stalked toward the door.

"I'm leaving," he called over his shoulder. "You *explorers*," he emphasized the word bitterly, "may explore all you want.

Reluctantly the four filed after him, casting helpless glances over their shoulders as they made their way away from the dome toward the edge of the cliff. By this time Wons had also slowed his pace; the anger had apparently left him and been replaced by dejection.

Wonina now took the lead as they moved toward the cliff's edge, and as she reached that precipice over nothingness, her agonizing scream pierced the others. When Front and Nash reached her side at the same instant and, following her stare, their voices also rose in horror. From the black churning wall of storm that sliced the distant sea, an armada of ships was breaking through, a wedge of ugly, black, round-bottomed vessels, two perfectly straight lines of beetle like specks on the blue sea forming the point of a spear—*pointing directly at the heart of Sebasa!*

3

COUNCIL OF CHAOS
AND COERCION

Nash was first to recover. "Get your ropes on. Down the cliff! *Hurry!*"

Fyva and Front reacted almost simultaneously, reaching and grabbing for the frantic Nash.

"Don't be a fool, Nash," demanded Fyva, struggling to hold him back. "We'll never reach them in time."

Wonina, jerking her eyes away from the distant terror, pleaded, "But we must go. Our families are down there!"

"Yes, yes," Fyva reasoned. "But first we've got to plan. We can't go rushing off like wild animals. We've got to have a plan."

Nash was still struggling to get by Front. "We haven't time for planning. The Outhans are the wild animals. They'll destroy Sebasa. We've got to warn them!"

"Nash, Nash, listen to reason!" Front shouted back. "The Outhans will reach Sebasa it less than three hours. It would take us at least eighteen to reach there, if we reached there at all rushing off half crazy. Warning the people is not the important thing. Look, you can see the small sails of the fishermen already heading home. They know, they know."

"But at least we can be with our families," Wonina moaned.

"And we can fight with our families!" insisted Nash.

"And we can die with our families," concluded Fyva, then added quickly, "or we can come up with a plan that might rescue them."

Nash suddenly ceased his hazardous struggling. "Rescue them?" he asked with piteous hopefulness. "You have a plan, Fyva?"

"I have an idea," she ventured cautiously. "But first we must regain control of ourselves and start thinking straight rather than flying off like frightened goats."

The sun was declining, and a cool breeze now began to bite at them. Nash put his arm rather roughly around the quietly weeping Wonina and began escorting her back to the building. "All right, we'll plan!"

Front and Fyva quickly followed, while Wons trailed behind seemingly too stunned to care what they did. Front and Fyva, working without the others, did their best to replace the large front door to better break the increasing wind. At Fyva's suggestion they then gathered and seated themselves in a circle near the square box at the center of the building.

"I see it this way," began Fyva. "We can leave for home as soon as possible and hope to join in whatever resistance the people have been able to put up, or we can probably save ourselves for a while by heading northward to one of the other towns up the coast. We might even be the first to warn them of the Outhans' coming, though I would guess the Sebasans have already sent messengers north. Or..." and she paused, "we can really do something that might make a difference. We can seek out the weapons of the Angle Beings and strike back!"

The group broke out in a babble of confusion with Nash and Wonina asking rapid argumentative questions and Fyva trying to defend her plan. Front was as surprised as the others by Fyva's suggestion. It was hardly what he expected from the usually reasonable Fyva. He wanted to say something to get the group back on a more rational track, but he was at a loss for words. To his further surprise, Wons was the first to rise above the chaotic noise. His voice was characteristically loud, but uncharacteristically flat and feelingless.

"Fyva, you're insane. There are no Angle Being weapons." The others were suddenly quiet. "And as far as I'm concerned, there aren't even any Angle Beings. It's all just a stupid myth. I say we head back now. I say when we meet the Outhans we'll find they're just people like us. My father and the Officers' Council will reason with them. We're up on this silly mountaintop scaring ourselves like stupid children." He turned as though to rise.

Nash exploded. "Like hell you can reason with those murderers! Was Front's father able to reason with them? Were the other three fishermen able to reason with them? The Steward and that bunch of other snobs would probably sell us out!"

Wons turned back slowly to Nash, but before he could speak, Wonina screamed, "Stop it! Stop it, you two! Nash, you have no right to talk about Wons' father that way. He's a good man. They're all good men, and they're in danger just like we are."

Fyva, struggling to maintain a calm voice, broke in. "Wons, Nash, listen to me. We'll get no place fighting among ourselves." She turned to Wons. "I don't know myself if there were any Angle Beings, but I do know no one today could've constructed this building. The metal and stone here are so hard that it must have taken a tremendous force to cut them, and I have reason to believe that force still exists."

Nash eased himself back down, seemingly forgetting about Wons. "How do you know, Fyva? What've you learned?"

"Look at the plaque on the block above your head," directed Fyva. "I have no way of knowing for sure, but I'm convinced that's a map. Look here, this represents the sun in the west, and this round figure here, that's the dome we're in right now. If you follow these lines they all seem to lead generally in the same direction. Now we know that places having a lot of roads leading to them are seats of government, places of power. And look, the lines all go to one spot. Note the figure here," she pointed emphatically.

"Doesn't that look like a symbol for lightning? What could be more clearly an indication of power?"

Wons broke out laughing, a sneer on his face and in his voice. "What a bunch of mystical nonsense! You have no idea what that map means, or if it's even a map." He started to get to his feet again. "Come on gang, let's get moving."

Front finally found his voice. "Hold it, Wons! I'm not convinced that's a map either, but I know no one has offered a good plan yet, and I'm not leaving until I know where I'm going."

Wons looked surprised; he apparently hadn't anticipated resistance from Front. He sat down slowly.

Fyva used the momentary lull to continue. "Notice how the lines in the map moving toward the source of power make these little bumps over those going sideways. If my idea about the direction of the sun is correct, that would indicate the lines are moving to the southeast, down the back of this mountain, and that those humps are smaller mountains along the way. To reach the power, we must head southeast!" She finished quickly.

"But that's right in the middle of the great swamp!" Wonina said with alarm.

"How do we know that?" Fyva hurriedly countered. "When was the last time one of our people actually crossed these mountains? All we know are just legends from the remote past."

"We do know," cautioned Front, "the mist is quite heavy in that direction. Could we find our way?"

Nash, who had been listening intently, stated firmly, "If there are weapons in that direction, we'll find the way."

Fyva leaned toward Nash. "I'm really convinced the weapons exist, Nash. If we're together, we can reach them."

Wons, his voice more modulated and feelingful than before, seemed to intrude between what promised to become a two-way conversation. "Now look, gang, let's think on this more carefully. I admit I was probably premature wanting to rush off that way. Perhaps it would be a good idea for us to sleep on it." He smiled around the group. "We'll have clearer heads in the morning, and I'm sure we'll be able to see that the wisest plan will be for us to head back to Sebasa. Surely the Sebasans will have either fended off the Outhans or come to terms with them."

"Oh, do you think there's a chance of that?" Wonina asked hopefully. "When I think of my mother and father down there...." she broke off.

Wons put his arms around her. "Don't worry, honey. The Council will be able to handle this."

Nash glared at Wons, and Fyva looked disgusted. Front could see that the group was breaking up into two opposing camps, but he could think of no way to bring them back together.

Fyva raised her voice, irritation finally breaking through. "Look, Wons, my father's on that Council too. I know those people. They're not the nobles you make them out to be. They're just as self-serving as everyone else. If we're going to depend upon anyone in this, it'd better be ourselves."

"Fyva, how can you talk that way about your own father?" pleaded Wonina. "Your father's a good man."

"My father's a businessman," sneered Fyva. "He buys and sells. But at least he buys and sells fish and serpent skins. The other men on that Council, men like the Steward, they deal in people. If they have their way, the Sebasans will be sold to the Outhans!"

"Your father may be a thieving businessman," shouted Wons, his voice higher than usual, "but my father's the Steward, my father's a statesman, my father's the leader of the people of Sebasa, and he would give his life for them."

"Your life maybe, your mother's life maybe, but not *his* life," Fyva sneered.

Front wanted desperately to think of something wise and soothing to stave off this growing bitterness. He was further alarmed when Nash jumped suddenly to his feet. The stocky goat herder's voice was loud, but surprisingly steady, and Front was even more surprised at what Nash said.

"Enough of this! We're getting nowhere with you two bickering. Listen to me, it makes no damn difference what they're doing or not doing down in Sebasa. We're here, and we're going to do what we have to do. Wons, shut up about your father! And that goes for you too, Fyva!"

Wons started to rise, but Nash stepped over him, and Wons sank down again.

Nash then stared down at each of the others from his standing position while they knelt or sat below him, and Front was relieved by the sudden silence that followed. After all the squabbling, Nash's stern, clear voice seemed to be settling the chaos that had been rising within Front's mind.

The silence continued until Nash spoke again, his voice still stern but no longer hard. "This discussion's going no place. Here's what we're going to do. Fyva, I want you to study the map further or look for any other clues around this place that might give us some idea of where to go from here. Front, we're going to need something to keep us warm tonight. Gather all the burnable debris you can find. If you can reach them, pull down those birds' nests from around the edge of the roof. Wonina, we'll need food." He turned to Wons and his voice softened further. "Wons, you and I should work together. Let's explore the perimeters of this plateau and see if there's another way down."

Wons, still seated and looking up at Nash, seemed about to put up an argument, but Wonina rose and moved between them. She placed her head briefly on Nash's shoulder. "You're right, Nash, we've been behaving like children. I'll fix something for us to eat." She turned to Wons. "Give me your packs, all of you; I'll take a little food from each."

Fyva turned to the plaque on the metal square and began to reexamine it. Front, sensing that the breakup of the group would give Wons no audience for further argument, quickly rose and began gathering the few twigs that had fallen from the nests above. When he looked back, Nash had turned and was moving purposely away, and, to Front's relief, Wons was following, his shoulders stooped and his head down.

Front had finished cleaning the floor of likely fuel and had deposited his small supply in the room with the intact door when Fyva called him over to the block in the center of the floor.

"Look, Front, I've been trying to pry this plaque away from the stone. No matter how hard I try, my knife won't bend or even scratch it. Whoever they were, they certainly knew a lot more than we do to be able to create such metal."

Front nodded in agreement. It had not occurred to him to doubt that people further advanced than the Sebasans had build this structure.

"What do you think might've happened to these people?" Fyva asked.

Front guessed that Fyva already had her own answer to that question, but he welcomed the opportunity to share his own speculations. "This place looks like it was very carefully evacuated. Whoever they were, they left almost nothing behind. I'd guess the roof caved in much later." He stooped and picked a small scrap from the floor. "I don't believe this material from the roof will burn, but it's certainly not as strong as the stone or the metal."

"I don't think we should try burning it," Fyva recommended. "Who knows, the fumes might be dangerous."

Front hadn't thought about that, but he decided to follow her advice. He remembered then he needed more fuel, however.

"How about giving me a hand," he asked. "See if you can boost me up the side of that wall. If I can get a grip on that ledge, I can pull myself up and I'll be able to walk around and pull down most of those birds' nests."

She nodded, and he helped her to her feet. "By the way the temperature is dropping," she added, "we'll need as much fuel as we can get for tonight."

As they walked to the side of the building, Fyva placed her arm around Front's waist. "I really appreciate how you've conducted yourself," she said warmly. "While the others were flying off the handle, you always seemed to maintain your calm. You're someone who can be depended upon."

Front felt both pleased and uncomfortable with Fyva's compliment. "I'm calm because I can't think of anything to say," he laughed nervously.

"But when you do talk, you make sense."

"Yeah, I'm slow but sure."

She squeezed his waist and then released him to cup her hands in readiness to boost him up the wall.

Her height and surprising strength were more than adequate, and Front was able to reach the ledge and further hoist himself up. He then began working his way from the caved in edge of the dome around the back to the far side of the building, tossing down nests to Fyva who followed below.

When he reached the back of the building, he took time to examine the plateau outside. Through the gap in the roof, he could see Nash and Wons trudging along the outer perimeter of the ledge. As he let his gaze wander over the scene below, he saw something he might not have noticed from on the ground. Below him, off the side, there was a circle carved into the flat surface that surrounding the building. Radiating from the center of that circle were lines that stopped where they the met the circle. He realized instantly that he had seen this design before. Right in the middle of the Commons there was such a circle, though it was larger than the one he was now seeing, perhaps twenty feet in diameter compared this of twelve feet.

After he dropped down from the ledge he described his discovery to Fyva. They went outside and examined the circle, trying to slide their blades into the almost imperceptible slice in the stone. That proved futile; the similarity between this circle and the circle on the Commons also occurred to Fyva. But just as the people of the town had frequently tried to make sense out of the Commons, Front and Fyva were equally baffled by what they had discovered on Mount Stareye. They gave up when Nash and Wons came by, returning from their reconnoitering.

A thickening mist was now rolling in from over the backside of Mount Stareye. In unspoken agreement, the four of them trudged toward the front of the ledge for one last look at their world below. No one seemed surprised when the view from the front of Mount Stareye was also obscured by the thickening mist. Over that rising mist Front could barely make out the turbulent black line marking the edge of the storm that had come to dominate their world. Without words, the four turned back toward the dome.

Wonina had followed Front's lead and set up their evening meal in the same room as his kindling. Nash nodded his approval of the small but tidy stash of nests and twigs in a corner and at the tiny cooking fire Wonina had kindled in the middle of the room. He then shut and attempted to secure the door behind them. Front chuckled to himself at the futility of that gesture, but he sympathized with the feeling that must lay behind it. The Outhans were still far away and no one, not even the Angle Beings, were likely to disturb them on this lonely peak. Still, there was a need to shut out the misty unknown of the night.

They ate in silence their meal of fish pudding, dried fruit, and crumbly dry biscuits. Only Wonina and Nash seemed to be communicating as Nash occasionally patted the girl and as he accepted food she handed or even fed him. Front, who was seated across from the two, tried to avoid looking at them.

Wonina finally broke the silence. "Be sure you either eat all your food or save it. We're going to have to be stingy with all supplies from now on."

As the others carefully repacked their uneaten food, Nash spoke. "I believe we're all in agreement we must do something to help our people in Sebasa." Without waiting for reaction from the group, he continued on. "We've reviewed all possible plans. Although I know the risk, it seems the smartest decision is to find some way of striking back at the Outhans. I say we go in search of the Angle Beings' weapons."

Wons stirred but before he could speak, Fyva interrupted, and her words seemed almost a continuation of Nash's opening speech. "Front and I have further examined the map on the side of the metal square. We've agreed that only an advanced people could have produced such materials, and it seems logical that a people so advanced and with such skills could indeed have produced weapons with great power."

"But...." Wons attempted to speak again.

Fyva continued without breaking pace. "Front and I also discovered something else." This seemed to stop Wons. "There's a circular design up here on Mount Stareye, just like the one carved on the Commons. This means that the Commons must also have been constructed by the Angle Beings. It seems logical to assume that these are not the only Angle Being structures, that Angle Being outposts or even cities must have been built all over this area. If this is true, it seems only logical that the existence of the great source of power indicated on the map is a distinct possibility."

Front didn't remember agreeing with Fyva on any of the conclusions she was now presenting. He could see how their discoveries might have led her to her conclusions, but he wasn't sure he could go as far as she was going. Before he could object, however, Wonina protested.

"But we have no way of knowing if the map is accurate, and it's all so risky."

Nash knelt and put his arm around her reassuringly, before standing again. "Wonina, no need to worry. We're all in this together, and as Wons said, 'when the people go together, there's always fair weather!'"

"That wasn't me, that was someone who didn't exist, named Emanuel," Wons muttered bitterly.

"Emanuel might not have existed," Nash said, almost indulgently, "but we do know the Outhans exist." His voice became more forceful. "And we all agree we must combat the Outhans. Is there anyone here who is not against the Outhans?"

Even Wons remained silent at this question.

"Then it's agreed," Nash concluded. "Tomorrow we head down the back side of Mount Stareye, toward the southeast following the map that Fyva discovered." Without waiting for either disagreement or agreement, he began describing his plans, and giving orders. "Wons and I discovered that the back side is not so steep as the front of this mountain. We probably won't even need to use the ropes. Fyva, if you can't get that map off the wall, I want you to spend some time tomorrow morning memorizing it. Wonina, from here on out you take charge of the meals.

Each person will keep his own supplies, but you make sure that no one eats too much at any one time. Front, we're going to rotate the watch tonight; you're up first."

"The watch?" asked Front and Wons at almost the same time.

Nash continued as if he had not been interrupted. "Front, you did a good job in choosing this room. It will keep out the wind, but it's also almost airtight. We've got to make sure our fire doesn't go out or that we don't suffocate. Burn just a few twigs at a time, and maybe open the door occasionally. The order of the watch will be this; Front first, then Fyva, followed by Wons, and then Wonina. I'll be last. I want to be sure to get all of you up early in the morning. We've got to get an early start."

Wons' voice was almost petulant as he complained, "Why should I be the one to have to wake up in the middle of the night?"

Nash was already standing and moving to arrange his sleeping bag. He turned abruptly on Wons. "Damn it, I've had enough of your sniveling! You're either in this all the way with the rest of us, or you can damned well go back down to Sebasa by yourself!"

Wons, who had started to rise, sank down again.

Wonina quickly intervened, "Nash, please."

With one final glare at Wons, Nash turned almost jovially to Wonina. "Into your sleeping bag, honey. It'll be a cold night."

Front looked with concern toward Wons, but there seemed nothing he could say or do. Wons spread his palms outward and then dropped them in his lap. After a moment he too went to spread his own sleeping bag.

As directed, Front carefully stoked the small fire in the center of the room and then went to the door to reassure himself that there was enough air coming in. The small draft he felt entering beneath the door was enough to assure him they wouldn't suffocate. When he finished his few chores he wrapped his own sleeping bag around his shoulders and sat down before the fire, facing the door. The others had already arranged themselves for sleep, Nash flanked by the two girls and Wons an obvious distance apart from the others. Front noticed that Nash and Wonina's bags were so close together that they seemed to be in one bag. Front didn't like that thought, so he chose to think of something else. He listened first to the wind whistling through the partially destroyed dome of building. He could feel rather than see the mist swirling about and through the empty structure beyond the closed door. The small fire before him seemed to suddenly grow dimmer, and he hastened to add another small twig. The fire brightened, but the darkness still hung heavy around him, stretching out into the night beyond the edge of the platform, engulfing all he knew.

By now he realized the Outhans must be within sight of Sebasa. He forced himself to consider what defenses the townsmen might have been able to employ. Sebasans were certainly not warlike people. Mostly, they were simple fishermen, traders, and goat herders. The only weapons they had were their slings, their fishing gaffs, and an occasional harpoon for larger fish. From what the fishermen said, those who had seen the Outhans' ships, they were obviously armored, and each Outhan carried an identical short sword and a small spear. Their uniformity made them seem well trained soldiers, and Front guessed that's exactly what they were. As he thought about it, he presumed and even hoped that the Sebasans would merely give in to the Outhans so as to cause themselves as little harm as possible. He tried to think positively about what seemed inevitable. After all, what did they know about the real intentions of the Outhans? No one understood their oath. It seemed to be some kind of religious vow; there had been no indication that their intention was to conquer anyone. After all, wasn't religion a good thing? Wasn't a religious vow intended to achieve some good? He was almost beginning to feel better when he thought to wonder what the Outhans would have to do to fulfill their vow that they couldn't have done in their own country.

He shook his head. There was so little information about the Outhans. It seemed futile to try to figure out what they might do. He tried to turn his mind to something else. What about the Angle Beings? He couldn't reasonably go along with Fyva's conviction that the few clues they had discovered on Mount Stareye proved anything about those mysterious vanished beings. Certainly the evidence didn't convince him that they would find weapons or any legendary source of power by traveling to the southeast. He did, he realized, seem to be gaining faith that there had in fact been someone, by whatever name they were called, who had occupied this country before the Sebasans. The similarity between the stonework and the circles found on the Commons and at this outpost on Mount Stareye was too great to be ignored. With a start it occurred to him that there might be something underneath the Commons. Just as they had tried to pry beneath the circles here, with better tools they could do the same on the Commons. Could there in fact be weapons underneath the Commons? Just as a feeling of hope was returning to him, he remembered their predicament. The Outhans were probably going to occupy Sebasa, perhaps even camp on the Commons. What do you say to someone occupying your town? he wondered. "Pardon me while I dig beneath your feet for weapons to use against you?"

He got up and began pacing slowly about the room, as far away from the sleepers as possible. He even considered going outside, but reasoned it wouldn't be wise to open the door and let escape the little warmth that had finally risen in the room. He glanced into the shadowy darkness at the huddling figures of his companions, particularly at the blending forms of Nash and Wonina. Though his feelings didn't agree with his thoughts, he reminded himself that those two were in fact appropriately together. It was none of his business that they chose to be intimate. He was the outsider, the one without rights, and he resolved again to maintain his proper distance from Wonina.

As he continued his pacing, however, he couldn't ignore his confused feelings about Nash's recent behavior. He had come to like the steady, grumbling, but dependable Nash, and he was certainly pleased that Nash had settled the petty bickering that was going on earlier in the evening. He was not sure, however, he altogether liked this new Nash. Surely with Nash's new firmness there was no more arguing, but there was very little diversity of opinion being expressed either. He paused in his pacing. He suddenly realized that he was the only one who had voiced no opinion. Wons had tried to disagree; Wonina had questioned; and Nash and Fyva apparently agreed. Only he had remained entirely silent.

But then what was his opinion, he sighed. I certainly feel it would be pointless to go back to Sebasa now, and I don't want to run away to the other towns. He thought of the swirling darkness beyond the door and shuddered. I'm surely not going to stay up here. So where else? Nash did say that descent would be easier down the backside of the mountain. Perhaps the wisest thing, he concluded, would be to use that back slope as the safest way to descend at least on the upper part of the mountain. Then, if the mist were indeed too thick for safe navigation, they could always skirt around the edge, back to the front of the mountain.

Even as he settled on this plan, Front was not entirely satisfied. He felt he was deciding by failing to decide. But how was he to know what was wise? With so little information, on what basis does one make a decision? Reasoning gave him no assurance, and he found himself peering into the flickering gloom at the shadowy form of Wonina. He was taken by a desire to be close beside her, enclosed in her gentle warmth, no longer alone. Chances are Wonina would follow Nash, he realized, and chances are he would follow Wonina. He signed, perhaps that was all the assurance that reasoning was going to give him.

4

You Must Build Boats

Front was awakened by Wonina's protest.

"Nash, not now. I just got to sleep."

Nash responded gruffly but good-naturedly. "Come on, baby, move it."

Front had to fight down a feeling of outrage, reminding himself that their affair was none of his business. He felt a little foolish, however, when Nash began shaking each of the others in the sleep bag clad group. It was apparently morning and, true to his sword, Nash was getting them off to an early start. The group was groggy, though compliant, whereas Nash seemed almost jovial. He went from person to person, jostling and encouraging them in a playful manner.

It seemed no time at all before they had finished their morning meal and were trooping out of the dome into the fog filled semidarkness. The thick mists through which they were moving reminded Front of his lack of conviction about their plan, but not wanting to risk spoiling Nash's playful mood, he found himself putting off mentioning his alternate strategy of skirting the mountain should the back way be too difficult.

The boulders on the back of the mountain were slick with moisture, but the incline was such that they were able to descend face forward, mostly on their bottoms, sliding down from perch to perch. It was a good test of the durability of the hard gray nodules on the sea-serpent pants they were wearing. After a time of bounce, slide, and perch, however, those same hard nodules began to test the durability of their bottoms.

Nash had taken the lead and instructed Wonina to follow him. With Front in the middle, followed by Wons and then Fyva, it seemed an unusual order. The sense of it came clear to Front when he heard Fyva alternately prodding and urging the sluggish Wons.

Eventually the sloping lessened to the point where they could begin to use their feet rather than their bottoms.

"Use your walking staffs now," Nash directed, and they unstrapped from their packs the staffs they had not been able to use since beginning the steepest part of the climb the previous afternoon.

With the descent less arduous, Front was able to take more notice of his surroundings. Their gray world was brightening, and patches of color began to appear in startling contrast to the grayness. His eyes were first drawn to yellow and blue lichen sprouting from crevices in the larger boulders. Then small trees began to appear out of the mist, dark green evergreens, a species that was relatively rare on the western slopes of the mountain.

As the incline further lessened, the trees grew larger, and the group was soon moving in and out of darkness among taller, mist shrouded trees. The fog diffused light beclouded his sense of direction, and Front was gripped by a strange sense of familiarity as he descended slowly into this moisture laden atmosphere. In fact, he was so involved in experiencing his senses that when a right angle turn around to the front of the mountain became possible, he was no longer interested, preferring rather to follow Nash, giving over responsibility to the leader to guide him safely down the mountain and into his future.

As the trees grew even taller, the mist seemed to lift above them, and the blue and yellow lichen gave way to a thick green moss that now began to cover the trunks of the trees and spread over fallen logs and boulders along the way. Soon their whole world became a rolling carpet of soft lumpiness. The downward slope and the spongy turf were making Front's steps springy and his head light, and this lightness seemed to affect the whole group as they bounced down the slope at an increasing pace. It seemed to Front he was gliding over the ground, covering territory with unreal speed as green softness floated by his almost blurred vision.

It finally dawned on Front where he had experienced such otherworldliness before, as he swam alongside and through algae covered reefs caves, gliding along in the soft quiet world beneath Sebasa Bay. The bright fog diffused light above him was now the same as the silvery reflection of the sky on the undersurface of the sea. He expected any moment to see fish or sea-serpents dart out from the many dark holes and caves that speckled the reef. With the familiarity of this new world no longer a puzzle, Front now allowed himself to go along with his illusions, and he even began to see dark movements at the corners of his eye.

He wasn't sure just when, but after a time the friendly, familiar illusion began to feel less comfortable. He began blinking his eyes and reminding himself there were no fish out of water, no reefs on mountain slopes. The illusion faded, but the uncomfortable feeling persisted. His mind now clearer, he came to recognize the feeling; it was a feeling of being followed—of being watched. Soon Front was stumbling where he had formerly glided over moss covered stones, as he turned his head from left to the right, spying for what he thought must be there.

The feeling was so strong that without further delay he quickly moved ahead to whisper his suspicions in Nash's ear. Nash was instantly alert, as if he might have had similar feelings just below the surface of his consciousness.

"You watch left, I'll watch right," he responded, also whispering. "Stay alert!"

Almost imperceptibly Nash began to slow the pace of the group so that they began to close ranks. The others, apparently without knowing quite what was happening, also began peering to the right and left. It seemed to Front that the bright soft greenness about them became darker and the ceiling of mist above them, which had been rising, now began to descend and close in. The softness under foot that had bounced them along seemed suddenly soggy and treacherous, and he found that he was crouched and heavy as he picked his way along.

Time ached onward, time to fill with new suspicions. In each new dark gaping hole in the moss-encrusted rocks, Front's imagination created greater dangers, until finally that last lurking fear was allowed to emerge. He denied the thought as soon as it came. Those dark shadowy glimpses could not be Outhans! It was not possible for those monsters to have come so far inland in so short a time.

It was Nash who saw it first. With more of a hiss than a bark, he commanded, "Load your slings! Front, to the right!

"Wons, to the left. Girls, get close to me!"

Without even bothering to look where Nash must have seen something, Front jumped to his position and fumbled a stone from his stone pouch to load his sling. He didn't know how effective his hunting weapon would be against whatever might be lurking beyond that green menace, but with Nash at his back, he felt almost ready for the challenge. They waited in silence broken only by the breathing of five anxious people. Nothing moved and nothing else sounded. Only the clawing mist above them seemed alive in their suddenly deadened world.

Front's readiness for action was almost affronted when he heard Nash's sudden laughter. He turned to look where Nash was pointing. There, peering cautiously around a tree trunk was a face with large yellow eyes. Almost as if encouraged by the laughter, the animal moved into full view.

"It's a little dog!" giggled Wonina.

"No, no," corrected Fyva. "I believe it's a bear."

"What's a bear?" asked Front, never having seen anything quite like this plump, fluffy creature.

"They're more common up on the North Coast," Fyva explained. "They apparently live in the mountains or in colder country. I think they're harmless, at least until they are much larger than this one."

The whole group relaxed as one, and Wonina even went forward to try to pet the creature. The temporary courage the animal had displayed at the group's first stillness apparently left him, and he scurried off out of reach and then out of sight.

Nash wasted little time in reasserting his discipline over the group, but his voice was now almost fatherly as he insisted, "Okay, people. Let's hit this soggy trail again." He moved ahead without looking back. The others obediently fell into line and trudged after Nash.

Nash now set a less demanding pace, and a new mood of lightness seemed to permeate the group. Wonina called ahead to Nash, commenting on new sights that came into view. Even Wons responded with agreement or disagreement to Fyva's speculation about the origins of many of the new species they were seeing. The stillness about them began to be interrupted by other sounds, particularly and persistently the sound of babbling water. They soon encountered a small stream that cut a speckled black and silver pathway through the green carpet. After pausing to drink, they replenished their water flasks, which had been depleted during their stay on Mount Stareye. This fresh water was cold, crisp, and refreshing, and it seemed to Front there was even a greenness in its taste.

Nash allowed them only a brief rest. He turned to Fyva. "It seems the stream moves in the general direction we want to take. Better check your mental map. What do you think?"

"I've been noticing. We've been moving slightly to the right of our southeast direction. In fact, following this stream should correct that drift."

"Good. Let's move on."

They were already under way before it occurred to Front that he hadn't felt the slightest inclination to doubt Nash's confident tone. As he thought back on the recent events, he reasoned that the firm, sure way Nash had commanded the group in the presence of their supposed danger was very reassuring to experience. Front imagined that Nash's behavior must be very much like that of any military commander, with quick decisive commands that stimulated instant responses from his troops, precise responses that were needed in the face of sudden danger. It was very reassuring and comfortable to accept without questioning such sure commands. There was a lightness in the absence of responsibility accompanying such acceptance. As Front's mind further considered the military analogy, however, and particularly when he remembered that he had associated the alleged danger of the dark furry bear with the Outhan menace ever lurking on the edge of his consciousness, he no longer felt so comfortable. He remembered the Outhans were also militaristic. He recalled the fishermen had said there was always only one person who spoke for all of the armor clad ships' crews. After making this association, Front resolved not to give in so easily to the temptation to mindlessly follow Nash's orders.

The stream they were trailing beside grew wider and straighter. It was shallow, and here and there flattened boulders broke the surface. At times those flat rocks were close enough together to make a pathway across the stream. Front's mood was now such that he had to resist a temptation to bounce across the stream on those inviting pathways.

Nash kept the group moving ever downstream, however, and soon, up ahead, the trees seemed to be parting, revealing more of the bright gray sunless sky. The stream beside them lurched into action, and the babble and gurgle of its voice became a hiss and then a roar, and suddenly the stream itself disappeared into that gray sky. Nash held up his hand to halt the group, and then moved cautiously forward. He moved to his left at a slight angle, and the group followed. He then stopped abruptly, and knelt on the edge of a broad ledge. The others did likewise, and crept forward beside him. Front heard gasps around him, and he felt his own breath taken away. That gay stream he had moments earlier wanted to spritely prance across poured forth from its bed and dashed into space, dropping down, down, into a swirling mist of endless nothingness.

Front's feelings on recovering his breath were awe and fascination, until he imagined himself, having slipped on those slime-covered rocks upstream, sliding down, shooting forth into space, and falling with that endlessly falling water. Then his fascination changed to fear.

He heard Wonina's voice, sounding like a whisper above the roar of the falls. "What do we do now, Nash?"

Nash, who had reached the falls first and was seemingly less in awe than the others, had apparently already examined the surrounding terrain. "We simply walk back up the trail thirty to forty yards," he answered, "and then head off to the left. The slope is nowhere near as steep in that direction, and we'll meet up with the stream again down below."

Front, trying to be true to his resolve not to follow Nash's commands instantly, checked for himself and found that in fact Nash was right. Off to the left it was obvious that the slope would be much more manageable. They backtracked briefly and again fell in behind Nash.

They soon discovered, however, that although the slope was manageable, it was not easy. The evergreens were now interspersed with small bushy trees that seemed oddly twisted and which flattened themselves against the slope, allowing good handholds, but also making themselves into nuisances as they blocked the way and hooked and tugged at the knobs on their serpent-skin clothes. Fortunately, the thick moss of the evergreen forest they were leaving seemed to have difficulty in growing on the slope. The way was therefore not so treacherously slick. Nevertheless, the way was tiring, and after a time, Front began to find that his mind was slipping into thoughtlessness once again. He had to concentrate entirely on gripping one bush after another and then sliding downward and then catching himself again. More than once he bumped into Wonina who was just ahead of him, and likewise he was prodded by Wons who was behind him.

It was a tired and relieved crew that finally reached the bottom of the slope. Wonina, the food keeper, suggested that it was time to eat, but Nash stated they would press onward. Too much time had been lost in descending the slope, he insisted.

After a time, Front was struck by the silence of the new forest they had entered. Eventually he realized it was the sound of the stream he missed. Where was the stream? Surely they should have crossed its bed by now, a bed that should be considerably broader below the base of the falls and thus impossible to skip over, even in the mist.

Apparently the group was beginning to miss the sound as well. Finally, Wonina voiced their concern. "Nash, have we gone too far? Shouldn't we have met up with the stream by now?"

"Just a little further ahead," he called over his shoulder.

"But it's way past time for our noon meal and all of us are getting tired and weak."

It seemed to Front that Nash's tone displayed less confidence, that the missing stream was disturbing him as well, but he still insisted, "Not yet," and strode on, moving even further ahead of the group.

The others began to string themselves out, and Nash turned back with annoyance. "Catch up there! This is no time to get lost."

Obediently the group closed ranks and trudged ahead. Nash now lengthened his stride and set a steady cadence that reminded Front of his earlier disturbing thoughts about Nash's militaristic manner. As they pressed onward, Front was becoming exhausted. His earlier doubts about the wisdom of their decision to head down the back of the mountain began to creep back into consciousness. Where was Nash taking them anyway? He was stalking ahead as if he knew where he was going, but the very insistence on this straightforward direction further increased Front's doubt. He was about to demand a halt himself when Fyva spoke up from the rear.

"Nash," she called ahead. "If I remember correctly, we're veering away from the path our map directed. I suggest we halt and eat while I rethink our direction."

Nash stopped and paused, still staring ahead. Eventually he turned and barked, "All right, all right, let's stop! Wonina, make sure you check to see no one eats too much." With that command, he unstrapped his pack and sat down somewhat apart from the rest of the group to eat his noon meal.

Front noticed the others in the group also took seats separated from one another. As he unpacked and began eating his own food, he was sadly amused to see Wonina peering through the gloom, apparently checking each person's food intake to see that they were not excessive. He caught her eye and smiled, trying to show that he understood, but his smile only seemed to make her unhappier.

After hastily eating her brief meal, Fyva went to where Nash was brooding, and they entered into a hushed conversation. Fyva would point and talk, and Nash would shake his head. Eventually, however, Fyva seemed to win her way. When Nash ordered the group again to its feet, he dictated a change in their direction.

"We all know we left the bottom of the slope going in the right direction. My guess is we must've crossed over a natural bridge in this heavy mist, and the stream passed underneath us. At any rate, we'll head back at an angle to the left, and that way we'll probably meet the stream as it comes out from underneath the natural bridge. All right, let's move." This time Nash waited until the entire group was on its feet and assembled before he took off ahead of them.

The natural bridge explanation was one possibility, Front conceded. It must have been quite a wide bridge, however, since he recalled at no time hearing the stream ahead or behind them.

But then, after pondering this mystery for a moment, it occurred to Front that it could all be irrelevant. Even if they reencountered the stream there was no guarantee it would lead them to what they hoped to find. With that thought, his former doubts began to return, and as the way dragged on, those doubts had ample time to gnaw at him. Nor was the changing terrain any encouragement that they had made the right decision. The lush carpeting of greenery had now given way to patches of dark earth and decaying leaves, the slippery greenness had changed to slippery brownness, and mud was beginning to thicken on his boots.

He tried to ignore this new discouragement by studying the changing flora around him. The trees were again growing taller, but now the evergreens had been replaced by a more familiar sight—familiar and yet unfamiliar. More and more he was seeing his old acquaintance, the boat-bark tree, but such boat-bark trees as these he had never seen. It was typical for boat-bark in the moister hollows on the dry side of the mountain to have trunks of up to two feet in circumference. When the bark was stripped smoothly from the trunks, the two-foot wide pieces could be used in overlapping strips to cover the frames of their fishing boats. The boat-bark trees in this lush, dank forest were almost big enough for one tree to provide the continuous skin for a single fishing vessel. Front estimated that some of the tree trunks he passed were as much as eight feet in circumference. He was already considering the contribution such trees could make to the ease of boat building back in Sebasa when he felt Fyva at his side.

"Have you ever seen such trees?" Fyva exclaimed. "Think what a profit we could make from harvesting in this area. What fools we've been for not exploring back here more thoroughly. There's a crop here for a whole new industry for Sebasa. My guess is these great trees only grow in our southern reaches of the coastline, that up north the altitude and the cold would not allow such growth."

Front notice that there was almost passion on Fyva's face and in her voice as she continued. "We could become the boat materials center for the whole coastline."

Front smiled and started to raise the question of how they would transport the material back to the coast. It would be necessary to find a less arduous route into these forests than the one they had followed, and the mountain ridge to the immediate east and north of Sebasa was said to be impassable. But Fyva had already bounced back to her place in line before he could voice his reservation about her fancied scheme. Front was then left to ponder a new concern. How indeed could they make it back to Sebasa without once again going up that long slippery slope If there were another pass through the mountains, surely earlier explorers would have found it, and these trees would be common knowledge among the fishermen in Sebasa. He guessed that the Sebasans, content with their prosperous coastal existence, never had much incentive to stray across the high passes of the Up-back mountain range to descend into this constant muck.

His thoughts of easy prosperity became even more remote as the boat-bark trees were soon joined by gnarled, barkless trees, and the mucky ground beneath their feet changed to a shallow floor of water, a dark pungent leaf smelling water oozing out in all directions as far as Front could see.

Nash hesitated only briefly before trudging ahead in his constant straight line. Front shook his head and followed. Although Nash's imperiousness was becoming more irritating, Front had to admire his tenacity. Their insistent leader had maintained his straight line by blazing a trail on almost every tree he passed and then by constantly checking the rear to line up the harsh gashes he had inflicted on the trees.

Those gashed trees were now growing further and further apart, however, as trees became scarcer in this shallow bog. Front began to wonder if they had at last wandered into the great swamp, the legendary dismal swamp of the east and south. After a while he even started to amuse himself by looking for those monsters he had heard of since childhood. Soon, at each new splash and ripple ahead of him, he looked and then came to half expect the awesome sight of a slithering, bejeweled giant serpent rearing to engulf them in its fang-filled jaws. He knew the image was absurd, but eventually he found it necessary to remind himself that the serpents he knew of were not amphibious, that the water here was so shallow it could barely cover a good size worm. In spite of his fleeting self-induced fears, he continued to carry on his fancied encounters. It seemed better to be mildly afraid than to allow his mind to dwell on the constant sloshing and oozing and sucking of the mud about his exhausted legs.

He realized the others must also be feeling that exhaustion. Ahead of him he saw Wonina as she struggled to catch up to Nash and place a restraining hand on his waist. Nash merely shoved her hand away and continued on. Wonina looked back and, realizing that Front had observed her interaction with Nash, quickly looked away to plow on with more determination. From behind him, Front also heard Wons mumbling and, although he could not make out the words that were swallowed by the sloshing water, Wons' meaning was clear.

Front's mood and his steps were suddenly lightened, however, when there was an uptilt to the land, and again boat-bark trees and drier earth appeared. Nash's mood seemed to change also as he slowed and allowed Wonina to catch up with him. When he put his arm about her shoulder, however, her stony stiffness was apparently enough to re-dampen his mood, and he moved on again alone.

To their right the land sloped slightly, and to Front's surprise, Nash now veered in that direction.

He soon learned why. A small sluggish stream had begun cutting its way in the general direction they were going, so Nash had apparently rediscovered his stream.

As the stream continued to cut more deeply into the gradually elevating terrain, it gained more life. Nash called over his shoulder, "We're back on course again. Okay, gang, let's pick up the pace."

There was not much response to Nash's command, but he did not repeat his insistence.

The stream soon broadened into a smoothly flowing brook that, before long, poured into a broad pond, the far side of which faded away into the mist. The group began skirting this pond, looking expectantly for some new change in terrain. What they finally saw was not what Front had hoped for. There was a unanimous groan, and they all stopped abruptly. Oozing out of the mist, and beginning to cut across the pond to their right was what appeared to be a wall of moss covered steps. It was obvious, however, that those steps quickly became giant steps and finally ended in a sheer uplifting tower of moss that faded into the nothingness of the gray sky.

"Oh, my God!" gasped Wons.

Nash turned on him. "I warned you, no more sniveling! You'd turn back at a goat fence. Now come on, let's explore before we give up."

He stalked off to his left, apparently looking for a possible route through or around the impasse blocking their way. The group again strung out behind Nash as, in his determination to prove himself right, Nash seemed almost to have forgotten the others. Front soon lost Nash in the haze ahead, and for a while he and Wonina walked side by side, but said nothing to one another.

Front was growing concerned about Nash when they abruptly came upon him standing still and staring up at the immense green height that climbed unchanging above him. This wall of green also continued in the direction Nash had been leading them and seemed to continue on in that direction endlessly.

Nash turned and brushed past the others. "All right, let's go back. We'll head off to the right of the pond. But hurry, time's running out."

They returned to the pond, but by peering across they could see the immense moss wall merely continued on from the right side of the pond just as endlessly as it had from the left. "We can't waste anymore time," Nash growled. Savagely, Nash turned to the moss barrier and began clutching at the soft turf, pulling himself up the steep slope. He had gone no more than ten feet, however, when he came tumbling down with a handful of moss in either fist.

Wons laughed sardonically, but the others were silent.

Nash started to lunge to his feet, but Fyva quickly moved to restrain him. "Nash, you've been pushing us too hard, and you've been pushing yourself even harder. It's time now to stop and rest...and think. These people will never get there at this pace, and we're going nowhere until we come up with a better plan."

Nash continued to glare at Wons, but he remained seated.

All right, rest!" he barked. "But don't get too comfortable."

All but Fyva threw themselves on the soft ground and sought to stretch and relax their taut muscles. Fyva moved along the edge of the pond peering across at the wall. After a moment, with the new silence brought on by the cessation of their sloshing feet, Front thought he could hear a rushing noise. He studied the surface of the pond and saw that in fact the water was moving rapidly toward the wall. He guessed that Fyva was also aware of the moving water as she studied intently the face of the distant wall across the pond.

"There's a cut in the cliff," she reported. "The stream flows on through what looks like a narrow channel. There's a way through this embankment if only we can follow that channel."

She reached gingerly down into the pond, and Front could see her arm disappear into the depth. She turned back and announced with chagrin, "Well, we won't follow on foot it seems."

Nash was instantly on his feet. "Then we'll go by boat!"

"What?" they all asked at once.

"I said, we must build a boat!"

"Build a boat?" Wons asked incredulously. "Are you out of your mind?"

"Look," continued Nash, hastily. "No problem. We're surrounded by material for building a boat, and we have our own seaman." He turned to Front, "Right, Front? It can be done," he insisted, "it can, can't it?"

Front had to admit that in this forest of boat-bark trees they had the basics for building boats, but they would need binding material.

Fyva was already thinking ahead of him. "Look, this long marsh grass is tremendously tough fiber. We merely have to braid three strands together, and we'll have as strong a rope as we'd ever need."

"But you can't make boats watertight with binding cords," objected Wonina.

"They don't have to be watertight," insisted Nash. "You all know boat-bark floats. It's mostly air pockets covered with fiber. And look, you've never seen boat-bark as thick as this!" He pounded one of the trees with his fists, and turned again to Front for confirmation.

"Yes, I suspect you're right," Front agreed. "A boat made of this would float, even without being watertight."

"Then it's agreed. Here's what we do."

Before he could continue his commands, Wonina again protested.

"I don't like this, Nash. Even if we do build a boat, how do we know the stream goes through this barrier? How do we know anything but the water's cold and the boats will be flimsy, and I'm tired, and all of us need rest?"

"Look, my pretty friend," growled Nash. "I'm getting tired of your complaining. We haven't time for rest. It's late afternoon now, and we have to get these boats built and through that pass before the sun goes down. If we wait any longer, we won't be able to see our way. We're not wasting time here when we could be moving."

Wonina didn't seem to be impressed by his logic, so Nash raised his voice. "Have you forgotten what we're up against? All of you, remember Sebasa? Remember the Outhans? Do you remember what those monsters are doing to our people right now? Your damn tiredness and complaining can wait!"

At the mention of the Outhans and the people back home, the obstinacy on Wonina's face changed and etched into concern. She bit her lip and turned away.

Nash took advantage of the silence to continue his orders. "Fyva, you and Wonina begin cutting blades of grass and plaiting them into cords. You two," he motioned to Front and Wons, "let's select the best looking tree and peel the bark."

Front struggled to his feet and glanced around. He had no trouble finding a tree that was approximately eight feet in circumference. He drew his knife and began studying the shape and condition of the bark. Nash was already beginning to cut into the tree.

"Wait! Wait, Nash," he cautioned.

"No time to wait!"

"You'll waste more time if you don't plan ahead," said Front firmly.

"This is my game, remember? If you want to build usable boats, you have to build them right."

Grumbling, Nash pulled back his knife.

"The first question is, what kind of boats are we going to build?" mused Front.

"Just a simple boat that will carry us till we can get through that short passage."

Front shook his head. "There's no way we're going to build one boat big enough to carry all of us. I suggest we make individual boats. They'll be much sturdier and more durable."

Nash looked at Wons, but then turned away without waiting for Wons to comment. "All right, then it's individual boats. Where do I cut?"

"Wait a minute. You're still in too big a hurry. Think about this problem. Even though I said this material would float, I really don't think that we're going to be able to make even individual boats that will be stable enough to hold a person sitting high and dry inside. My guess is we're going to have to build something more like a small raft that will hold most of a person's weight and leave his lower legs free to paddle."

"What?" gasped Wons. "I'm not going any place half submerged in that cold water!"

Without even looking at Wons, Nash growled, "You'll do what you're told," and barely changing his tone of voice, he asked Front, "You're sure that's the best way?"

"No, I'm not sure of anything, but that's what I recommend."

"All right, just tell me where to cut."

"The useable bark starts about a foot above the ground. Below that point it's too gnarled with root knots."

Front began a cut around the tree at about face high. "Wons, you're the tallest. You should do this. Nash, you cut around the base, and I'll cut a straight vertical line from where you gashed the tree."

Nash began savagely and finished first, while Wons and Front were being much more careful.

"All right. Now slide your blade underneath the vertical line and...No, wait," Front restrained the impatient Nash. "I'll do it myself. You two pull the top and the bottom while I shear the bark away from the tree. It comes easily. Don't jerk."

This time Nash was more careful, doing as he was told. As Front had predicted, the bark came away smoothly and easily.

The girls had already cut and braided several strands of cord, and now Front stood back to observe his material from a distance. All they had was a sheet of boat-bark, cord, and their knives, but he thought it would do.

Nash began, without conferring with the others, to try to bend the bark in the middle of its longer length.

"No! No," insisted Fyva, even before Front could correct him.

"Can't you see the bark's too thick and you're bending against the grain?"

"She's right, Nash. It looks to me like we'll be able to cut this piece vertically again and make two boats out of it. We'll bend it with the natural curve of the bark, and then we can lash up the front to make the bow of the boat."

Wonina studied the project while her hands continued automatically to braid the rope. "You'll need to shear off the top of the bow so you can see over," she recommended.

"And then we'll bind up the rear too," said Wons hopefully.

"No, we'll have to leave that open so that your legs can dangle out," Front reminded him.

"And the cold water can drool in."

Front ignored Wons and continued his planning. "And either we make the sides shallow or we cut arm wells so that our arms can paddle and guide the boat."

"All right, all right, let's get to it," ordered Nash.

"Not so fast," Fyva tried to stop him again. "Let's think this thing through one more time."

"Enough thinking! We need action. Look, the sun is sinking."

Front automatically looked up. Of course he could see no sun. Still the growing dimness was apparent, and he began to feel some of Nash's sense of urgency.

Front pointed out where he wanted the bark cut, and they quickly slashed the larger piece in half.

"All right, Wonina. You get in the middle here and we'll bend the front around you while you hold it apart with your knees."

Wonina placed herself carefully while two of the men held the sides together at the front. Right after Front had punctured each set of holes, Fyva forced the cord through and tugged fiercely to secure each knot. When the binding of the bow was completed, Wonina eased herself out, and to their relief, the natural resistance of the material enabled the bark to retain a presentable boat-like arch.

Before the others could spend much time admiring their work, Wonina insisted that they double bind the front of the boat, and Fyva, and Nash complied with her recommendation, while Front cut the arm wells, and then sheared off some of the bow for better visibility.

"All right," ordered Nash. "Let's cut some more bark and finish the rest of the boats."

"Wait, wait," insisted Wonina and Fyva almost together. "It needs to be tested."

Nash scowled, but voiced no objection. Fyva dragged the small craft toward the pond, but after they had all gathered on the bank, no one moved. Finally Wonina grinned at the others, peeled off her jacket, and began positioning herself in the boat. "All right, slide me and the boat into the water," Wonina instructed.

Front and Nash edged the boat forward, and they all held their breath as the boat floated only briefly and then began to settle. Wonina shuddered and gasped as the cold water poured in from the back of the boat. "Come on in," she chattered. "The ice is fine."

But only about one inch of Wonina's front side sank beneath the dark water before the boat reached its point of buoyancy. Gingerly Wonina began experimenting with propelling herself with slight paddling movement of her arms through the notched sides of the boat. It was awkward at first, but she seemed to be gaining skill.

"Hey," she cried cheerfully. "This is fun. I can't wait till you join me." She gave a laugh as she propelled herself back to the bank.

Now that the basic design was settled upon, the work of building the remaining five boats moved quickly. Nash continually reminded them of the sinking sun, and Front soon forgot himself, his concerns, and his doubts in his own growing need from speed. Nash's conception of how fast the sun was sinking seemed to be exaggerated, but nonetheless Front realized Nash was probably right; it was necessary to work as quickly as possible to get the job done so there would still be enough daylight for the passage through the cliff.

"Wear your packs and use more cord to lash your walking staffs to the inside of your boats. We're still going to need them when we get beyond this cut," Nash instructed.

Front had been so involved in his own labors that he had failed to notice at first that Wons had gradually slowed his involvement in the activity. For the last several moments he had been standing aside doing nothing. When the others stooped and began positioning their boats for the take-off, Wons remained standing.

"All right, Wons, what's with you now?" sneered Nash.

"I'm not going."

Front expected Nash to be furious, but instead the tone of the goat herder's voice was controlled. "All right, Wons," he began slowly. "You haven't really been a part of this group for a long time. So if that's your choice, fine. We'll go ahead and do our duty for Sebasa. You crawl right back up the mountain. You crawl back down the other side so you can lay yourself at the feet of your Outhans and lick their boots. We don't need a coward with us anyway."

"I'm no coward!" shouted Wons. "I'm no fool either! You're the fool, pushing these people off into that cut, not knowing what's on the other side. And what proves you're so brave? You're the one who's running away from danger. You're the one who's afraid of the Outhans, not me."

Even though Front expected Nash to retaliate, he was shocked when the stocky goat herder lunged forward, and slammed his fists into Wons' middle.

Wons doubled up groaning.

Wonina screamed and rushed to throw herself between the two combatants, but Nash shoved her roughly aside. Jerking and dragging the gasping Wons, he pushed the fellow down into his boat and shoved the boat into the water.

Front hurriedly launched his own boat into the iciness and paddled rapidly to catch up with the drifting Wons. While steadying the two boats, he awkwardly reached to hold Wons' head above the surface. By this time, however, Wons had recovered enough to hold up his own head and gasp for breath.

"Oh, that bastard, that bastard," he groaned.

Front felt the urge to return to shore, to hurl himself at Nash, but Wons clasped his wrist and mumbled, "I'll be all right, Front. Just a little longer, I'll be okay."

Front looked back to the bank and saw that Nash had herded the two girls into the water and was now launching himself forth.

"Front," he bellowed. "Leave that coward and follow me. It's time that men took the lead here. Fyva, you follow Wons and see that he keeps moving. Wonina, in the middle! Move!"

The current was already beginning to carry Front along, and it seemed the wisest thing now was to get this trip over with as soon as possible so that they could get out of this cold water. He would deal with Nash later, he told himself. He followed after Nash, but not before assuring himself that the others were also following.

When he was fully under way, Nash was already rounding the gash in the sheer wall of moss and stone, and their leader seemed to be sucked in as the water picked up speed on entering the narrow confines of the passageway. Front also experienced that sudden surge as he maneuvered into the cut. He struggled to master the bobbing and twisting of his small craft by gently fluttering his legs and by shifting his weight for better balance and by guiding with his hands, and soon he was making excellent progress through the passageway. He glanced up to see that the thick moss on the face of the cliff also coated the upper walls within the cut. Overhead, the walls faded out of sight in the haze of the growing darkness. The ceiling of haze above and the sheer almost perpendicular walls made him feel that he was in a tunnel rather than in an open cut. Only occasionally did Front flow past a sharp outcropping of rock, suggesting the cut was natural rather than man-made.

Now that they were on their way, Front began to relax a little. Except for the cold water, the smooth, gliding, boat ride would have been almost pleasurable. Front now had his craft under control and he edged himself over toward the side to verify his suspicion that the sides were as smooth as they appeared. The slickness indeed allowed no grasp by which he could hold himself back if he chose to. This seemed unimportant, however; at the speed they were traveling, they should soon be through the cut. Front centered his craft again in the narrowing waterway and flowed smoothly onward, concentrating on steadying the boat and listening to the quietly rushing water.

After a time, however, the hissing swoosh of the water against the walls seemed to be growing louder. It took a while for Front to realize the louder sound was not coming from the walls but from up ahead of him. Front became more concerned when a vision of stone filled rapids began to come to mind. He glanced back to assure himself that the that the other three were still close behind him, and then concerned himself again with what might be ahead. He peered above the bow of his small craft. In the distance he could see that the water, which until this time had been dark to the point of blackness, was beginning to whiten in bubbles and foam. He reached out once again to try to grasp the wall to his left, but came away with nothing but an oily slickness on his hand. He saw that Nash was likewise trying to resist the rushing current, but the bubbling, churning water was now irresistible.

Front experienced a brief moment of hope as suddenly the walls parted and there appeared an opening ahead of him. He looked up frantically, only to stare into an endless expanse of greenness. Suddenly his stomach dropped, and then the boat seemed to be falling from under him. There was wild white emptiness whizzing by his eyes, and screams, and the constant roar, and then darkness.

5

POWER PULLS APART TOGETHER

Front lunged for his boat and clutched it to him; it was the only familiar object in this suddenly unfamiliar world. But the craft returned his embrace with a crushing blow and his face was smashed against the corky bottom of his boat. Water rushed over him, and as he opened his mouth to scream, he wished he hadn't—suddenly there was no air to breathe. He tried to let loose the boat to climb toward air, but now the boat was above him and blocking the way. He felt himself being yanked and pushed by the force of the water until he collided with something painfully hard and veered off to the left. Again he tried to abandon his boat, and swim frantically upward, but he reencountered the boat, though this time less cruelly, against a surface that seemed almost soft and yielding. Finally, shoving aside his boat, he clambered up that yielding surface to break forth into the roaring air. Gasping and choking and spitting, he sucked the precious essence into his lungs.

Only after he had regained his breath sufficiently could he hear above the now somewhat muffled rushing of the water, a moan of desperation. "I'm hurt, I'm hurt!"

Feeling around in the darkness, Front first pushed aside his boat and then another boat. A hand grabbed him and hung on, and he started to go under again. He clutched at the barrier against which the water was shoving him. His fingers encountered more slime, but enough of a handhold so he could draw himself back to the surface.

The clutching hand now became two arms and a body. "My leg—it's numb. I can't move it!"

Front recognized Nash as the clutching, moaning figure. He placed his other arm around the stricken fellow and, groping in the dark, found another handhold.

"Hold on, Nash. I've got you. Hold on."

He felt Nash relax somewhat in his arms.

"My God, Front, what happened? Where are we? I've hurt my leg!"

Front didn't answer. He had no answers. It was enough for the time being to be able to hold on and draw more air into his lungs.

After a moment, his breathing began to require less of his attention, and his mind became clear enough to register some of what was around him. With his arm and shoulder he felt a series of stone pillars through which the water was wildly rushing. He was clinging to and being shoved against a barrier of such vertical pillars, and he and Nash and the two boats were at least temporarily saved from following the wild rush of the water.

"Nash, grab the rocks behind you! You can hold on."

Nash seemed unwilling to release himself from Front's shoulders, but eventually he did as he was told.

Holding on with one hand, Front searched around him and over his head. The ceiling was out of reach. To the left at a right angle to the pillars was another wall that headed in the direction from which they had come. With considerable effort, and awkwardly against the force of the onrushing water, Front turned himself around to peer in that direction. He almost slipped under again in the process, but to his relief he could see light. From where they had come, in the haze created by the churning caldron, he

could see was a hole through which they must have been forced by the
water. His angle of sight was not too good, but he could tell it was brighter
beyond the hole. Forcing himself to think back on the terrifying experience
he had just undergone, he speculated that the stream on which they had
been traveling must have fallen through into an underground cavern, and
they had careened off the rocks below and been shunted aside to the left
into a narrow, partially blocked passageway.

The force of the water was so great he didn't even try to swim against
it. Instead, he worked his way across Nash and started to move perpendicular to the force of the water along the pillars and to his right.

Nash moaned, "Don't leave me, Front!"

"Hold on, Nash. I've got to learn where we are."

Struggling awkwardly, with only the slimy pillars against which to propel himself, Front continued his perpendicular struggle until he came to
the other wall of their stone chamber. He felt beyond the darkened corner
and encountered only another slick wall. Again he felt over his head. This
time, by pulling himself up the pillars and kicking against the water, he
encountered the top of the pillars and the ceiling—more slickness and no
opening over the pillars. There was no way they could continue with the
flow of the water. To escape this mossy stone trap, *they would have to swim
against the cruel current.*

He could feel the panic returning. Maybe not, he tried to tell himself.
In desperation he drew in a breath and pulled himself beneath the dark
waters, searching for another way, a submerged way that might promise
escape. The pillars continued downward into the blackness, and there was
still no escape between those narrow slits. He reached the bottom and
encountered a surface as smooth as the ceiling above. He wanted to search
longer, but by now his need for air was greater than his need to escape,
and he shoved off that smooth floor and struggled to the surface.

Clinging to the pillars and gasping again for air, he tried to calm his
pounding heart. He told himself, fear will accomplish nothing. He
breathed more deeply. Okay, okay, he pleaded with himself, calm down!

There's a way, there's got to be a way, but first you've got to calm down! He remained clinging there long enough for his ragged breathing to subside, but as he was regaining control of his emotions, he was also becoming aware of the growing coldness of his body. This rushing water was rapidly draining what little heat remained beneath his serpent skin garments. He tried to ignore his shivering as he worked his way across Nash again to the wall closest to the far opening. The light was deceptive, but he estimated the opening might be about eighteen feet away. Turning himself, he placed his feet against the pillars and, shoving with all his might, he swam fiercely against the current. The results were pitiful. Almost instantly he was pushed back against the pillars. Once again he chided himself, strength won't do it, stupid! Calm down and use your head!

Nash had now pulled himself over to Front, and except for an occasional gasp of pain, he seemed to be mastering his desperation, regaining some of his former assertiveness.

"You won't be able to swim against this current, Front. Is there anything we can hold onto on that wall?"

"No, it's too smooth. I couldn't feel anything to grab hold to."

"Maybe if I stretched out, pushing against the bars, I could push you forward."

"Maybe, but I don't think it would make any difference. That hole must be maybe eighteen feet away. Even together we're not tall enough to reach that far."

"How about the boats? Maybe we can pile one on top of the other and add to our length."

"We could try it, but I suspect the boats would just collapse."

"How about using the walking staffs—they're still lashed to the boats, aren't they?"

"Mine was. I guess it still is." Front pulled himself over to where the boats were pounding against the pillars. He felt around in the semi darkness and found that both staffs were still lashed to the boats. He started hastily to untie one of the staffs, but then stopped himself. Slow down,

Front! Think first! It wouldn't do to have the walking staffs washed through these slits and gone forever.

"Okay, they're still here," he called back to Nash. "But how do you think we can use them? Even if we could tie them together, that's only about ten feet, and there's no way we could lash them together tightly enough so they wouldn't bend and break if you were trying to push me forward with the pair of them."

"I still have the rope on my pack," said Nash hopefully. "It's about twenty feet long. If there were some way we could get the rope around the bend, maybe the other end would catch onto something and we could pull our way out." He paused, apparently realizing their two staffs wouldn't be long enough. "If only we had the others' staffs, we'd at least have a chance."

With a rush of shame, Front realized that during all this time he'd not even thought of his other three companions. "Oh my God, Nash! What's happened to the others?"

"Never mind the others," Nash replied distractedly. "They couldn't be any worse off than we are."

Ignoring Nash's comment, Front tried to think back. What might have happened to them? Why didn't they get forced into this same cave? Wonina was right behind them, in the middle of the stream, and he and Nash had been over to the left. He vaguely recalled that Fyva and Wons were clutching at the right wall of the channel when he last saw them.

Despairingly he concluded the other three would have been carried on downstream, probably beyond help or hope. He tried to force himself to think no more of them, but the thought of Wonina's soft body being torn by cruel rocks as she was pummeled through those dark waters left him weak and clinging again to the pillars. If only I'd taken her home like she wanted. If only I hadn't been such a coward. If only I'd resisted the others and refused to go down the back of that cursed mountain. She was always fearful of the risks, but they forced her. No, damn it, Nash forced her. Was there any goal so important, is anything so important, that we should've caused this to happen to her? He tried to shut out his shameful failures, but he could almost hear her sweet voice calling his name. She seemed totally desperate, but he could only cringe helplessly against the pillars.

Nash was shaking his shoulders. "I think I hear something!"

"You're crazy, you bastard! You caused this!" Front muttered bitterly.

"Listen, Front! It sounds like Wonina. She's calling us!"

Front fought down the anger rising within him. With the little strength he had left he wanted nothing more than to crush the life from Nash. He reached toward the shadowy figure, only to have himself pulled closer.

"That way, Front. It's coming from that way!"

The insistence in Nash's voice began to break through to Front. Without much hope, he began to listen.

Could it be true? Was there a faint voice riding on the rushing water?

"Front! Nash! Where are you?"

He fumbled to release himself form Nash and, pushing his feet against the pillars, he stood out against the current. Groping along the wall, his hand clutched another small pillar about a foot above the water line. He pulled himself forward until his face was against a set of three such pillars. A little light was coming through, not enough to see by, but just enough to show him a hole went through the wall.

"Here, Wonina! Here!" he shouted joyously, "We're behind this wall."

Front felt Nash clutching his leg, using the leg to pull himself along the wall.

"Get her walking staff, Front. Get her walking staff!"

"Wonina, are you all right?" Front called again. "Are you hurt? Can you hear me?"

Wonina quickly responded, and there was also joy in her voice. "Oh, Front, I hear you, I hear you. I was so worried."

"Hold on. I'm coming." Front tried to drag himself further along the wall, but Nash was holding him back. He tried to kick Nash loose from his leg, but without success.

"You can't get up here too, Nash. Wait! Shove against my feet so I can see better through this hole."

With some relief he felt Nash pushing awkwardly against his legs. It helped, and he was able to shove his face against the small opening. He was tiring rapidly, but he held himself there, hoping to get a glimpse of Wonina.

It seemed an eternity before her voice came again, this time much closer. "Are you all right, Front?" she pleaded. "Are you hurt?"

It was a moment before Front could talk. "No...Yes...I mean Nash hurt his leg, but we're okay. Are you hurt? What's over there? Are you safe?"

"No, I'm not hurt," Wonina broke into a burst of information. "I'm in a large chamber, lying on a ledge right now. I can hear you through a small series of slits in the rock wall, but I can't see you."

"Are the holes big enough to put her staff through?" Nash urged from below.

The center hole seemed big enough, Front realized. "Yes, yes," he called back impatiently and then tried to ignore Nash.

"Are you alone?" he asked Wonina. "Have you heard from the others?"

"Over there."

"Where over there?" He stared hopelessly into the light coming through the pillars.

"Back along the ledge I'm lying on, there's a series of flat rocks that rise above the current. My boat and I got wedged in between those rocks, and I was able to pull myself up on top. After a while I heard Wons calling. I jumped across the stream to a much larger flat surface, and then I crawled out on another ledge just like this one I'm on now. There's a hole there too. They're okay, but they're trapped, and they need Nash's rope and your walking staffs. Can you get out and bring them with you?"

Her last question brought him crushingly back to their desperate situation. For a while it had been enough just to know that Wonina was safe, but again, he recalled their plight. But now, somehow, he couldn't feel quite so helpless. Just knowing that she was safe made a difference.

"No. We're trapped just like they are, but we'll find a way, darling, we'll find a way."

He finally remembered Nash's request and realized that it was in fact important. "Have you got your staff, Wonina? Can you get it to us?"

"No. It's gone," sighed Wonina. "The boat and the stick washed away when I shoved off against them to reach the top of the rocks."

"Damn!" he heard Nash curse behind him. "Then get the staffs from Wons and Fyva!"

"Can you get the staffs from Wons or Fyva?" relayed Front.

"I just said, that's what they want from you, Front. After I found them, and I went looking for you, they shouted to me to bring back your walking staffs and Nash's rope."

"Damn," he heard Nash curse again and felt him tugging at his legs.

Front wanted to stay close to Wonina, but his arms were now tiring, particularly with Nash's insistent tugging.

"Hold on, Wonina. My arms are getting too tired. I'll have to let go."

He tried to let himself down easily, but his arms were now too weakened, and he was dashed painfully against the stone pillars as Nash moved out of the way.

"Why the hell are you pulling me, Nash?" he gasped.

"Don't trust them, Front. As soon as they get our staffs, they'll get out and leave us behind."

"Don't be a fool. What's happening to you, Nash? They'd never do that. They're our friends."

"Friends, hell! You heard that slimy snob squirming out of everything we did along the way. Just because he's the Steward's son and I'm a goat herder, he thinks he's better than me. He can't wait to get back and cozy up to those stinking Outhans so his kind can stay in power."

Front wanted to argue further with Nash's irrational accusations, but the fury in Nash's voice seemed insurmountable. He tried another approach. "Well, how about Fyva? You and she were certainly working together."

"I don't trust her either. That bitch isn't concerned about people like us. All she wants to do is find some way to make money out of this trip. You can't trust them, Front, you can't trust them. We've got to get those staffs for ourselves!" Even though his voice was raised over the noisy rushing water, his tone became suddenly confidential. "Here's what we'll do. We'll promise them that as soon as we get out, we'll get them out."

"If you don't trust them, Nash, why do you think they'll trust you?"

"Well then we'll promise them...no, we'll trade them our length rope for their staffs."

"But we need both lengths of rope." It had occurred to Front what the others' plan must be. If they could tie both ropes together, the total rope would be long enough to reach around the bend and back to the pillars through which he had talked to Wonina. Wonina could tie it there and they could pull themselves hand over hand around the bend and out into the larger cave.

He explained this plan to Nash and the other agreed that it would be pointless to try to bargain with the rope. Still, he wouldn't relent. "I don't care what you tell them, Front, just don't let them have the staffs."

Without a clear plan in mind, Front struggled again to the small pillared opening.

"Wonina, can you go back to the others and see if they'll give us their rope and their poles. Tell them we have a plan. We'll get ourselves out, then we'll rescue them."

Wonina hesitated before speaking.

"Wonina, are you there?"

"Yes, Front. I'll do as you say."

Front let himself back down with the current. Now there was nothing to do but wait.

But Nash wanted to plot further. "We'll have to come up with a plan in case they won't buy our deal. Think, Front, think! What else can we offer them?"

"Nash, what's happening to you?" Front asked angrily. "They're going to give us the staffs. They know it's the only logical thing to do. Now shut up about it. We just have to wait."

Nash lapsed into sullen silence, and Front was left with his own thoughts and discomforts. He was growing even colder, and he tried to curl up in a tight ball against the pillars. The rigid tension seemed to make his thoughts tense and choppy. At least, I think it's the logical thing to do, he reflected. After all, Wons and particularly Fyva are levelheaded people. But then he checked himself. I used to think that Nash was levelheaded too, and now he's acting like a madman. And Wons certainly could be obstinate when he wants to be. His heart chilled further as he recalled Wons' recent behavior, the petulant child-like behavior, the whining, complaining, and sulking when his hopes about the Angle Beings didn't materialize. The longer he thought about Wons, the more concerned he became. Suppose Wons was being as obstinate as Nash. What then? Well, there's always Fyva, he tried to think hopefully. No one could be more levelheaded than Fyva. When she wanted something, she got it.

Somehow that last thought wasn't all that reassuring. What does Fyva want? There was some truth in Nash's accusation that Fyva seemed to want to make a profit out of this trip. Is it possible she would try to cut us out of... No, no, Front dismissed that idea as foolish. One thing he was sure of, Fyva is practical, and it is only practical that she would try to save the two of us; she still needs us. It was a cold but nevertheless reassuring thought.

Still, as the time wore on, even that small reassurance began to fade. He thought of Wonina. There was the one warm spot. He knew he could trust her....

But why the hell hadn't she come back? What could be keeping her? The longer he waited, the more annoyed he became, even with Wonina.

Nash voiced the same concern. "Where the hell is that bitch?"

This time Front didn't bother to argue with Nash's words. Yes, where the hell is she?

When Wonina's voice finally called, he felt an irrational urge not to answer her. Shaking off that petulant feeling, he scrambled once again to reach the small opening. He noticed that his arms were even weaker, but with Nash's help and extra effort, he made it.

"Front, they won't give their things to you. They don't trust you. They say that Nash can't be trusted any more."

"Oh, my God," Front mumbled to himself. Then louder he bellowed, "Why didn't you convince them? Why didn't you say the right things to them?"

"Front, don't yell at me, I did my best."

The anger left Front. He believed her. It wasn't Wonina who was the enemy. It wasn't Wonina they were against, it was this cursed place, this freezing water. No, he began to realize, *it was they themselves.*

"Look, honey, I know you did your best. Hold on. I've got to get back and talk to Nash."

He dropped back again, this time purposely letting his weight crush against Nash before the man could get out of the way.

The other gasped and held on. "Watch what you're doing!"

"Listen to me, Nash. You heard what she said. They don't trust us, and I don't blame them. Our first thought was to save ourselves, and then we tried that stupid bargaining. There's only one way we're going to get out of here, and that's by cooperating with them."

"I'd sooner cooperate with Outhans!" growled Nash.

Front was stunned. He didn't quite believe what he had heard. The grip Nash had taken on his arm slackened. After a moment, Front controlled his voice enough to ask, "Did you hear what you said, Nash?" and he fought down the urge to shake the man.

But the message had gotten across. "Yeah, yeah, I heard...Okay, Front, what do we do?"

"We do what we should've done all along. We do exactly what they ask. We give them the staffs and our rope, and we trust them."

Front thought he could hear Nash's sigh, even above the rushing water. "Okay. I'll unlash the staff from my boat. You do yours."

Nash climbed over him to reach his boat, which was pushed against the far wall.

"Okay, but be careful, don't drop it, Nash."

"Front, trust me." There almost seemed to be a chuckle in Nash's voice. After a short time he thrust his staff into Front's hands. "Here, hold this while I take the rope off my pack."

Nash struggled briefly and then turned his back to Front. "Better yet, you take it off. I can't reach it. I trust you." This time Front was sure Nash was laughing.

The next task was awkward but necessary. While Nash held Front's feet, Front pushed the loose end of the uncoiled rope through the pillars to the waiting Wonina. It took two or three attempts because the rope kept bending and getting jammed. Finally Wonina suggested they shove the rope through with one of the poles. Once the rope slipped loose from Front, and Nash desperately lunged to catch it before it snaked through the pillars behind them. Cursing and threatening, he returned the loose rope to Front. This time the rope got through, and Wonina pulled it the rest of the way.

"Don't drop it, Wonina," Nash bellowed.

"I'm doing my best, Nash. You'll have to trust me."

"Yeah, yeah," both Nash and Front chuckled together. Finally, Front pushed the staffs through. The hole was barely large enough for their thicker ends.

Again, they had to wait. And again, the doubt set in. This time Nash was quiet, and Front's doubt came from within himself. He began to realize that he didn't really trust Wons or Fyva. Wons' behavior had proven him undependable. Fyva's motives, however accurate his assessment of them might be, somehow lacked something that made her trustworthy.

As the time wore on, and his body became more sapped by the cold, he even began to wonder about Wonina. She had been awfully tired the last time on that ledge. Maybe her strength would give out. Maybe, even if she wanted to come back, she couldn't make it. No, no, he tried to reassure himself. Somehow that girl always came through.

He felt Nash pressing against him, and soon they were clutching each other for warmth and perhaps reassurance. He heard himself say, "She'll be back soon, Nash. Hold on."

Nash mumbled almost incoherently, "That bitch, you can't ever trust a woman."

In spite of his misery, Front laughed at the absurdity of what Nash had said. What had any of this to do with Wonina's being a woman? Right now, they were five desperate people in need of each other, and Wonina's gender had no part in it. If they ever got out of this, he swore to himself, he was not going to let anything, not even his sexual attraction for Wonina, get in the way of their working together as a team. *We need each other, we really need each other!*

When Wonina's call finally came, Front thought at first he was too cold to move. The shock of uncoiling his body and letting in the slightly colder water was unbearable. His muscles were now so rigid with the chill he could hardly control them, but he forced himself back along the wall to reach Wonina's voice.

"Here's what we're going to do, Front. I've got the four poles tied together with strands I've taken from the rope. I'm tying one end of the rope to the pillars here. I've tied a chunk out of Fyva's boat to the other end, and I've coiled the rope and hooked it loosely on the end of the pole. I'll shove the pole forward until it comes to the bend and then try to work it around the edge by leaning out from the edge here. If it works just right, then the current should catch the boat piece and carry it back to you. Then you can pull yourselves out."

Front listened to this complicated plan, and after he was sure he understood, he thought to ask, "Where's Wons? Aren't they already out? Why didn't he come? Why isn't he doing this instead of you?"

It took a moment for Wonina to answer. "This ledge is too small for him. Now don't argue with me, Front. This is how Wons and Fyva got out, but I've got to do it just right."

Front could hear Wonina scraping and gasping as she struggled behind the wall. Once he heard her give a small scream, and he held his breath, but then her squirming and scraping started again.

"There," she gasped, and the rushing water mercifully brought the chunk of boat and the end of the rope to Front's grasping, clutching hands.

After the first rush of relief, he realized there was still desperate work ahead of them. Front's own muscles were tired and numb, and he could tell, now that rescue was almost here, Nash was near the end of his endurance. Front forced himself to try to think clearly. He could afford no false starts. He had only energy enough for one try at getting around the point of the wall. He started to worry whether or not Wonina had tied the rope securely on the other end, but he dismissed the thought. Wonina had done her job. Now he must do his. He struck upon a plan that he hoped would work. The rope was long enough to secure a loop around Nash's upper body and then to leave additional line to lash through the ties on the bows of the two boats. He reasoned that they would need the boats once they got into the main stream, particularly if his fear was confirmed that there would be no returning upstream.

"I can't feel my leg any more, Front. Don't leave me! I don't think I can make it on my own."

"None of us can, Nash. But hold on, I've got to work myself around the point and back to that ledge on the other side. Then I'll be able to pull you out with the rope."

"Okay, friend. I trust you," Nash's voice was now barely audible.

Front began his arduous hand over hand climb up the rope. It was worse than climbing the mountain. His freezing hands had difficulty in feeling the rope, and the water seemed to fight his every attempt to find the next handhold. He worked his way slowly toward the dim light ahead; reaching that light became the most important thing in his world. Only when at last it seemed likely that he would make that hole did he begin to change his goal. He now wanted to see Wonina. It was a pleasant thought, but fleeting.

When he finally reached the edge of the hole, the current was particularly fierce, and it took several attempts to reach around to the other side. Suddenly the situation was reversed. He felt himself desperately clutching to hold onto the rope, as the fierce current began tearing him away from the direction that moments ago he had wished so desperately to go. At that moment, he felt his head bump against an object behind him. Desperately, he clung to the rope, trying to clear his thoughts. When he was finally able to think again, he realized he had bashed his head against the ledge on which Wonina had traveled to reach them. Looping his arm across the rope he rested momentarily. Then he threw his leg over the rope, and struggled to raise himself to the ledge. The ledge seemed so narrow there couldn't possibly be room for him to sit there. How, he wondered, could Wonina have traveled this narrow strip of stone? With one final pull on the rope, he surged backward and caught his hand on one of the pillars in the small opening. It was again a while before he could think what to do next. Carefully, and holding on to the pillar behind him, he slid to a standing position. Then he squatted back down with his back to the pillars and, loosening his leather belt with one hand, he awkwardly looped the belt through the pillars. After several attempts, he was able to grab hold of both ends of the belt in his hand. Teetering dangerously, he tied the belt securely about his waist. He reached down and grasped the taut rope and then shouted back through the hole in the wall, "Okay, Nash. I'm pulling."

There was no response from Nash, so he began pulling, struggling with all his might to make some headway on the rope. Through his gasping, he shouted for help from the others, but he was afraid to turn to look for them for fear of losing his grip on the rope. There was nothing to do but breathe more deeply and pull, and pull, and pull.

There was nothing in his life now but pulling. He never knew where the power came from, but he pulled. Suddenly he was pulling on nothing, and he jerked backward, then dangled forward on his belt, suspended from the pillars behind him. He gagged from the choking belt about his waist, and then struggled to pull himself back up onto the ledge. Somehow he managed to reach behind him and grab hold of one pillar, but now his arms seemed unable to make that last effort of pulling himself back to a squatting position. He hung there breathing, gasping, and let go again. With his second attempt at pulling himself backward, he was able to manage the feat. Through blurring eyes into what seemed to be growing darkness he looked about for Nash. He could see two figures above the waterline off to his left, and he made out Wonina pulling Nash from the water onto shallow rocks. The rushing water broke over the rocks and over the two figures like the oncoming waves on a stormy night on the beach of Sebasa. Regaining some of his strength, and reassured that Nash at least had been pulled from the water, Front further examined the area about him. To his right was the cascading and now gray foam of the incoming falls. At the point of the wall he had just rounded, rocks were being pounded by the incoming water. Across the channel, he could barely make out a similar outcropping of boiling rocks and a wall. He guessed it was behind that wall that Fyva and Wons had been carried by their branch of the current. Following that far wall backward into the gloom he saw two more figures huddled on what appeared to be a more expansive stone ledge in the far corner. Between that ledge and the lower grouping of flat rocks onto which Wonina had now pulled the floundering Nash, there ran a clear channel into a black hole. Moving his eyes further to the left, Front spied the long narrow ledge on which Wonina must have had to crawl several times in order to reach the small pillared hole to which he was belted. He marveled that she could have managed that feat without falling.

He realized with sudden concern that the same challenge now confronted him. Some of the exhaustion had left his arms, and he fumbled to disengage himself from his belt. That task eventually accomplished, and without bothering to retie his belt, he first tried to walk along the ledge, feeling for something overhead and in front of him on which to grasp. There seemed to be nothing, so he went to his knees, pressing himself as close to the wall as possible, and began edging forward. His knees were too large and the ledge began cutting his kneecaps. He slid his knee over a particularly jagged spot and gasped in pain. Without thinking, he reached down for that wounded joint, only to reach into nothingness, and found himself tumbling off the ledge.

Once again the cold blackness met him, drawing him under. It was now almost not worth effort to struggle to the surface again, but it was the cruel current itself that buoyed him up as it shoved him along.

He heard Wonina's scream above the rushing water, and it seemed that reaching her was worth at least one last effort. Feebly he began kicking and struggling to resist the pull of the current. He felt his arm strike something hard. He was twisted around and his hand grasped nothing. He reached again and this time grasped something soft and yielding. His body was carried along but remained secured to that one soft object that now tugged and yanked at him. Pulling his head above the surface, he breathed, and gasped, and reached with his other hand for the wall.

He found a rocky hold, slick but jutting out enough for grasping.

Pulling now with both arms he was able to loop a leg over another rock and draw himself from the clutching blackness. Wonina grabbed him under both arms and pulled backwards, and they both floundered up the slippery rocks beyond the reach of the current.

He lay there in her arms and chose not to move. It felt as though he was at last home and nothing else mattered.

Finally, he heard Wonina's voice and felt the warmth of her tears. "Front, Front, you did it! We're okay. We're okay. Don't move, just let me hold you."

Front had no intention of doing otherwise.

Finally it was Wonina who released him and pulled herself to her feet. "Okay," she ordered gently. "Let's get us all together. Come on, on your feet now. You too, Nash."

"Right," Front heard Nash reply. "I think I can make it now if you'll give me a hand."

Front didn't want to let go of Wonina's other hand, so he pulled himself to his feet along side her. Leaning down, he assisted her in pulling Nash to his feet. The three of them hobbled and stumbled across the perilous rocks until they came to the edge of the swiftly moving channel where it entered that black hole.

Front looked across to the higher ledge on the other side and gasped. "There's no way across!" He turned and clutched Wonina to him. "How did you make it over there?"

"I jumped. How else?" she replied.

"But I'm not even sure I can jump that far. You must have gone across once, twice, three times. How could you possibly have done it?"

Without hesitation she answered, pulling the two men closer to her and hugging them, "You needed me. I had no choice."

6

WE MUST STAND STILL
BEFORE WE CAN MOVE

After testing and flexing his legs, and after a few false starts, Front was able to overcome his initial uncertainty and make the jump across the stream. It was necessary to take a brief running start over the slippery stones and then, being sure not to jump too high and hit the low ceiling, to hurl himself toward the slightly higher rock ledge where Fyva and Wons were able to catch him.

For Nash it was a different matter. He tried to hobble along for a running start, but it was obvious to all he would never make it. It was equally obvious that Wonina wasn't going to let him try again anyway. He halted at the brink and then backed up for a second attempt, but Wonina clutched him and forced him down to a seated position. "I didn't risk my neck rescuing you to have you swallowed up by that black hole, Nash. You just wait here."

Front watched anxiously while Wonina scrambled back over the slippery boulders, to the wall behind her and then slid herself once again across that perilous stretch of narrow ledge. He marveled at how she seemed to flatten herself and cling like a limpet to that slippery wall.

Then, having found her balance, she shuffled her feet along the ledge in what was now an obviously practiced method of locomotion. When she reached the pillars where the rope was tied, she slid down the wall to a prone position on the narrow ledge and untied the rope. After carefully coiling the rope, she stood and shuffled backward to the boulders.

With the recovered rope and tied to Nash, Front and Wons were able to haul Nash through the rapidly moving water of the cut and hoist him up the bank. Wons dropped his share of the sodden and trembling Nash in a decidedly ungentle fashion, then moved away. Front bent down and put his hand on Nash's shoulders and began trying to massage some warmth back into the fellow. He glanced across the cut and noticed that Wonina was winding up for her jump over the stream. He left Nash and hurried to the edge, wanting to be sure he was there should she need help. His protectiveness was unnecessary. Wonina demonstrated the skill and style she had learned in her many flights across that perilous cut. Apparently knowing just how high she should jump, and how fast she needed to go, she hurled herself expertly and nimbly across the wide gap between the boulders.

Without even slowing down, she went directly to Nash and began removing his pack. She shook out the bedroll and checked inside. "Just as I'd hoped," she announced. "The tight roll kept the goat hair inside as dry as you please."

She spread the bedroll in a dryer corner to the rear of the platform and, without consulting Nash she then began to remove his outer garments.

"I can do it, I can do it," Nash complained.

Wonina merely brushed his hands aside and continued her work. After removing his undergarments, she wrung them out and then used them to sponge him dry all over. Helping Nash back into his jacket, she steadied him as he hobbled to his bed. Before assisting him into the sack, she tore a part of her own undergarment from around her waist and began cleaning and bandaging his upper leg. This intimate ministering to Nash's needs, particularly the practiced and familiar way she went about her loving care began to make Front uncomfortable. He turned away and tried to examine the cave from his new vantage point.

Over his shoulder he heard Wonina's encouraging report, "Clean. Clean as a baby's bottom. I don't think we'll have to worry about the wound's getting infected. Our icy stream's washed your wound and all the rest of you as clean as you've been in years."

Front caught himself wondering how she knew his usual state of cleanliness. He dismissed the question as unworthy of him.

Wonina's voice lost some of its cheeriness. "You've lost quite a bit of blood, though, Nash. What you need is food and rest. Into your sack now."

Front could hear that she now turned to address the rest of the group, "And that's what all of you need, food and rest. Don't just stand around looking foolish. Off with your packs and start feeding yourselves."

Front chose to ignore her instructions, and he began pacing along the edge of their platform, trying to get a better view of the distant opening in the ceiling through which the water was loudly cascading. It was considerably darker now, but he reasoned there was still light enough for them to attempt an escape if he could find some way to make it back to the sides of that waterfall.

He could hear the others rummaging through their packs, and he was surprised to suddenly feel Wonina at his side.

Her voice was low. "Front, darling, I hope you're not planning to go back into that icy water."

He was startled by her closeness as well as by her endearment, and the sudden warmth of that closeness brought vividly to mind the icy water he had recently left. All of this was indeed a powerful argument against an immediate return to that torturous cold.

Nevertheless, he drew himself away from her. "But there's still light, Wonina. We've got to take advantage of this light while there's still time."

She moved even closer and pulled him away from the edge of the platform. "Front, there'll be time enough tomorrow. Time we have; energy and strength we don't have. Do as I say. Take off your clothes and get into your sack. Just curl up and get warn. I'll even feed you so you won't have to have your arms uncovered."

The offer was delightfully compelling and repelling at the same time. All the while he had felt it his duty and desire to care for Wonina, and now she insisted on caring for him. The temptation of her soft caring was tantalizing, but somehow the idea of being helpless, even with her, was not to his liking.

He went as far as allowing her to help him remove his pack, but when she began to unbutton his jacket, he insisted that he could continue undressing alone.

The others were already eating, without first removing their sodden clothes, so after she left, he stopped undressing and followed their example. Wonina returned to where she had removed her own pack, and after extracting her food, she placed herself next to the cocoon shape of Nash.

Front found that most of his food was still in reasonably good condition. The hard biscuits were no longer hard, but soft and mushy as fish pudding. Out of the growing darkness he heard Wonina caution, "Don't throw away those biscuits anyone. They're still good."

Dutifully he tasted a few bites of the slush and then restored the rest to his pack.

He heard Wons grumble, "Damn, this mush is nothing but fish food." He paused and then laughed bitterly, "Just as well. Fish food for foolish fish. Soon we're all going to be food for some kind of fish eating monster down in this black cave." He raised his voice and slung his bitterness toward Nash, "I hope you're happy with the mess you've got us into!"

Front could see Nash struggling to pull himself to a sitting position.

Wonina leaned against him and forced him again onto his back. "I'll have no more of that, Wons. Whatever Nash did, he did because he thought it was right. Now eat your food. Fish food or not, it's good for you."

The meal continued in silence. Wonina ate quickly, and began massaging Nash through his serpent-skin bag. Front could hear the fellow groaning, and he couldn't determine whether those groans were of pain or pleasure. Although very little distance separated him from the others on this stone platform, the spray and the haze spreading from the wall of water behind him and the fading light made them seem far away. He felt a sudden return of his former aloneness. He shuddered. Although the air of the cave was certainly not as cold as the water had been, still the dankness of the place was heat sapping. He guessed he hadn't fully recovered from his recent ordeal. The meal had helped, but he realized it would probably be wise to follow Wonina's suggestion, to strip, sponge off, and crawl into the potential warmth of his sleeping bag. Still he sat there, listening to the sounds of pain or pleasure barely audible above the rush of water and wondering why he was torturing himself by trying to see Wonina more clearly, trying to see exactly what she was doing with Nash.

Finally, with a sigh, he rose and began removing his clothes, primly turning his back to the rest of the group. The current of air created by the falling water was sharp and unpleasant on his exposed skin, so he quickly sponged himself off and crawled into his sack. He heard the others removing their clothes as well, and he fought the urge to peer behind him in the gloom to spy on Wonina. He felt mildly ashamed of his childish curiosity. After all, he reminded himself, it wasn't too long ago, when he was trapped and near drowning, he was admiring that girl's selfless courage and pledging to ignore her sexuality for the solidarity of the group. Funny what a little food and warmth will do to one's need for solidarity with a group, he mused, and the humor and irony helped him fight his urge to peek.

He was surprised moments later by a pat on his shoulder, and after half turning around, he turned away quickly. Wonina was apparently checking to see that he was properly covered by his bag. He couldn't be sure in the gloom, but it appeared that she had already removed. her own clothes. He was instantly freezing and burning. He had a sudden return of the trembling he had experienced in the cold water.

He heard Wonina whisper softly in his ear. "Good night, precious Front. I was so worried when you were missing. I'm so glad to have you back." Then she kissed him lightly but warmly on the cheek.

Before Front could move again, she was gone. He was left aching with a half glimpsed image of soft rounded breasts. After a moment he thought he heard Nash recommence his moaning, and he hated to think of all that loveliness caressing someone else. Instead he clung to the memory of that silvery image, tempting and tearing at him, until eventually the pain was too unpleasant to bear. He took a deep breath and let the air seep slowly from him in a helpless sigh. As he did so the warmth now growing in his moisture proof sack and the exhaustion of the day began to overwhelm him. Even his dream of Wonina would have to wait for sleep.

Sleep and dreams—violent, tumbling, repetitive dreams—he tumbled down green moss covered mountains and sank into gray foam that engulfed the light. Everywhere he touched slime, and nothing could hold him back from his rushing, endless flight through the darkness. Wons was there, and he sat on top of a mountain, dressed in the town Steward's regalia, reading booming words from a great open book. The mountains began to crumble beneath Wons, and Front was once again falling, rolling, tumbling and wrestling in a careening heap with Nash, alternately pounding him and hugging him, and then his combatant became smaller, softer, and more pliable. He found himself wrestling with Wonina, and then burning with guilt. He pushed her away, only to find it was Fyva who was standing back and shaking her head and saying, "That's not logical, Front. There's nothing to gain from this childish play. Now get back into the water," and she tumbled him briskly, head over heels, into the cold blackness. He was swimming furiously upstream toward the foaming mountain when suddenly the water began to sparkle with brightly colored lights. In a fountain of foaming water the lights merged, and he rose up within the fountain, and the fountain became a jeweled robe, and then he was rising from the middle of a mountain of people who curled and writhed at his feet like billows of foam. A multitude of people in a great circle about him fell to their knees on the turf-covered Commons and chanted, "Oh, save us, Angle Being, save us," and Front felt all powerful as he looked far below him to see Wonina's nude back, her head bowed toward him, touching the ground, and her tempting rear raised in the air. He raised his great jewel-headed scepter and beckoned her to dance for him. She flowed sinuously from the ground like a silvery snake and glided temptingly, tauntingly toward him. He could hear cries of, "No! No!" coming from the crowd as he opened his robe to engulf and press her naked body deliciously to his own. But the crowd was looking behind Front, and with annoyance, he turned in that direction to see a horde of great black insects hovering over the surface of Sebasa Bay, descending and crushing the small fishing vessels beneath them, grinding toward the shore and the Commons. The multitude screamed for Front to use his weapon. "Kill the Outhans! Kill the Outhans!" But when he tried to open his robe to draw his jewel headed weapon, it was crushed between him and the clinging Wonina. He tried to pull away, only to find that he was now beneath her, and he didn't want to pull away. He turned back to the Outhans and shouted feebly, "Go away, go away"...but the closer they came, the more feeble he became. There was a great crunching sound, the whole Commons shook, and Front started up in his sleeping bag, his heart pounding, the goat fur about him matted and damp with perspiration.

With a groan he sank back down against the hard rock beneath his sweat soaked sleeping bag. He lay for a moment, feeling his heart pounding, wondering how long he had been asleep, not wanting to open his eyes, but not wanting to risk falling asleep and returning to those pounding dreams. The most vivid image that remained was the sparkling, jeweled robe. When he reluctantly opened his eyes, it seemed he could still see those bright lights. He bellowed a short whoop, and shoved himself up to stare into the darkness. One hand slid from under him and he flattened himself quickly on the brink of the platform and but still teetered precariously over the water. During his tossing sleep he must have rolled over several times and brought himself dangerously close to the edge.

He squirmed cautiously away from the brink. When he stared again over the water there was only the dark grayness of the mist filled cave, a grayness that was just now growing lighter in the direction of the waterfall. For a while he lay there quietly, his heart still pounding, more from the real peril he had just experienced than from the imagined peril of his dreams. This day will be bad enough, he sighed. I really didn't need that dream. He forced himself to forget the dream and to think of the coming day. There had to be a way out of this cave. Use your head today, and keep your mind on the task, he cautioned himself.

He pulled himself to a sitting position, but remained inside of his bag for its warmth. As well as he could, in the semidarkness, he examined again the walls on either side of the cave. The two ledges upon which Wonina had crawled ended abruptly before they reached the openings into those side caves. Beyond those two openings the walls continued on to the falls; there were no ledges on those walls beyond the openings, and they appeared to be as smooth and slick as the walls within the side caves. Scattered out from those side caves were widely spaced boulders, most of which also looked treacherously smooth and awash.

Front then looked above the farthest of those boulders to where the ceiling ended abruptly and the light began. The edges there were jagged, and Front could only imagine that rising above those jagged edges would be that wall of green moss he had glimpsed just before he shot over the falls. That wall of moss had seemed immense, but still, if he could somehow make his way to one of those boulders and then toss a line up to one of those jagged edges on the roof, perhaps it would be possible to shinny up the rope and somehow climb that wall of moss. It seemed almost hopeless, he realized, but at least it was a hope.

The others were beginning to stir in their sacks, so still wishing to be modest, Front quickly extracted himself from his own sack, gathered up his serpent-skin jacket and pants, and began looking about for his undergarments. Against the back wall, neatly arranged, were all of their underthings. As he hastily recovered his own and turned his back to the others to begin dressing, Front wondered when Wonina had accomplished this motherly chore. He gasped as the cold cloth hit his loins, and he heard Wonina's bright laugh behind him. He started to turn around accusingly, but thought better of it, and quickly completed his dressing. While the others were still groaning and stretching, he returned to the front of the shelf and continued his examination of the rocks and falls.

"What are you up to, Front?" Wonina's voice came from just behind him. He turned, and she slipped her arms around his waist.

He found he had trouble answering her immediately. "I'm...I'm figuring how we're going to make it back up the falls."

He could feel Wonina pulling him gently away from the edge.

"Well, all that can wait until after you've eaten."

"Wonina, we can't go on waiting...."

"We can wait at least until after breakfast. You still need strength if you're planning to have a second go at drowning yourself. Besides, there'll be more light soon."

She was right of course. Unlike last night, time and the growing light were on their side this morning. She led him back toward the center of the group to where he had left his pack.

"Now let's all eat," she directed.

"But not too much," Nash ordered hoarsely, coughing as he talked. "We still have a way to go to get where we're going."

"Who are you to give orders?" sneered Wons as he rose to his knees. "If it wasn't for your stupid orders, we wouldn't be down in this ice hole."

Nash, apparently stronger this morning, also struggled to rise, but Wonina moved smoothly in between the two men.

"The more chewing and the less talking you two do, the better off we'll all be. Now come on, fellows, why don't you two leave each other alone?" She diverted them further by turning to Front. "Why don't you tell us what you plan to do, Front?"

Between bites and swallows, Front outlined his plan. "It might take a number of tosses, but I think I can loop a rope onto that most jagged of the boulders sticking out above the rapids. Once I pull myself there, I should then be able to make a toss to one of the jutting rocks on the broken edge of the roof. Once up there, I'll start gouging out holes. That moss shouldn't be too thick, and there has to be some crevices underneath it or the moss couldn't catch hold so readily."

"And then what?" asked Fyva.

"I'm not sure," Front admitted. "The rope should be long enough to stretch back to the small set of pillars. I know it will be hard, but you could hand over hand, or at least shinny up the slope of that rope, and then I could get each of you started up the cliff."

"Oh, Front, that sounds so dangerous," Wonina's voice had lost its recent firmness.

"No more dangerous than starving or freezing to death down here!" Wons countered harshly.

No one refuted Wons' bitter argument, and the silence continued until Wonina finally took the lead again. "Well, at least this time let's prepare you a little better for the water."

She rose and approached Front, tearing away more strips from her undergarment as she came. "Shove your shirt inside your trousers and then lash your waist tightly with your belt. I'm going to tie your wrists and your pants legs with this cloth. Then, with another strand about your neck, you should be able to keep most of the water out and some of the heat in."

It seemed a good suggestion to Front, who complied readily. Then, taking the rope that Wonina had neatly coiled, he looked once more at the small group about him. He wasn't sure he could read their expressions, but only Wonina's seemed anywhere near hopeful.

He decided on the ledge on the far side. As narrow as it was, it was wider than the one on this side of the cut. Not being so exhausted now, he figured that he could do a better job of balancing on the ledge this time. His legs were also were stronger this morning, and the leap across the current was much easier. Wonina followed immediately, and he found himself foolishly worrying about her safety after she was already across. Moreover, he reminded himself, she had already proven herself more agile than he. She followed him to the ledge and helped him hoist himself up.

As he again crawled awkwardly along the narrow ledge, and he recalled how quickly and often she had made this same passage, he was further convinced of Wonina's superior agility. He drew in a deep breath as he finally edged his way to the small opening in the wall. After he tied one loose end of the rope to the stone pillars, he tugged to test their strength; perhaps yesterday's pressure might have loosened or broken the slender wedges of stone. When he was assured of their sturdiness, he coiled the rope about himself several times, allowing just enough slack so he could stand up and lean slightly forward away from the wall. Then he began tossing the other pre-looped end of the rope at the deceptively distant up-jutting boulder he had already chosen.

The first toss brought suddenly to mind the pier on Sebasa Bay and the many times he had tossed his painter to secure his boat to that dock. The water churning below him was hardly as warm and welcoming as Sebasa Bay, and he cringed at the painful comparison, but still his mind didn't want to abandon that reassuring image. Then the image changed unbidden, and there flashed across his mind the picture of swarthy Outhans swarming over those same familiar docks. His next two tosses went wide of the mark, and he had to calm his agitation before he could at last make an accurate toss. He felt the satisfactory tautness of the line as he tested it. Snatching loose the other end of the rope from the pillars, he glanced back one more time at Wonina, wringing her hands and leaning forward from the slippery rocks behind him. Looping the rope around his upper arm, he launched himself once again into the frigid current. There was a sudden jerk as he sank beneath the water and the current slashed his body. His face and hands were stinging with the cold, but he was gratified to feel how slowly the water was seeping beneath the binds that Wonina had placed around his limbs and neck. He then began the hand over hand pull along the rope. At least his arms were stronger than they had been for that dreadful pull of yester evening—at least they seemed that way for a while. All too soon, he began to tire, and he was reminded of his recent tumbling, pummeling dream. Those fevered images seemed to further weaken him, and he raised his head above the water to sight for his goal and gain a firmer grip on the real world. With relief he realized he had only several more lunges before he would reach the longed for boulder. In his new eagerness and hope, however, his hands slipped temporarily from the rope, and he had to caution himself to be more careful. Finally, hooking his hand over the loop that encircles the boulder, he breathed deeply and then lunged forward to grasp the other side of the rock. The effort had cost him, and he had to fight to hold on while at the same time trying to regain his breath and strength. While he did so, he glanced up and saw to his relief that the slope of the moss covered cliff above him was not so precipitous as he remembered. It was less reassuring, however, to see that the heavy mist was hanging so low he had no way of learning just how far up the cliff they would have to climb.

Drawing another deep breath, he kicked his feet and pulled with all his might to drag himself up on the rock. As he did so, he arched his back and brought his chest perpendicular against the onrushing current. The full force of the water struck the now greater resistance of his body, and there was a sudden lurch of the boulder, and Front had time for no more than a short scream as the rope and the boulder seemed to rise up from the water and lunge toward him. He was struck painfully by the pointed boulder, and he let go of the rope to clutch his chest. Suddenly the rope whipped out of his hands as the great boulder tumbled by him. Forgetting all else, he struggled desperately for the air above him, only to be dragged beneath the water by a jerk of the rope that had coiled itself around his leg.

He doubled up to grapple with that entangling, dragging rope, and managed to free himself enough to churn again to the surface. With one gulp of air his panic eased a bit, and he was able to remember to re-grip the rope before it slipped completely from his hands. Then swimming ferociously toward the wall and downstream, he had just begun to inch toward safety when the boulder-entangled rope snared his arm and dragged him under again.

Then the boulder must have caught along the edge of the rock-strewn bottom, for the rope went slack, and Front was able to swim again to the surface and make his way more quickly to the bank.

Wonina was there, pulling him forth and clutching him to her. "Oh, Front, Front, my poor darling, I thought you were lost you for sure."

Front held her with one arm, but made sure he had the end of the rope in the other. "I'm all right, I'm all right. Here...help me pull the rope in."

They tugged several times before they were able to disengage and recover the precious rope from the submerged boulder. Wonina then helped the exhausted Front back to the flatter boulders further from the water.

When they had again leaped over the cut, it was Nash who came forward, limping stiffly, to put his arms around Front.

"My God, boy, I thought you were a goner for sure."

"And if we had lost him, we all know whose fault it would be," Wons called out accusingly.

Front felt Nash's body stiffen, but Nash said nothing as he helped Front over to where he could sit against the back wall.

"Now what do we do?" Fyva asked.

Front was still breathing heavily, and Wonina responded first. "Let him rest, you people. Can't you see he's been hurt?"

Front wondered, had he been hurt? No, he realized, just scared.

"I'm all right, Wonina, just tired. Just let me rest." He turned to Fyva. "I'll try again in a moment."

"You will not," pleaded Wonina. "You were almost killed. I won't let you do that again!"

He patted her on the leg. "I wasn't hurt, Wonina, honest, now don't worry."

Having now sufficiently regained his breath, he raised his voice to address the others. He described what he had seen while briefly dangling from the line on the boulder. "If I can find another boulder to toss my line to, I'm sure we could make it up that cliff."

"If, if, if," cried Wonina. "And why should you be the one always risking yourself? It's someone else's turn to be a hero. If you're so eager to go back up those falls, Wons, why don't you try it this time?"

Wons moved slightly away, and Wonina seemed to catch herself. "Oh, Wons, I'm sorry. I didn't mean that. I'm just upset. What I mean is no one should risk himself like that."

"But, Wonina," Fyva said patiently, "you do realize we can't stay here forever."

"We don't have to leave this moment," Wonina's voice was becoming shrill. "And next time someone else really should be the one to take the risk!"

Nash saw his chance to return some of Wons' sarcasm. "How about it, Mr. Steward, sir. You're so good at picking mountains to climb, why don't you show us how to climb out of here?"

"Oh, but you're much better at stumbling down holes, Mr. Goat...excuse me, Mr. Goat herder. Why don't you lead your flock back up the mountain you made us crawl down?"

Nash's voice grew harder. "The only one who crawls around here is the one who wants to crawl on his knees to the Outhans."

"One more crack out of you, slime, and you won't even be able to crawl."

This time it was Wons who surged to his feet and lunged forward. Front was so startled by Wons' movement that he was too late as he swung his arms to restrain Nash. The tall and the stocky two scuffled only briefly on their feet before the slimy footing brought them both down with a thud.

Front struggled to stand, and before Wonina could also rise, Fyva was holding her back. "No, Wonina. Let them have at it. This has been a long time coming. Let them get it over with."

Front now also held himself back, feeling there was wisdom in what Fyva said. Instead of interfering, he hovered over them, wanting to make sure there was no real damage done.

"No! Stop it!" screamed Wonina. "This is wrong! Stop them! They'll hurt themselves. Please, let me go," and with an even greater effort, she yanked free of Fyva and threw herself upon the tumbling, flailing combatants.

Wonina's intervention stilled the battlers, but not before a random blow slammed against her head. She sat back hard on her bottom. The two men, seeing what they had done, disengaged from each other and hovered around her. Holding her bowed head, Wonina whispered in a tired voice, "I'm all right. Please, just please stop fighting."

Both men, with an arm about Wonina, glared at one another, but Wonina had won her way. Wons backed off and sat down again. Nash helped Wonina against the wall and held her in his arms, her head cradled on his shoulder.

After a while Wonina spoke into the unsettled quietness, "That's better. Now we're all calmed down. Promise me there'll be no more fighting."

When no one answered, Wonina pleaded again, "Please, you promise, don't you? You won't do anything like that again, will you?"

Still no one spoke, and Front finally pulled himself to his knees. "Well, I think I'll have another go at roping a boulder."

"You will not, Front!" Wonina's voice instantly took on that shrill pitch.

Front couldn't understand the intensity of her objection; he figured she would at least be pleased at his intervention to divert the combatants from further bickering, even though he knew she didn't want him to be the one to take the risk. Patiently he tried to explain, "Wonina, we all know I'm the best one for the job. I'm best with the rope, and I'm the best swimmer. Since I'm the lightest male, I'm probably even the best climber. I'm not being a hero, I'm just being practical."

Nash put a restraining hand on Front's leg. "And I'm not being a hero either, Front, but if anybody goes this time, it'll be me. I've gotten enough sympathy out of this leg anyway. I think I'm ready for a little exercise."

"Well, well," said Wons sarcastically, "the heel's healed."

This time it was Fyva who barked, "Enough, Wons! We'll get no place if you two start bickering again."

Front, who had been touched by Nash's willingness, felt his own annoyance at Wons' behavior. "Damn you, Wons! If you can't offer any worthwhile suggestions, keep your mouth shut!"

Wons looked shocked, but he recovered quickly, and was starting to reply when Wonina screamed. "No, no, not you too, Front! I can't take any more of this! It's just like at home, always shouting and fighting. I can't take it, I can't take it." She buried her face in her hands and sobbed.

The others looked at one another, dumbfounded, as Wonina's sobbing became even more uncontrollable. "Damn you, damn you all! "she shouted through her sobs. "Go ahead and kill yourselves for all I care!"

Finally Fyva moved over and put her arms around Wonina. "I'm with you, Wonina. I agree, we've got to stop squabbling among ourselves. Now come on, calm down, honey. Get a hold of yourself."

Front wondered why he hadn't been the one to reach out to Wonina. She was always so quick to come to his aid. But he still knelt there, baffled at her new behavior. He had to quickly reconsider all he knew about her so as to understand what was happening. Lately she had been so strong, the solidest member of the group, the one who risked her all for the others. He remembered now that she was also the one who seemed the first to be frightened. And her allusion to fighting at home, apparently no one else was aware of her family discord. That seemed to explain her fearful sensitivity to fighting in the group. Her risk taking, in spite of her fears, or because of her fears, nevertheless now seemed even more admirable to Front. He finally overcame his shock and belatedly moved over to comfort her.

"Oh, Front," Wonina whimpered, "what are we going to do? What are we going to do?"

But it was Fyva who quietly answered. "It seems only logical, if we can't go backward, and we've certainly stood still long enough, it's time we go forward."

Involuntarily, they all turned toward the black hole of receding water that stared threateningly from behind them.

7

COUNCIL OF COMPROMISE AND COLLUSION

Wonina voiced the fear they were all undoubtedly feeling. "But we can't go into that hole. It pours into the ground, and we'll never come out."

"Now, now," Fyva soothed. "You're letting your imagination run away with you, Wonina. If this cave is a natural phenomenon, then this stream is merely a continuation of the stream above. Though it seems like miles and years ago, we were heading along this same stream because it cuts through the mountain hanging over our heads. It's still cutting through the mountain, and it'll eventually come out the other side."

"Are you sure about that, Fyva?" Nash asked eagerly.

"Relatively sure. We know the terrain here is gradually sloping downward toward the great swamp. Now a swamp is always situated on top of very spongy ground. There can be no caverns beneath a swamp, so this stream must break out of the mountain again before it reaches the swamp."

Front was impressed with how calm and sure Fyva seemed of herself. He wondered, however, where she had learned about underground streams and swamps. Her information seemed reasonable, but he wasn't entirely convinced. He started to ask about the possibility the stream might eventually just ooze into the ground beneath the swamp rather than breaking out above ground when Fyva continued smoothly, "I say all these things will be true if indeed this is a natural cave, but that's a big 'if'."

Nash, who had seemed satisfied with the information he had already received, was suddenly concerned again. "What do you mean, 'if'?"

"Just look about you. Does it seem reasonable to you that a natural cave, a cave that for so many years has been carved by running water, would have so many sharp angles?"

The others began to reexamine the cave about them.

"And those two side passageways, notice how they're almost identical—two openings ending in partially blocked pathways, and notice those two identical grates that Wonina used to talk to us. Isn't that too much of a coincidence to be natural?" Fyva paused to let this new information sink in, then continued dramatically, "People, we left Mount Stareye looking for a road we'd seen on a mysterious map, hoping it would lead us to the Angle Beings. I think we've found that road."

"Oh, come on, Fyva," Wons interrupted jeeringly. "We're not back to that Angle Being garbage are we? Haven't we had enough stupidity?" He turned to Front. "Let's you and me work on your plan, Front. If these others want to listen to fairy tales...."

Fyva seemed unruffled by Wons' interruption. "And another thing. If you really want to go backward, I'd say stop trying to go up the falls. Go under them."

That stopped Wons, and now Front was even more interested.

"Notice all these unnatural lines," she stressed the word, unnatural. "Notice how they head straight for the falls and disappear underneath them. My guess is this underground channel we're in now wasn't originally filled with water. Through the ages, the stream broke through the roof above and filled this roadway with water. Before that time, it was the very roadway we saw on the map, stretching from Mount Stareye to the great source of power."

The others were quiet when Fyva paused again. She took her time and looked at each one before continuing. "My guess is if you followed the roadway, or now waterway, beneath those falls, you'd soon start sloping up the mountain, probably eventually on a dry roadway. Eventually you'd reach whatever was underneath circle in the platform on Mount Stareye.

That idea was definitely intriguing to Front. He turned and examined the falls more carefully, trying to peer beyond them. Even trying to see what he hoped to see, however, he wasn't able to make out any indication there was a continuation of the stream behind the falls. Still, it might be possible, once behind the falls where water pressure wouldn't be so fierce, it might be possible....

Fyva seemed to be reading his mind. "But why go against the current when you can go with it? Why not go downstream to get where we originally wanted to go? Need I remind you of our primary purpose in making this trip?"

This time it was Front who interrupted. "My primary purpose at the moment, Fyva, is to get us out of here alive."

"Exactly! And the surest way of doing that is to go downstream." Front apparently looked unconvinced, and Fyva pressed on, "Look, Front, you've tried making it up the falls. You tried your very best, and I admire you for that. It was a courageous thing you did, trying to find a way back, risking your own life for all of us. But it's time now for another kind of courage—courage to face the unknown." She laughed quickly, "And frankly that unknown takes a lot less courage for me to face, since I'm convinced that not only will we reach our hoped for goal, but we'll reach it much more safely."

Again Front had to admire the smooth way Fyva had countered every argument. Though not totally convinced by her reasoning, he was relieved at how quickly she had calmed the seething animosity within the group. He noticed that Wons and Nash were no longer glaring at one another. In fact Nash seemed almost content, apparently satisfied with

Fyva's new suggestion. Even Wons looked partially convinced. Only he and Wonina were still holding back.

"I don't know, Fyva," Wonina shook her head, glancing again at the dark opening in the back wall. "I've looked into that hole. Shouldn't we be able to see something, at least some light, at the far end of the cave? I haven't seen anything back there."

Fyva responded quickly, "That's probably because there's too much light here in this cave. If we were to go further into the darkness, I'm sure our eyes would adjust and allow us to see light at the other end."

Wonina still shook her head, and Wons now seemed about to speak.

"Actually, that's something we can test," Fyva hurried on. "If one of us were to allow himself to be tied onto the rope and be let out into the cave, I'm sure he'd be able to see what I'm talking about."

"What do you mean 'he'?" Wonina quickly objected. "If you're talking about Front's going in again, I think he's had enough!"

"Well, of course it needn't be Front this time. In fact," Fyva smiled, "I see no reason why I shouldn't be the one to test my own theory."

Wonina hastily changed her tone. "Well, I didn't necessarily mean you, Fyva...."

"Oh, come on, Wonina. You're the one who's been taking risks for the rest of us. I say we girls are just as tough as the boys." She put her arm around Wonina. "Now it's my turn to show the rest how tough we girls are. Besides, there's really no risk. The fellows will just hold the rope, and let it out slowly until I say stop, and then pull me back after I've seen light at the other end." She jumped to her feet. "Come on, let's get the rope."

She seemed to notice that Front was still hesitant. "I mean, this does seem reasonable to me, Front. You tried your way, now I'll try mine. If mine doesn't work, then we'll try yours again. That way, we're both getting our way, and we both stand to win. Now isn't that reasonable?"

"All right, Fyva," Front laughed. "Whatever else, we can always depend upon you to be reasonable."

"But before you go into that water," Wonina interjected, "I want you to bind your ankles and wrists like Front did. If you're going to be a heroine, you might as well be a warm heroine." She pulled up her outer jacket, and then quickly pulled it down again.

"I guess we'd better tear off a part of your undergarment this time, Fyva. I've already gone about as far as I can go in that direction."

The others laughed, and Wonina hurried to help Fyva tear off the necessary binding material and to secure her ankles, wrists, and neck.

Before the three men lowered Fyva into the water, Wonina quickly scampered across to the other side of the stream. Once again Front's heart lurched as Wonina leapt across that perilous space. It seemed to him that she was becoming almost carelessly casual in her hurried leaps. She then stretched out on the damp boulders on the other side. "I'll have a better angle of sight from this side," she explained.

"Wheee!" Fyva shivered as she hit the water. "This hero bit is no fun after all."

The rope jerked taut as Fyva was caught by the current.

"Let it out easy," Wonina cautioned from across the stream. The three men worked together to allow the current to take Fyva away and into the darkness. Front and Nash had already checked the rope carefully and made sure the two parts were still securely tied together. They had looked for a place to fasten the end of the rope, but there was nothing protruding, nor were any of the cracks in the platform narrow enough even to allow for wedging a knotted end of the rope. They had to be satisfied using a knotted end to at least give them a firmer grip.

"I can't see her any more," Wonina shouted.

The men quickly halted the rope, but then Fyva called from the cave, "I'm all right. Keep letting out the line. Hey, this is fun! I feel like a kite on a wet wind."

The three men laughed. Only Wonina seemed unamused.

They eventually let loose most of the rope, maintaining only line enough for the three of them to grip. The drag on the rope was strong but not so strong as to cause undue concern.

There was silence for a time, and then concern began to grow again.

Finally Fyva's muffled voice was heard calling excitedly, "I think I see something. I'm not sure, but I think I see light!"

"All right, pull her in," Wonina demanded.

With relief, the men went along with Wonina's insistence and quickly, though with some effort, retrieved Fyva from the dark cave.

As Fyva clambered up the slick side of the platform, there were eager questions.

"What did you see?"

"What was there?"

"Are you sure you saw light?"

"Let her get her breath, boys," Wonina called from across the stream. "Are you all right, Fyva?"

"I'm all right, Wonina. It's not bad. It's not half bad. I got used to the water and the darkness in no time."

"But what's back there?"

"Well," Fyva struggled to calm her voice. "At first, of course, there was nothing. As my eyes slowly adjusted, I could see that the walls of the cave beyond this barrier seem to be straight and smooth, just like along the walls here, only the two walls back there are much closer together. I seemed almost to have reached another small platform of rocks when you stopped me. I closed my eyes, hoping to let them adjust even more to the darkness, and when I first opened them and looked downstream, I'm sure I saw light."

"And what then?" asked Front.

"Well, I'm not quite sure. I was bobbing about in the current, and sometimes my head would sink a little low, and then I'd get water in my eyes, and I was splashing, and then the platform seemed to have gotten in the way of the light, but I'm still sure I saw it."

Front's first exhilaration was beginning to fade, slowly being replaced by some of his old doubt. "But you're not absolutely sure, Fyva?" he asked.

"No." She shook her head slowly. "But I am sure someone who's a better swimmer could have fought the current and moved over more to the other side of the channel. There, I'm sure you could have seen clear to the other end, and seen the light."

"There you go talking about Front again," cautioned Wonina. "Remember your promise! We're to test your way and then get back to Front's way."

"But it'll be so much easier and far safer for Front to at least test the cave one more time before he tries what he tried this morning. It'd only take a few moments, Wonina!"

Front had to admit the effort of dangling on a rope and letting someone else do the pulling was certainly more pleasant to contemplate than the agony he had undergone last evening. "She's right, Wonina. It wouldn't hurt for me to give in just a little more. After all, we all stand to win if she's right. And maybe especially me," he chuckled, and raised his arms. "Okay, tie me up."

"Oh, please be careful, Front!"

"What's this, Wonina," he chided reassuringly, "don't you think that I'm just as tough as Fyva?"

As Front turned to clamber down the sides, he noticed that Fyva had taken a place at the end of the rope, and this time Wons had moved to the front of the platform. The cold blackness rushed over him, and he struggled quickly to the surface. He was staring into the light, and his vision was further impeded by the spray breaking across his face. Slowly that amorphous light dimmed as he was pushed farther into the cave. He gripped the rope firmly in front of him, not trusting the knot on the loop underneath his arms. When he felt the rope jerk tautly, he struggled to do as Fyva had suggested, swimming across current to come as close as possible to the opposite all. Turning and churning upward, he peered into the darkness.

It's there, he started to shout, but then checked himself. For a moment he thought he had seen light, not white light as he had expected, but it seemed almost a series of colored lights. He thrust himself outward and upward again, but this time there was nothing. The next time he tried, he thought he saw a white light, but he now guessed it was light from behind him reflecting off the splashes he was making. He peered again into the somewhat lessening gloom. He saw to his left the small outcropping of rocks that Fyva had mentioned. Perhaps if he could stand upon those rocks, he would have a better view.

"Can you let me out further?" he called back, "I'm heading for the platform," and began swimming to the near side again.

He had almost reached the platform when he heard a scream and then Fyva's wail, "It slipped, it slipped! I couldn't hold the end!"

Suddenly Front was terrifyingly free; the rope pressure against his body was relieved, and he was flying. His first lunge, however, was so desperate that he indeed flew out of the water and flopped onto the edge of the platform.

Crawling up the rest of the way, he then heard Fyva pleading for forgiveness, "Front, I'm sorry...I tried to grab the rope...I lunged into Nash and Wons...Front, forgive me, forgive me."

"I'm safe," he called out to reassure them, "I'm on the small platform."

"But they shouldn't have dropped the rope," Fyva complained.

"You bitch, you almost shoved us in to the water," Wons countered. "Who could think about the rope?"

At the mention of the rope, Front remembered he was still being tugged by that dangling tail. He began to draw in the line as the voice in the distance continued trying to explain. Staring in that direction, he caught a glimpse of a shadow breaking the light as Wonina flew again across the opening. When she spoke, her voice was louder and firmer than the others. "Never mind your stupid explanations. What are we going to do about Front? We've got to get him back!"

The others began to offer suggestions, but not so loudly as Wonina had been, and the noise level settled to a lower pitch and became inaudible. Having pulled in the line, Front could think of nothing better to do than to begin coiling it carefully about his waist so at least to get it out of the way. Then he wondered if perhaps he should leave it uncoiled. Perhaps then he could cast it back toward the others...No, the distance was obviously too great. Just to be sure, however, he rose cautiously to his feet and considered the distance again. No, obviously too far. He then began checking the walls. He was not surprised to find the same slickness he had found everywhere else in these caves, but he could see, silhouetted against the light, no indication whatsoever of a ledge upon which he might crawl back to the others. He turned to peer, though with little hope, in the other direction. Unhappily, he was again not surprised; his eyes met only darkness, no promising light to show the way to salvation. Perhaps there are other barriers jutting out from this wall that is blocking the light, he tried to reassure himself. Leaning out over the water to check, however, was out of the question. The footing was too slick. He squatted down, a small feeling of despondency beginning to seep into him.

He was relieved to eventually hear Wonina's voice. "Hold on, Front, we're coming. We're coming to you."

He started to protest, "Coming to me? Wait just a minute...."

But Wonina continued, "We've decided, we've all decided, it's the best thing to do."

"But I don't see a light," he called out.

"Never mind. We know it's there. Now, I'm going to come first. I'll be in your boat and carrying your pack. I'm going to paddle over to where you are, and then somehow we've got to get into the boat together. The others will be waiting to start as soon as we join up."

"But the boat's too small," he shouted back.

"Now, don't argue, Front. There's no other way. The boat will hold us until we get to the other side of the mountain. Don't worry, we've thought of everything." Front settled back somewhat heartened, but hardly convinced of the wisdom of this latest decision. He chuckled wryly to himself, it's strange how it worked out. I was the one most resistant to Fyva's plan, and here I am the instrument that's forcing the group to follow that plan...He quickly shoved aside the unpleasant thought that Fyva's losing her grip on the rope might not have been all that accidental. No, her voice was just too forlorn and penitent when she begged forgiveness.

"Here I come, Front," he heard Wonina's shout, followed by a splat. Against the backlight of the cave, he could then make out Wonina's ferocious splashing. He held his breath and reached. Almost too quickly, she was upon him. Her own efforts got her to him, however, and she banged solidly into the rocks in front of him. He grabbed the boat and pulled it up sharply, almost slipping himself and tumbling her back into the water. Desperately, with his other hand, be grabbed her by the back of the jacket and yanked, and then they both sprawled together onto the slippery platform.

"Oh, Front, Front," and she clutched him so convulsively he had trouble holding onto the boat, which was now sliding off the platform. He felt like laughing and crying, and he wanted only to hold her, but as the boat slipped further, he thought better to push her aside slightly and grab the boat instead.

"I think you're crazy. I think we're all crazy," he laughed, "but before your whole plan goes down the stream, literally, help me get the boat in."

When the boat was also on the platform with them, Wonina shouted to the others, "Okay, we're just about to get started again. Is everyone ready?"

They shouted back their readiness.

"I think it best if you get in first, Front. Then I'll lie on top and hold onto you."

The thought crossed his mind that he would rather be on top, but then he felt rather silly, considering their current desperate circumstances.

She steadied the boat, and he crawled in. As she edged it into the water, however, she must not have anticipated the strength of the current, and the boat was ripped from her hands.

"Wonina!" he screamed.

Wonina threw herself from the platform, landed on top of him, and grabbed for his neck. They both went under. With one hand Front grabbed back for her, and with the other he clutched the boat.

Thank God for boat-bark, Front marveled, as the little craft bobbed sluggishly again to the surface.

Wonina was scrambling to perch more securely on his back, and though the boat seemed to ride precariously low in the water, they were still afloat.

"I'll have to move more forward in the boat," he shouted through gulps of water. "My arms won't be able to fit into the arm notches, but I'm high enough to dangle them over the sides of the boat."

As best he could, he slid forward, and she slid further down his rear with her hands about his neck.

"Don't choke me, Wonina."

She eased her grip slightly. Arching his back, he was barely able to peer into the darkness above the bow of the boat. It was obvious they were moving rapidly into the darkness. He looked hopefully for a light ahead, but as yet there was nothing. His arched position was awkward, but he found that by lifting and lowering his head regularly, his neck didn't get too tired. It took quite a bit more squirming and positioning before they could properly balance the boat and keep the bow pointing forward.

All that squirming was tiring, but Front realized it was rather pleasant in its way. Wonina's body working against his was almost enough to compensate for the discomfort. Unlike the others, at least he was not alone in this rapidly closing darkness.

It suddenly came to him he had almost forgotten about the others. The frightening thought occurred that they might not have left at all, that he and Wonina were alone in this ever-increasing darkness. He jerked his head to the side and looked backward. The cave opening was growing smaller, as it faded in the distance, but before he could distinguish anything else, the boat lurched to the left, and he had to turn his head quickly to redirect their craft.

"Front, we're going to collide with something!" Wonina screamed, and he felt her head duck beside his. He scrunched down further, his face in the water to allow her to press even closer to him. Wonina quickly raised her head again.

"What was it?" he asked, spitting out water.

"I don't know. It seemed like something was stretching across the stream."

He could feel her looking backward.

"It's fading fast, but it almost looks like some kind of ramp...No, it's too irregular for that. Like something has fallen across the stream, like a water tower base, maybe."

Damn! We should've grabbed for it, he thought to himself. Maybe it was a bridge across the stream. Maybe it led somewhere. Where else he wanted to go, he didn't know; he only knew he could still see no light in the direction the stream was taking them, and he wasn't happy about going further into the darkness.

But the darkness and the rushing hiss of the water was all there was for them. He looked back again briefly, because that was all he could manage. That object, whatever it might have been, seemed to have further blotted out the greatly diminished light far behind them.

They rushed on. The darkness was becoming so intense he could no longer see the sides of the walls, and after a while, even the noise of the water swishing along those walls began to fade. He guessed the channel was widening, or perhaps the pace of the stream was slowing. Whatever was happening, the blackness was becoming larger. He sensed that Wonina must also be depressed by that blackness. He could feel her body pressing closer to his and her clutching hands were again beginning to cut off his air. He was even reluctant to ask her to let up the pressure, since that pressure was the only reassuring thing he felt at the moment.

"Wonina, you're choking me again," he gasped finally.

She let up, but whispered in his ear, "Front I'm scared."

"So am I, honey. But at least we're moving again. We'll get there...we'll get somewhere."

Somehow she drew her body even closer to his, and there was now only the vast blackness that Front's imagination soon made into a towering, yawning cave, a terrifying subterranean sea, into which they were sailing rapidly and alone. The rush of water seemed now only a whisper, a whisper from some great distance. To either side of them, the vastness became so great he was now afraid to move for fear of disturbing that eternal blackness.

But eventually he felt their boat had turned sideways to the current, and he was forced to flutter his legs to redirect the boat. He was relieved to hear his splashing echoing immediately from the two walls, and he realized their familiar walls had never left them. Immediately he could feel that they were in the same narrow channel, and he knew it was only his imagination that had created that other even more fearsome world.

Relief quickly turned to concern, however, as Wonina "Wooped," and he felt the boat jar. She pressed down against him, and then let go with one of her hands.

Quickly he grabbed back for her, but then she explained reassuringly, "I just bumped my head.. We passed under one of those things again."

Hastily, Front tried back paddling, but the current was still too rapid. Then, with Wonina trying to be more cautious of her head, they continued downstream. Wonina kept one hand in front of her head, and Front kept his own head down most of the time. The quietness settled about them again, and now for the first time during this new day's ordeal the chill of the water reasserted itself. His body remembered that earlier agony in the narrow corner cave yesterday when he and Nash were struggling to survive against this same heat sapping wetness. At least, he mused, it's more fun being squeezed by Wonina. He imagined there was a growing spot of warmth between them, almost at the point where the middle of her body met his buttocks, and every so often she squirmed and the warmth seemed to increase. He was amused at his own pleasant absurdity. No heat could be transmitted through their double thick serpent-skins and the cold water. He realized he was creating his own heat, and not sharing Wonina's, but it was a pleasant thought nonetheless. Then every time she moved to adjust her position, the thought reoccurred.

"There's light ahead!" Wonina shouted joyfully.

At just that moment, Front's face was down below the water in their boat, and his eyes were closed. When he jerked upward, he could see nothing.

"There were colored lights. The whole ceiling seemed to light up!"

"I saw it too," came a small voice to the rear of them—Fyva's voice. "It was beautiful," she marveled.

They're still with us, Front sighed, but he didn't allow himself time experience his relief. He could see nothing. He wanted to know more, "What happened to the lights? I don't see anything."

"They just flicked off as quickly as they came on."

"Colored lights?" he asked.

"Red, blue, green, yellow—it was like carnival on the Commons!"

The whole picture brought back to Front the crazy dream he had last night, when he had seen himself wrapped in a jeweled robe, and he recalled now he had thought he had seen those same kinds of lights upon wakening.

"It must be your imagination," he suggested, hoping he was wrong.

"But Fyva saw it too. You heard her."

Fyva! He heard her! Of course. Now he allowed himself to fully realized what that meant and experience his relief. The others had been following them all along. "Are you all there?" he bellowed. "Wons, Nash, are you there too?"

He moaned happily when he heard the two male voices answering from the darkness. At least we're going together into this unknown blackness. But then he remembered, unknown *colored* blackness...What could that mean?

He looked ahead again, but there was no color, only blackness, and he lowered his head and went back to contemplating the warmth between himself and Wonina.

"More light! More light!" Wonina suddenly shouted.

"Colored?" he asked, raising his head.

"Well...blue," she answered.

Lifting his head again, he stared, and in fact there did seem to be a vague bluish glow shimmering in the corridor ahead of them. He tried to raise himself even higher, but Wonina started slipping backward. The brief glimpse he had caught, however, indicated they were rapidly approaching that blueness.

"On either side, under the water," Wonina pointed.

He jerked up again and experienced a flash of brightness, and then it faded behind them.

"Did you see it? Did you see it?" Fyva called excitedly. "Now do you believe me? I told you these weren't natural caves. That was some kind of artificial light under the water."

"Light? Under water?" Front wondered. "How could there be artificial light underneath water?" He wanted to argue with Fyva, but it was too difficult to speak with a craned neck. The only light under water he knew of was natural—sea creatures gave off such light. Suddenly that thought was rather disturbing. It would have been quite a large creature to have put out so much light, and he hadn't before this time thought about the possibility these waters might be inhabited by anything other than themselves.

"Not just the lights, I'm not just talking about the lights," Fyva broke into his thoughts. "Just above the lights, there seemed to have been another platform."

"That's right. I saw it too," agreed Wonina.

"Front," Fyva directed, "if we come to another set of lights, do your best to grab hold of something and stop. We've got to find what those lights are."

In his rational mind, Front agreed—that is, *if* they came to another set of lights. But the unpleasant imagined prospect of investigating some charged up, and maybe charging underwater creature, was not agreeable to contemplate. Still, the two lights they had apparently passed had seemed to be stationary. Perhaps it was a sedentary creature, a sponge or a hydra of some kind, attached to the sides of the walls. At any rate, he eagerly looked forward to at least a return of any kind of light.

Fyva further directed, "Some of us should stay to the left of the cave, and others to the right. That way, we'll have more of a chance of grabbing hold."

Dutifully, Front guided his craft over to the left.

"There! Just ahead," Wonina shouted, and she started thrusting and paddling against the wall.

All too quickly they pounded against a bright object. Both he and Wonina were clutching at that slippery object. By reaching a bit higher Front was able to place the flat of his hand on its surface, and there was enough friction there to slow their progress. They slid to a halt, and he was then able to reach up an elbow to gain more fastness.

"There seems to be a little lip along the edge here. I've got a good hold," indicated Wonina. "I think I can pull myself up.

"Wait!" Front pleaded.

Wonina was already shoving down on him, and he suddenly felt her weight lift from his body. He felt much lighter, and much more alone. Hurriedly, he grabbed for a better grip himself, while at the same time trying to hold onto the boat.

He remembered then he could probably see what he was doing if he only opened his eyes. When he did so, he could see Wonina already on a platform above them, and he felt her holding on to him. He pulled himself out, and pulled the boat up after him.

"We did it, Front, we did it!" Wonina was clutching and squeezing him.

Yes, but what, he thought. He was already reasonably sure they had not been tangling with some undersea monster, but then what was this thing they were sitting on?

"Nash, Fyva, Wons, are you okay?" Wonina demanded.

Wonina loosed him, and he also became concerned about the others. But even before they called back, Front could see in the dim glow coming from the water and reflecting off the slimy walls that there were three figures perched on a ledge directly across from them. The light from below the water cast them in eerie shadows.

"Good! You made it," answered Fyva. "Let's investigate what this thing is."

"No," corrected Wonina. "Let's not investigate. Let's rest!"

"But..." Fyva started to protest, then changed her mind. "Yes, you're right, we do need rest. Also, I think it'd be a good idea if we break out some food and replenish our warmth."

That was the best idea Fyva had had all morning, Front grumbled to himself. Secure on their lighted platform, however, his feelings were warming again toward Fyva. He didn't yet know where they were, but they *did seem* to be moving toward some definite goal, and under her direction the group had become more organized. Furthermore, he was thankful the others had come to his rescue, and he guessed that Wonina and Fyva were responsible for that quick decision.

"Eat, Front," Wonina urged him, and he needed little further urging.

As he prepared his food, by feel and memory, he was also checking the amount of food he had left. Perhaps one or two more days, by stretching it, he estimated. And then what? Maybe it wouldn't be such a bad thing to find that there *were* creatures in this blackness. If they went beyond another day or so, before reaching the surface, they would need to try to fish these waters. With those thoughts in mind, he cut short his eating, and repacked his food.

Wonina had done likewise, and now she moved closer to him, placing her head on his shoulder and her hands in his lap. She squeezed her hands down between his thighs, and although he realized she was probably just warming her hands, her positioning was definitely arousing. He slipped an arm around her shoulder, and then almost withdrew it as he remembered to glance across the stream. What am I doing, he thought accusingly? There's Nash, not more than twenty feet away, and here I am thinking of fondling his girl. Already, half our time is being spent trying to keep Nash and Wons from killing each other. If I don't leave Wonina alone, Nash and I will be at it too.

He was still there, frozen, unable to either further embrace Wonina or to withdraw his arm, when Nash called from across the gulf. "Are you all right, honey?"

"Yes, yes, I'm fine, Nash. Just cold."

Front felt even guiltier, and he was relieved when Fyva called again for investigation. "Front, after all you've been through, I don't want to ask you to take any more risks, but you've got the rope over there. What I'd like for you to do is have Wonina lower you into the water by the rope. We've just got to find out what this light source is beneath these platforms."

Not relishing sinking, even into that lighted depth, Front reasoned, "My guess is, Fyva, it's a natural phenomenon. I've often seen sponges and corals on the reefs at night that light up like this. It's part of the way they attract other species for food or even for mating with their own species."

"You mean those things are alive?" gasped Wonina. "Oh, no, Front's not going down there!"

"Come now, Wonina. Obviously these things haven't moved. Besides they're not things. They're some kind of artificial light, and we've got to find out what they are. The more we know about this place, the more we learn about the Angle Beings, the sooner we'll be able to get to the source of power we must reach if we're to fight the Outhans. Front, if you'll just do this one last thing, I promise the next risk will be mine."

"You're always promising something, Fyva," Wonina challenged.

"Girls, girls, enough!" Front intervened. "Wonina, it's no big thing. Don't worry, I won't get hurt. Come on, tie the rope about me. Let's get this over with."

"But, Front...."

"No buts. Just tie it."

"Why are you always the one to give in?"

"Wonina, Fyva's right. We've got to do what we've got to do if we're ever going to get back home." He dismissed her further argument by gesturing toward the rear wall. "There seems to be a small crevice where the platform meets the wall. Wedge the knotted end of the rope in there."

Mumbling, Wonina did as she was told.

Breathing deeply, Front lowered himself into the glowing water. With one last breath, he ducked beneath and headed toward the brightness below.

He kept his eyes closed at first, but he could tell the brightness was increasing—a bluish glow, growing whiter as he descended. Finally he opened his eyes, and struggling to maintain his position against the current, he cautiously felt before him. All he could see was blurred distortion, and his hands met a slick but rough surface, which seemed to be between him and the source of light. The glowing object appeared roughly round, almost like a half of a globe, and the rough surface changed to mere slickness where it met the wall.

He was about to submerge even deeper, for it seemed to him there was a break in the wall just below the light, when he felt something bump his back. The bump was slight, but his breath almost left him. In panic, he struggled to the surface and lunged up onto the platform.

"My God, Front! What happened?"

Drawing in a deep breath and struggling to relax, he lied, "Nothing, nothing. I just came up for breath."

Wonina hovered over him, obviously unconvinced, but waiting for him to catch his breath.

He guessed it was a lie. Had he in fact been bumped by something? Or was it his imagination? As he had twisted away from the glare, it almost seemed he had seen a long black object slithering away into the darkness. Such wild imaginings would do no one any good, he realized, and lie or not, he certainly didn't intend to scare Wonina with what might just be imagination. She was already concerned enough, and soon she would have to be back in this fantasy provoking water.

"What was it? What did you find, Front?" Fyva called.

Drawing in another breath, he described what he had seen, but not what he thought he had felt.

"Could you pull it off the wall, Front? If only we had something like that to take back with us."

Front was sure there was no way he could possibly have even gotten a grip on that thing. "I still don't know whether it's natural or artificial, Fyva. Either way, if it's dislodged, I suspect the light would die."

After a moment's thought, Fyva agreed reluctantly. "I suppose you're right. But it would've been nice...All right, let's get started again."

"In a minute, Fyva. I want to do some work on our boat first to make it more comfortable for the Wonina and me."

"All right, but hurry up. Remember our mission."

Front started to be a bit irritated at Fyva's constant reminder of their mission, but before he could develop his irritation, Fyva called out again.

"Forgive me, Front. I'm sorry I'm so impatient. I know this mission is just as important to you as it is to me. It's also important that you make your boat as comfortable as possible. Take whatever time you need."

He felt somewhat better about Fyva, but only somewhat. He put it out of his mind, however, as he explained to Wonina what he planned to do. "I'm going to cut another set of arm holes a little further toward the front of the boat. Then I'll be able to help more with the paddling and guiding. I'll wear my pack in the front, and that will prop my chest up just a bit, so my neck won't get so tired. What do you think?"

"I think you always think of everything, precious."

Front felt himself flush, and then he felt silly when he caught himself looking across the stream to see if Nash had overheard. To cover his embarrassment, he quickly pulled his knife from his side sheath and began to carve the arm slots.

He reversed his pack, and this time their embarkation from the platform was far less hazardous. It took very little repositioning to discover that his makeshift work on the boat had greatly improved his comfort and also his ability to maneuver the boat.

Quickly the five of them were away again, four small boats heading into a new darkness. This time, as the warmth between himself and Wonina returned, he tried not to dwell on it. Instead he concentrated on what might lay ahead of them. In spite of his reluctance to believe that the lights behind them were artificial, he was becoming more convinced that this channel could not be natural. This stretch of water seemed perfectly straight, and, as Fyva had said, such straight lines were not typical in nature. Surely a stream would have met some obstacle that would have forced it into bending and changing its course. But, on the other hand, what kind of force could have carved such endless straightness beneath the earth? If those were indeed artificial lights, how could they still be glowing after what must have been ages since this cave or channel was carved? There seemed no answer to these questions in the simple technical knowledge of the Sebasans. Wons, he remembered, used to have an almost religious reverence for the Angle Beings. He now began to wonder if perhaps the power they were seeking might be something other than advanced knowledge—something other...other worldly. On the other hand, he quickly reassured himself, why would supernatural beings need to carve roadways through rock? Surely a god or even a demon would merely move himself from place to place by magic and not have to go to so much effort. Whoever those Angle Beings were, he concluded, it certainly would be nice to have them as allies against the Outhans. However better prepared the Outhans were, with their swords and spears, the weapons and ships he had heard described would be pitiful against whatever weapons the Angle Beings must have used. The hopeful thought then occurred to him that if those lights were artificial and still burning, then it might just be remotely possible, if they did find weapons, that those weapons would still be serviceable.

All this fanciful speculation was beginning to raise his hopes, and when Wonina shouted again, and he opened his eyes to a new brightness, he almost expected to see a great chamber spreading before him, filled with marvelous magic swords and spears that flew by themselves.

At least he was not totally disappointed when he discovered the new light source was different from that they had left some time ago.

"Look at that!" he heard Fyva exclaim. "Now tell me that's not artificial light!"

They were rapidly approaching another platform, this time only on one side of the channel, but stretching in an arc for at least forty feet. Also it seemed to Front this new light was closer to the surface of the water.

"Hurry, hurry, paddle for it!" Fyva shouted excitedly. "We've got to get onto that platform."

The group needed little encouragement, and this time, since the platform was barely jutting above the surface of the water, they had little difficulty in quickly clambering aboard. They pulled their small boats back from the edge, and for the first time, the formerly continuous walls indented, creating a platform that was about fifteen feet deep and forty feet long. The ordinarily calm and steady Fyva was eagerly moving about the platform, examining the walls and then rushing back to the edge to look down at the water.

"Oh, no, this isn't natural. This has got to be something built by the Angle Beings. Hurry! Help me check the wall! See if there's an opening."

Fyva's excitement was contagious, and Front found himself sliding his hands carefully over the wall, looking for any kind of break or indentation. Several sweeps of the wall, however, were enough to dash their hope that something might lay behind that wall.

Fyva was now leaning out over the brink and stretching her arm downward. "Those lights are just out of reach. Oh, I'd love to get a hold of them." She turned to Front. "Front, do you think maybe you could...?"

"Fyva!" Wonina cautioned.

Fyva laughed, "Yes, you're right, you're right, It's my turn. All right, I really don't mind anyway." She leaned over the edge again. "It looks to me like this ledge indents quite a bit before it abuts the light. I can't wait to see what's underneath this ledge."

The curiosity of all seemed to have been piqued by this new observation, and they all leaned out, trying to glimpse beneath the ledge. The spreading glare was such that no clear view was possible, but it did appear that the platform they were on jutted unsupported from the wall, as though it was a the roof over something below the water, perhaps the true platform. Then the light would be on the back wall, lighting that submerged platform.

Fyva was already uncoiling the rope from around Front's waist. Her hands fumbled in her excitement, and Front pushed her gently away and finished the task himself. He then tied a careful knot, and slipped it over her shoulders and secured it under her arms.

"Okay, we'll let you down from upstream. The current here isn't that strong, so you shouldn't have too much trouble working your way below the surface. Once you get under the platform, don't try to swim back up the rope. Rather, swim out to the current and that should pull you out from under the platform."

"Okay, okay, I just wish I were half the swimmer you are, Front, but it is my turn, and this is one time I don't believe I really want you to take the risk. It's my show the whole way. I just know there's something down there!"

Front took the front position at the edge, with Nash just behind him and Wons wrapping the other end of the line around his waist. Wonina knelt and peered over the edge as they lowered Fyva into the bright water. It seemed to Front that Fyva took too few breaths before she dived quickly below, but he tried not to worry. He played the line out to keep up with her progress, and then when the slack came, he held tightly. He began counting under his breath and trying to check his own impatience and concern as he kept his eyes sharply downward.

"Oh, look," Wonina gasped, almost pleasantly, and then screamed. "The lights! They're coming this way! They're coming toward Fyva!"

Front turned, staring first at Wonina to his left and then over her head to a shimmer of color just below the surface of the water, a riot of blue, green, yellow, and red, flashing and sparkling in a sinuous, squirming curve, heading from downstream right toward the platform, rapidly pulling abreast of them, and right out from the point where Fyva must be.

"Oh, my God! Do something, Front! Do something!"

What the hell am I supposed to do? he thought foolishly as he began tugging at the rope to haul in Fyva. At the same moment, the rope snagged, and Nash lunged forward as if to throw himself into the water, bumping into Front. Then Front found himself arching outward and clutching the air just above that gorgeous and terrifying shimmer of lights slithering below him.

8

FALL BACK FORWARD

Front just couldn't believe his new predicament. One part of his mind knew that he hit the water and that almost immediately he felt a second impact of his body against a slick surface, peppered by hard, bright knots. Even while he closed his legs and arms about that sluggish flashing object, another part of his mind was bemused by the absurdity of his situation— one just doesn't go around leaping into underground streams and riding gaily flashing carnival poles. And why me? Why am I always the dumb one tumbling into this damn water?

So, what am I supposed to do now? He recalled stories of fishermen trying to fight off sharks with only their hand knives. Most of these stories, however, generally made clear the futility of such efforts. Nevertheless, Front fumbled to draw his knife. Without expecting much in the way of results, he positioned the weapon just in front of his face and plunged the blade downward. To his surprise, after an initial snag, the knife sank completely to its hilt. The creature beneath him gave a shudder and seemed to pick up speed.

The full reality of the situation then began to sink home. It didn't appear the monster had intended attack Fyva after all. Now, however, as the beast began to squirm to dislodge the knife, Front became more concerned for himself. The monster's only reaction, so far, to its new traveling partner was a shrug of its none existing shoulders, but somewhere beyond those metaphorical shoulders was a head—and presumably a mouth full of teeth. Furthermore, he and the monster were both moving rapidly upstream, away from any hope of help from the others.

Still feeling somewhat absurd, Front felt he had no choice but to pull out the knife and plunge home again. This time the beast shuddered more violently and began squirming. The slick surface of the creature promised quick dislodgement for Front, but then the lumps on the creature's hide caught on Front's lumpy sea serpent skin clothes. With each thrust of the knife, Front was pulling and working himself forward. His arm was now tiring and, although he frequently broke the surface, he had no time for a gulp of air. His arm was jarred when, with his last thrust, he struck solid bone, and his knife caught fast. The animal gave one final violent shudder, this time almost dislodging Front, then its movement ceased.

Apparently the blade had broken through the skull and entered the brain. The two of them bobbed to the surface, turned lazily, and began floating back downstream.

Still clinging to the back of what he now suspected was one of the legendary swamp serpents, Front drew near the glowing platform where his four friends were waiting and shouting. Front suddenly felt like a celebrant on a gaily-decorated carnival boat, returning from a procession about the bay. He started to slip off the back of the serpent, but his knife wouldn't be dislodged.

As he tried pushing his knees against the creature's back and yanking at the handle he heard Fyva calling eagerly, "Hold onto it, Front! Don't let it go!" She hastily cast the line she had just taken from her own waist.

As Front grabbed the line that was flying over his head, he realized she had intended the line more for roping the beast than for rescuing him. He wondered about that, briefly, as he held onto the line and his knife and allowed the others to draw him and his former mount to the platform.

Wonina and Nash were trying to pull him out while Fyva was pleading with him to wrap the line around the now lifeless serpent. They were both pulled forth, though the serpent cost them considerably more effort. After Front was out of the water, he joined the other four in dragging the twelve-foot long, three-foot wide, greenish white and still sparkling monster from its icy home.

"Look at it, oh, look at it!" marveled Fyva. "It's beautiful!" She ran her hands over the slick surface and fondled jeweled nodule after jeweled nodule. When she came to the gashes in its back, she worried, "I only wish you hadn't cut it so badly, Front."

Front shook his head and laughed, but Wonina admonished sternly, "Fyva, how could you? Front just saved your life. You were almost killed by this dreadful monster, and now you're worried about his having damaged its silly hide."

Front interrupted this scolding. "This dreadful monster, as you call it, Wonina, wasn't going to harm anyone. I feel like a fool—and a cruel fool at that. Sea serpents aren't dangerous, and I suspect, regardless of its size, this swamp serpent was no fiercer than our sea serpents. All the poor thing was trying to do was get me off its back. If I'd been thinking clearly, I'd have merely let go, and that would've been all there was to it."

"But those teeth, it would have torn you apart!"

"What teeth, Wonina?" With some further effort, and the aid of the others, he turned the serpent on its back to expose a curved and sad looking mouth. When he opened the jaw there was a series of flat, smooth ivories, aptly suited for grinding mollusks found in the mud.

"He might've cracked my bones but not torn my flesh very efficiently," Front insisted.

"I wouldn't want your bones cracked either," Wonina was even more insisted, "but that still doesn't excuse you, Fyva, for being more concerned about your new plaything than you were about Front."

"You're right, Wonina, and I'm sorry, Front. I guess I just got overly excited at seeing this fantastic creature. I do appreciate what you did for me, and I am glad you're all right."

Wonina seemed somewhat mollified, and they all turned to examine the creature. While Front struggled and finally succeeded in pulling his knife from the creature's skull, Fyva pulled forth her own blade and positioned her knife, apparently to make a slit from the serpent's gullet to its anus.

"This is the way you start to skin the animal, isn't it Front?"

"Skin it?" gasped Nash, more amused than surprised. "Why in the world do you want to skin it?"

"To take the skin back with us, of course. You don't suppose I'm going to leave this fantastic treasure to rot underground, do you? What a price this hide will bring—not that we'll ever sell it, of course—but what a trophy!"

Nash's pleasant tone became suddenly bitter. "Damn it, Fyva, you aren't going to weight us down with trophies. The only skins we're after are Outhan skins."

No one responded to Nash's outburst so, after scowling momentarily, he grumbled to himself and pulled slightly away from the group.

Perhaps to avoid further thinking or the difficult mission of which Nash had reminded them, the others began to assist Fyva in skinning the serpent. Even Nash eventually joined in.

Front took charge, because he was the only one with experience in skinning a similar creature. The closer he examined the body, the less doubt he had that this was indeed a close relative of the familiar sea serpent that provided them with their sturdy clothes. It was obviously male, and then he guessed the creature that had bumped him further up the stream was the darker, non-jeweled female of the species. It must be these serpents are attracted to light, and this poor fellow was merely dropping by the platform, just as they had, for the comfortable familiarity of its underwater light. That thought made him feel even guiltier.

Since the skin could practically be peeled from the flesh Front decided the gut slit wasn't necessary, so the skin was left in one piece. There was also very little scraping, therefore the skinning was accomplished rather quickly. Fyva then began thrusting her hands deep within the neck cavity to scoop out the creature's brains.

"You're not thinking of keeping the skull too," Front asked.

"Of course," she commented matter-of-factly. "Can't you just see that head mounted on a stand outside my father's store? It'll bring him customers by the droves."

"That's all well and good," he shook his head, "but just how do you plan to transport your enticing display back to Sebasa?"

"In my boat, right along with me. How else?"

Before the others could argue with her, Fyva explained, again rather matter-of-factly, "If you and Wonina can fit in one boat, surely the serpent and I will have no difficulty. Look, once the brain is fully removed, the skull weighs little more than the skin, and the skin weighs almost nothing."

Front had to admit she was right. The great value of serpent skin was its strength despite its lightness.

Nash darkened the mood once again by quipping, "And maybe you can frighten the Outhans away with it."

Front quickly changed the subject. "Well, at least we've replenished our food supply."

"What do you mean?" they all turned toward him suspiciously.

"I'm sorry I had to kill this poor thing, but maybe it was a stroke of luck for us after all." He stooped down again and sliced off a sliver of the firm raw meat, thrust it into his mouth, and chewed gustily. "Delicious! Why this is even better than sea serpent. Not salty at all. Sweet in fact."

"Ugh," the others made faces.

Even Fyva, who was coated up to her elbows in the animal's brains, voiced her disgust. "How can you eat that, Front?"

"Don't be silly, Miss Practicality. When we're out on the ocean all day long, we often eat raw fish. You certainly don't think I have a cooking fire on my small boat, do you? You get your food and drink all in one. And as you know, sea serpent is a delicacy. Furthermore," he smacked his lips again, "this is much better than sea serpent." When the others were still unimpressed, he added, "Besides, the last time I looked at my food supply, it was getting rather low."

Fyva then quickly changed her mind. "He's right. In our circumstances we can't be squeamish. I'm sure we'll soon be reaching the Angle Being home base, but we've still got to conserve our supplies." With a little less enthusiasm, she turned to Front. "Cut me a piece, Front. My hands are a little messy right now."

Front cut a small sliver and put it in her mouth. She chewed gingerly at first, seemingly trying to keep the flesh in contact only with her teeth, but soon her expression changed to genuine surprise. "Hey! This isn't bad at all. In fact, it's good. Sort of like a cross between fish and fowl...though just a little rubbery."

"That's why I cut such slender slivers. Okay, fall to, gang. Dinner's served."

When the others began eating, it was apparent that they not only found the flesh palatable, but that they were quite hungry, so there was little conversation for a while.

After her own meal, and having finally washed her trophy, Fyva was giving herself a final scrub. "Okay, gang, it's time to get under way again. We still have our main mission."

Before the others could rise, Front intervened. "No, Fyva. It's not time to get under way."

"But..." she started to protest.

"I don't know about the rest of you, but I've had a full day. I have no idea what time it is, but my body tells me it's time for rest. Who knows how much further we have to go before we reach another platform. I say we call it a night here."

The others had plopped back down. Looking about her, Fyva shrugged and began busying herself again sponging off her prize.

Wonina helped Fyva brush the remaining debris from the platform. "What about the carcass, Front?" she asked.

"Leave it in the corner there. That's our breakfast."

"But won't it begin to smell?"

"Eventually, but we'll be gone by that time. And I don't want to dump it off the platform. I don't like the idea of meeting the creature I murdered further downstream."

They all laughed nervously, but Front's unpleasant witticism was not enough to dampen the group's mood. They were well fed and at long last surrounded by enough light for reasonably good visibility. The mood was optimistic, and the conversation turned toward the hopeful future.

Front was surprised, however, that it was Wons who began the discussion. "Think back, Fyva. Did you see anything down below to tell us more about the Angle Beings?"

Fyva didn't seem to notice that Wons was again showing interest in his formerly disavowed preoccupation. She responded almost as if she had been waiting for her cue. "There did seem to be another opening down there, one that might be right below the slight depression in the wall behind us. Of course I didn't go in there, but is there any doubt now that this is an Angle Being artifact? You've got to believe now we're heading the right way."

"And you really believe we'll find the weapons?" Nash asked eagerly, his dark mood no longer evident.

"The people who could make lights that last for centuries can make whatever we need."

Front didn't want to undermine the renewed confidence of the group by bringing up his lingering doubts. Even if this channel was manmade, he still didn't know for sure that the lights were artificial. Even if they were, it didn't prove they would find anything ahead to aid them against the Outhans.

As the others continued to enjoy their increasingly fanciful speculations, Front remained silent. There was something about this platform

that bothered him, and it took him a while to discover what it was. At first
he thought it was the closeness of the platform to the level of the water,
but then it dawned on him that the problem was with the ceiling, not the
water. They were now too close to the ceiling of the cave. He became suddenly chilled when he realized what that might mean—either the water
had been rising or the ceiling had been getting lower as they traveled down
the channel.

Furtively, he glanced downstream. The diminishing light in the distance did not allow him to confirm his chilling suspicion. The others paid
him no attention when he walked to the far edge of the platform to peer
into the darkness. Still nothing. He studied the angle of the ceiling and
the backwall. Still inconclusive.

"What are you doing?" Wonina called out.

"Nothing." He tried to sound casual. "Just looking around."

"Well, come back and join us," she patted by her side.

He did so quickly, not wishing to alarm them with his unsubstantiated
fears. Once seated, he looked casually at each member of his group. They
were certainly in a happy mood. It was the first time he had seen them this
way since the initial night out from Sebasa, when Wons had lectured them
on the Angle Beings. Now Wons was again on his formerly favorite subject. He and Fyva, particularly, were describing the benefits that might
come to their town from the learning they could discover from Angle
Being documents. Nash kept asking about weapons, and Wonina seemed
content merely to see the group happy.

That happy mood lasted for most of the group until they made ready
to get into their sacks for sleep. Nash alone seemed to slowly lose his
enthusiasm, perhaps because Wonina had spent most of the time sitting
close to Front. Only when he complained about his stiff leg did Wonina
volunteer to check on the wound and dry out the dressing.

Front suggested they rub the sea serpent's liver on the wound. He was
glad now that he had decided not to toss the liver over the side. He
described how fishermen accumulated the oil from sea serpent livers to use

as medicine. The liver might be of help in healing the cut, he speculated. Wonina allowed Front this strange custom, and Nash seemed further mollified by the attention he was now getting from the two of them.

When they all finally made it into their sleeping bags, Front was both amused and concerned about the new sleeping arrangement. He found his bag had been placed in the middle, with the two girls on either side of him, and the other two males to the outside. Wonina snuggled her bag up to his, and Nash snuggled his bag up to hers. It was pleasantly warm for Front, but something, and he was not quite sure what, was not altogether to his liking.

The next morning after a breakfast of swamp serpent and, over their amused protests, slivers of raw swamp serpent liver, they were once again moving downstream. There was joking about Fyva's new figurehead, as she had shoved the tightly rolled serpent-skin to the front of her small boat, with the serpent's head rearing above the prow.

"The flagship of the mighty fleet," she proclaimed. "Nothing can stop us now."

Nothing but the stream's going underground, Front mumbled to himself as the light faded behind them and the darkness reasserted itself.

After the light had entirely disappeared, it seemed to Front that the walls also vanished, and on that black subterranean sea they were sailing again into nothingness. This time, however, he had the awful feeling that the ceiling above them was going to fall and they would be crushed beneath its awesome weight. Even the warmth of that special spot between him and Wonina was not enough to dispel the descending gloom.

It must have been hours later, and it came as almost a relief, when Wonina called out, "Hey, another light...." Then her voice trailed off in an, "Oh, no...."

Front knew what to expect when he raised his own head, and heard Wons already bitterly complaining, "Oh, my God! I told you so, I told you so." The dull lights they could see barely rising from the surface seemed to be on both walls and also directly in front of them and downward, much further downward than before. There was only a slight rippling of the water ahead of them as the ceiling finally met the wall and disappeared beneath it.

The four boats struck the roof before they reached the point of vanishing water, and they bobbed and bounced impotently.

"Now what, Fyva?" Wons asked sarcastically.

"Well, I'm sure we'll just be logical about this."

"Oh, shut up," growled Nash.

Front, who had been anticipating this, was obviously the least distressed of the group. "Fyva's right. It's not a time for us to start bickering again among ourselves. Fortunately the current is not so strong now that we're forced to do something immediately. Let's calm down and try to think about this."

Fyva took over from Front, her voice now weaker, however, suggesting she was no longer so confident. "There is one thing different here. Doesn't it look as though there's a light also in the center of the channel? Now I can't be sure, but it could be that means just beyond this point the stream might come to the surface. Doesn't it seem the light in the center is brighter than the ones on the side, and also a different color?"

Front now noticed there was something different about the light in the center of the stream; it seemed more diffused and not as blue-white.

"Front, I hate to ask you to do this, but since we still have the rope...."

"No, not again!" Wonina protested.

"Wonina, you know Front's the best swimmer. I'd go, but Front has the best chance."

"I'll go," growled Nash. "I'd rather go quickly than die waiting in here."

"No, Fyva's right, I'm the one to go," Front interjected quietly. "Come on, gang, we're all in this; let's work together." He gave Wonina a nudge. "Slide off the boat and uncoil the rope from around me. There's obviously nothing here we can tie the end of the rope onto, so I suggest we work it through the lashing on the front of all four boats. With the four of you remaining in your boats, that should be anchor enough."

Only Wonina continued voicing her quiet concern, but she did her part. The others then hastily drew the rope along and through the lashing at the bows of their boats.

"Make a larger knot after it's through the last lashings," Front directed. "Okay, Wonina, you loop it around my waist."

Treading water, Wonina did as she was told, and then threw her arms around his neck and pressed him tightly to her. She said nothing.

As he drew in deep breaths, Front looked at each of the concerned faces peering over the edges of their boats. Finally he helped Wonina back into her boat and squeezed her hand.

"I'll tug the rope if I need help."

He handed the slack rope to Nash in the nearest other boat and, with one last breath, he surface dived. Kicking smoothly, and alternately stroking with his arms, Front followed the slope of the submerged ceiling downward. Light to the sides and ahead of him grew brighter, but the further the gradual slope proceeded, the dimmer grew his hopes. His breath was also growing short and his heart was pounding fiercely. Just as he thought he would have to turn back, he felt nothing above him. Quickly glancing upward, he could see the silvery shimmering undersurface of the stream, and now the current behind him was pushing him upward and toward that blessed surface.

Joyfully he struggled upward and broke the surface gasping. The rope around his waist was just long enough to allow him to reach that surface, but only by tugging on it fiercely could he get his head above water. His eyes were still partially submerged, but he thought he could glimpse the stream parting just ahead of him, going at right angles to either side, and directly in front of him was the source of that bright light.

Just as he was letting out the first breath he had managed to take, the rope jerked him violently downward again. He struggled to return to the surface, but the rope was insistent. He was being dragged downward, without air. He had no choice but to follow the demanding rope and to desperately hurry the process by pulling himself hand over hand and kicking fiercely under the bend and upward along that slow, eternal slope. He wasn't sure he was going to make it, when he finally broke the surface in the darkness.

He could hear the others shouting, "Oh, Front, you were gone so long!"

"We knew you couldn't hold your breath that long...."

"When you finally signaled us to bring you back we thought it would be too late...."

Clinging to the side of Wonina's boat, it was a while before he could finally speak. By that time the group was silent, until Wonina asked quietly, "Front, is there any hope?"

Still a little annoyed at having been jerked back and almost drowned, he was tempted to delay telling them the hopeful news, but he really didn't want to prolong their agony.

"We can make it through. There's a continuation of the stream and another chamber on the other side."

They broke out cheering, and again the group was together.

"It's a long swim, gang, though probably not as long as it just felt—I was so scared I used up all my air worrying. Nevertheless, it won't be easy. How about it? Anybody here unsure about being able to make it that far under water?"

Nash was the only one to speak. "I hate to admit it, but I'm not too confident. My goats and I don't do much swimming on the slopes of the mountain."

"Okay. If the others are sure you can make it alone, here's what we'll do. I'll take the end of the rope back with me, while I help Nash along underwater. I'll give the rope a jerk when I get there—and this time, don't anyone jerk back! Then, one by one, follow the rope, pulling yourself as you go. You shouldn't have any trouble. When we all get on the other side, I think we'll be able to pull the boats after us."

"But what about my serpent skin, I don't want to lose that."

"Right now I'm more concerned about our own skins. But don't worry, Fyva, I think we'll get it through."

"Okay, Nash, into the water. Oh, yeah, it might be a good idea to make sure your skin is tied in securely, Fyva. And all of you, just before you go, turn your boats upside down so the bottoms will slide on the ceiling. We're sure to get the boats under and through that way."

The two of them turned Nash's boat over and wedged it against the roof. After both breathed deeply, Front churned under, dragging Nash with him. The trip this time, even towing Nash, seemed infinitely quicker. After bobbing to the surface, Front pressed himself against the wall for support and gave the rope a jerk. The wait for the others was much longer. Was it because they were slower swimmers, or that waiting was worse than doing? A large portion of his worry was relieved when Wonina bobbed to the surface, although she obviously wasn't taxed by the trip. He was surprised that Wons came next and, this time it was Fyva who was last in line. Front suspected she had been reluctant to leave her trophy, even to swim to her own safety.

It took the combined efforts of the five of them, feet propped against the wall, holding onto the rope against the current, to pull the four boats down the slope where, once they made that bend, they all bobbed rapidly to the surface. Frantically they floundered toward their receding boats and tried to scramble aboard, until Front gave the command to swim instead, dragging their boats behind them. Directly ahead of them, about a hundred feet and within easy swimming distance, was the source of light, a brightly lighted platform against the right wall that beckoned them invitingly.

As they swam Front reared his head out of the water briefly he saw what made the platform and light look different. In addition to the platform's being larger, stretching for forty feet or more on either side above the underwater light, the light itself had a red glow. Intrigued, he realized he wouldn't need Fyva's encouragement this time to investigate that red light. And right away, he told himself, as he continued stroking toward the platform with his small craft and the dangling rope.

They all needed a rest before exploring, however. Eventually Fyva and Wons were the first to rise and begin examining the walls to the back of their new cave. As he lay prone on the platform Front peered across the stream. The water was rising to the surface from under the far wall they had just left. The current seemed to flow first toward their platform and then bear to the right along a new, much broader channel that ran almost perpendicular to the incoming flood. A second, similar channel bore to the left. The light underneath the platform almost faded when it reached the downstream end of the platform, but as he had seen from their approach, a narrower ledge continued on into the darkness, along side the right bearing channel. The ceiling of this central chamber was gratifyingly high, and even though it lowered abruptly at the beginning of the new wider channels entrances, with relief Front noticed no downward slope in the ceiling of those receding cannels.

Fyva and Wons returned to the others, apparently having found nothing they hadn't seen before, but not having lost too much of their enthusiasm.

"What now, Front?" Wons asked.

"Time for another underwater investigation, and I won't even need to be volunteered for this one." He smiled at Fyva. Fyva returned his smile with feigned innocence.

"Untie the end of the rope from the boats," he ordered. "I'm going down to see what's causing that red light, and this time, Fyva, don't let go of the rope!"

"Oh, Front, you know that was an accident. Besides, the current here's too weak to wash you away."

"I'm only kidding. Come on, tie it around my waist. I'm eager to go."

The considerably lessened current gave Front little trouble. Diving downward and sharply toward the back wall, he stroked toward that crimson brightness. It was further than he had thought, and his chest was already paining him by the time he reached the wall. There, approximately waist high from the bottom, he encountered an oblong retangle of white light, framed by a band of red. He felt cautiously along the surface of the object, but as with the previous lights, the surface gave off no heat. This time the whiteness, however, rather than being rough, was slick and smooth. He risked pressing his face against the glassy surface and was not altogether surprised to see that the light behind the surface allowed him to peer within. By this time, however, his air was used up, and reluctantly he shoved himself away and strove purposefully toward the surface.

"What was it, Front? What was it?" they all asked eagerly.

Catching his breath first, he answered, "Some kind of glass box. I only got a glimpse inside before I ran out of air, but there's definitely something in there."

"What?"

"What? Describe it."

"I really didn't get a clear view, but it seemed like a long blue banded tube."

"Just a tube?" Nash sagged a bit.

"What do you mean, "just a tube?" barked Fyva. "That's proof. That tube proves everything. Even Front has to admit that nature or even swamp-serpents don't make glass boxes and put tubes inside them. We've found it! This is definite proof that the Angle Beings existed! Wons, Wons, you were right all along!"

"Fyva, control yourself," cautioned Wonina. "Let's let Front get another look before we jump to hasty conclusions."

Front looked around for anything that might be hard enough to allow him to break that glass. There seemed nothing available, so he drew his knife, hoping that the metal end of the hilt would do. After breathing deeply again, down he went, this time swimming directly and rapidly to the box. Without hesitation, he pounded away with the hilt, pounded away until he was exhausted, but the smooth surface was impervious to his pitiful efforts. He was forced to return to the surface with only a battered knife handle to show for his efforts.

They were all also disappointed, but obviously they expected him to keep trying, and he admitted to himself, even though it was more difficult this time to regain his breath, he expected to return.

"Use your head," Fyva suggested. "This time look for some kind of latch. I'm sure the Angle Beings didn't force their way into their treasures."

"But if it is a treasure, then maybe the lock wouldn't just announce itself," Front gasped, trying to sound sarcastic.

"Well, look more carefully."

This time he did look more carefully, and to his chagrin, Fyva was right. Just to the side of the box was a definite, large round knob, about the size of the palm of his hand. He first tried turning it, but it wouldn't turn. He tried sliding it up and down or sideways, but still nothing happened. Finally, in his frustration, he slammed the palm of his hand against it. He was startled by a muffled clanging noise, and even more startled when he was thrust backward and then sucked forward as the front of the glass popped open and the water rushed forcefully in. Without thinking of what dangers might lie within, he thrust his arm into the box, grabbed the tube and yanked. It came away easily from the box, and he surged to the surface, holding the tube above his head as he lunged into the air.

Fyva, Wons, and Nash all struggled to be first to pull it from his outstretched hand. Only Wonina ignored the prize to assist Front onto the platform.

"You three," she laughed. "You look like a bunch of kids, haggling over a toy."

Nash, with his powerful short arms, won the prize. The others gathered around as Nash turned it one way and another, peering critically at the three-foot long, inch and a half wide tube.

"All right, I give up," he grumbled disgustedly. "What in hell is this thing?"

"Not from hell, I'm sure," Wons said, finally rescuing the object from Nash's now indifferent hands.

Wons' handling of the object was far gentler than Nash's. In fact, Front could clearly see that Wons was quite reverent in his careful examination of the tube. Since the tube was no longer being thrashed about, Front could also see there seemed to be a green band, about the size of a knife handle grip, adjacent to a smaller red band, almost in the center of the tube. On one end, beyond the green band, the tube was blunt, and the other end tapered into what appeared to be a nozzle. The nozzle end gave no access to the center of the tube, however. Instead, immediately within was a cluster of pinpoint-size crystal heads. More careful examination showed that extending forward from the red band was a series of red dots.

Carefully Wons passed the tube to Fyva, whose inspection became less reverential and more matter-of-fact. Fortunately the tube was pointed, nozzle end toward the water when, after Fyva had pressed each of the red buttons, she carefully turned the red center band. Neither the tube nor Fyva's hands were jolted, but in the water where the tube had been pointing, there was a thunderous churning, a white hot hissing, and one frightful clap.

The silent moment of awe following that fearsome display was broken by Nash's whoop. He snatched the tube from Fyva's frozen hands.

"This is it!" he bellowed. "This is it! This is the weapon! My God, we've found it! We can stop the Outhans!" Eagerly he pointed the nozzle of the tube across to the far wall and harshly turned the red band. This time an even greater thunder and clash echoed off the far wall, and the stone ceiling hissed and evaporated in a white-hot hole of destruction, seemingly no bigger than the diameter of the tube.

"Did you see that? Did you see that?" and Nash aimed the tube on the far channel and rapidly turned the red band three more times, with three awesome claps of thunder following.

"Stop! Stop!" Wonina screamed.

Both Wons and Fyva grabbed and briefly struggled with the joyful Nash. By this time Nash was apparently satisfied and too happy to struggle. Wons won the weapon back and cradled it in his arms.

"Okay. You can hold it for now," Nash laughed. "But I get first shot at one of those Outhan ships. I'll cut the bottom right out of it, right out of every one of those stinking ships. I'll send all those slimy bastards to the bottom of the sea!"

"Okay, okay, Nash. You'll get your chance. Now calm down. We're all just as eager as you are to get rid of those Outhans. But before you rush off, half out of your head, it's time we did some planning." In her usual businesslike manner, Fyva was already calling the group together. They sat in a circle, with Wons still cradling the blue, red, and green banded tube in his arms.

"Okay," began Fyva. "We should carefully plan our next leg of the journey."

"But not before we stop and eat," said Wonina.

"Yes, yes, of course, we need to be sure we have plenty of energy. We have such fantastic things ahead of us."

"You know it!" grinned Nash eagerly.

"We'll still need our boats," continued Fyva. "Although there seems to be a wide pathway like ledge going in that direction," she gestured with her head to the left across the stream, "we don't know how far the pathway goes before we'll have to take to the boats again."

Nash began to frown, but Fyva continued on.

"We'll also need our boats to take back whatever treasures we might find when we get to the Angle Being city itself."

"Nash exploded, "What do you mean get to the Angle Being city! We're heading back to Sebasa. We don't need any damn treasures," he spit out his anger. "We've got the weapon. We've got what we came for, and we've got all we need. Now let's get started for home!" He rose to his feet.

"Sit down, Nash! You can't be serious," Fyva barked. "You can't expect to get the job done with that one weapon. We've got to find more and other kinds of weapons."

"Like hell you say! This is what we came for. This is why I followed you down that stupid channel. I'm not following you any place else while you grab and stuff yourselves with treasures. Now let's go, I say!" And he leaned toward the tube in Wons' lap.

Wons jerked away, protecting the weapon. "Not so fast, Nash. Who says you're the one to handle this thing? It's not a plaything for a murderous goat boy."

Front thought that Nash was going to lunge, but Wonina held him back with a quick grasping hand, only to turn fiercely on Wons. "That's enough of your sneering, Wons! He only wants to do what you all know we must do. I'm with Nash. It's time to head home!"

This time Fyva exploded. "Don't be stupid, girl. There's more at stake here than just our war against the Outhans. There are things to be discovered here you two haven't dreamed of." Now, she too came to her feet.

"Enough!" Front bellowed. The force and firmness of his voice startled even Front. The others turned with surprise on their faces, as his voice continued to echo down the distant channels.

"Sit down, all of you!"

Front was further surprised at how quickly they dropped in their places, continuing to stare at him. "I say we're going no place until we settle this." He had lowered his voice but remained firm and steady in his tone. He paused then, but no one else spoke. Somewhat more reluctantly he continued, "It seems to me that everyone wants to rush off someplace and do something. It'd help me decide what I want to do if we first look at why we are going to do whatever we're going to do."

They looked their puzzlement.

"What I'm trying to say is, one time I thought I knew why we were on this trip. When we left Sebasa, I thought we were out for a long holiday, with just the possibility of discovering something unusual on the top of Mount Stareye. Then ever since we left Mount Stareye, although I admit I didn't have much hope, I thought we were looking for the Angle Being weapons. After we fell down that hole, I was absolutely sure that the most important thing in the world was to remain alive."

Several others began to speak at once, but again he hushed them.

"It seems to me the first thing we'd better agree upon is our ultimate goal."

Fyva and Nash spoke at the same time.

"Our goal is to reach the Angle Being City!"

"Our goal is to destroy the Outhans!"

"Slow down, slow down," Front raised his hands to calm them. "You're still talking about what *you* want to do. Somehow it seems to me there's something even more important than that, something that will join those two goals together."

Again Nash, Fyva, and Wons all broke out talking at one time, and this time it was Wonina who calmed the group. "Quiet! Quiet, all of you. Let Front speak. I want to hear what he has to say."

The group grumbled to a stop.

"Okay. What are you getting at, Front?" Wons asked.

"I really don't know quite how to put it, but it seems to me we all have the same goal in mind. We all have the good of our people as the heart of our plans. Nash wants to drive off the Outhans. Fyva, and I guess Wons, want to bring back to the people the marvels of the Angle Beings, so they can increase the wealth, knowledge, and prosperity of the people. Am I right about this?"

Wonina was the first to agree, and the others nodded their heads somewhat more hesitantly.

"Then, if there is agreement on that, the next question is, how do we best go about doing what's the best for our people?"

Again the shouting broke out.

"But it's only logical we'd be more able to drive off the Outhans if we had more weapons."

"Damn it, the Outhans have already started killing the people of Sebasa!"

"Oh, don't be so bloody, Nash. We don't know the Outhans have any intention of killing the Sebasans." Wons showed his disgust. "They're not goat herders," he had to add.

Nash was sputtering as he came to his feet.

"Enough! Enough," Front called again for order. "We're getting no place this way."

They calmed down more quickly this time, and Fyva asked, "Okay, Front, what do you want to do?"

Front paused. It was not the question that surprised and stopped him, it was the realization that he wasn't sure what he wanted to do. He pondered while the group grew restless. Finally, he thought it best to say something.

"To tell the truth, I'm not really sure. Let me...let me just share with you the way I feel about things. Maybe if I think aloud, I can clear up some of my own confusion.' Hesitating only a moment longer, he continued. "I know I want to do what's right for Sebasa. Every time I think of my mother and sister alone with heaven knows what happening to them, I get cold and both angry and frightened. But I also get excited about the prospect of discovering whatever might lie in the other direction. I admit I was fairly skeptical about Wons' fantasies and then about Fyva's wild speculations regarding the Angle Beings. I admit I was wrong and you were right." He paused again, and both sides seemed at least temporarily placated. "But I think we're faced now with a question of time. Fyva, Wons, I sympathize with your desire to explore the unknown, but I really think time forces me to choose an immediate return, if possible, to Sebasa."

Again the conflict erupted.

"But we don't know that we can get back to Sebasa!"

"And we don't know that we can get to the ancient city either!"

"We need more weapons, Nash!"

"But we've got a weapon, and you saw what it did. It's all we need."

"Don't you two have any heart? Don't you feel concerned about your own families?"

"This is more important than families. This is vital to our whole civilization.

"Heartless!"

"Stupid!"

This time Front had to rise to his knees to get their attention. "Let's consider this," he shouted to override their bickering. "Granted we don't know that either of these channels leads to where we want to go. If I remember your map correctly, Fyva, up till this point we've been heading on an almost direct southeasterly course. Perhaps, I don't really know, but perhaps the channel running to our left does lead to your city. I am pretty sure, however, that the channel to our right leads directly toward Sebasa."

He quickly cut off the arguments that rose from Wons and Fyva. "You remember, Fyva, our speculation about what might lie underneath Mount Stareye? My guess is this channel leads directly to the Commons, and we'd end up in some kind of chamber underneath the Commons, right on the south side of Sebasa."

"But we don't know that, Front," Fyva protested.

"And we don't know that your Angle Being city lies in the other direction," Wonina countered.

"Hold it. Hold it. Let me finish. We're not sure of anything about either end of these channels, but I am sure that the stronger current is heading toward Sebasa, and that in itself is a pretty strong argument."

"Well, yes, but...." and even Fyva and Wons could think of nothing immediately to overcome that argument.

"Here's what I suggest then. We'll move off in the direction of Sebasa, and if we can get through, fine. If not, we'll head back in the other direction, and seek out your city. And even if we do reach Sebasa, and we manage to drive off the Outhans, I give my word that as soon as possible we'll head back up this channel. Next time, though, we'll be better prepared, perhaps with even more people, and we'll find your city."

"But that might be too late," Fyva started again. "We might run out of food before we can reach the Commons, and I'm sure we can find whatever we need at the other end."

"And who knows," Wons spoke, his voice now taking on some of its long absent firmness and strength, "it may be that the Angle Beings still exist and that they'd be willing to aid us."

"Oh, for God's sake," bellowed Nash. "Of all the stupid garbage. Haven't you learned anything from this trip, Wons? What are you, some kind of a holy fanatic?"

"At least I don't worship goats!"

"And smell like them," Fyva added.

"You bitch! Some of us earn an honest living. At least my family doesn't go around robbing other people of their hard-earned goods!"

"Who are you to talk?" Fyva rose up. "Your little girl friend here has a father who would sell his wife if he could make a profit."

Wonina was on her feet moving toward Fyva. This time Front had to move quickly to come between the two sides of the argument.

"Listen to me! Listen to me all of you! It's clear to me that we're never going to be able to think rationally until you people stop calling each other names. Sit down before I throw you down!"

He didn't really intend to use force, and he suspected that they didn't believe him either, but they did sit down.

Again, Front didn't know quite how to proceed. He was troubled by the number of unpleasant feelings bubbling to the surface. Every time they started to reason things out, the people always fell back into anger.

"All right," he started cautiously, "I guess the thing to do is just to get all this bitterness out in the open."

The others looked suspicious. "Before we get started, however, I want to tell you why I think this is important. I know that all of you are intelligent and reasonable people, but your feelings seem to be so strong you're not behaving as intelligently as I know you can. Maybe we could think more reasonably if we first spent some time either getting out all these angry feelings or, probably better yet, reminding ourselves of all the important things we've meant to each other—or, perhaps even more importantly, how much we need each other right now...."

Nash would have none of it. "You may need these two deserters, but I've had enough of them!"

"Who're you calling a deserter? Just because we don't want to rush out and butt our heads against a wall doesn't mean we're running away."

Front could see it starting again, and this time he jumped to his feet before the others could. His sudden action startled them. Then standing above them and also raising his voice, he stated firmly, "All right. You choose not to be reasonable. Now listen carefully to me. I've already said I believe we're all trying to accomplish the same thing, but it looks like I'm the only one who can get in touch with that thing. I'm tired of your bickering, and if I can't get your cooperation one way, I'm going to get it another way. I'm sorry if you don't all agree with me, but I'm going to do what I know is right for all of us. You all know I've been the one who's been taking the chances, and I'm the one who's gotten us through to where we are. If you still want me with you, you'd better get on your feet and get moving. We're heading downstream toward Sebasa!"

"Well, well," Wons leaned back on his hands, "look at the new "Nash"." He turned to Fyva. "We have a new goat boy whose going to butt us around and tell us what to do."

Fyva said with disgust, "Front, we don't need another dictator. We've been down that dark hole already."

"What do you mean, 'goat boy, dictator'?" Nash was up again.

"Sit down all of you." Front said quietly, "I've got one last thing to say to you." The tone of Front's voice had changed again, and they all seemed to recognize it. They quieted immediately. He had their attention again, and he spoke, standing before them. "I'm sorry you're behaving this way. I'm sorry I couldn't pull you together. I've tried everything I know how to do. You wouldn't listen to reason, and cooperate. You wouldn't even show each other a little kindness and respect. And obviously you don't plan to follow my orders. Okay, I'm going to follow my own orders. I know what I have to do for my people, and if you won't do it with me, I'll do it without you."

He moved too quickly for Wons to react. Snatching the weapon from Wons' lap, he turned and quickly grabbed the prow of his own boat. Then, turning his back on them, he stalked purposefully away.

At first there was only silence behind him. He heard only his own footsteps and the sound of his dragging boat. Then there was a hasty scurrying, and to his surprise, the people followed him.

9

THE LEADER IS TWO IS ONE

Front felt a bit foolish—not only had his grand exit seemed stagy, he had forgotten his pack. He was wondering whether to go back and get it when he was relieved by Wonina's tapping him on the shoulder and handing it to him. He was also grateful that she had made no issue of it. But he could hear the others trudging behind him, and the more he thought about his dramatic statements, the more he was concerned they might have found them amusing.

Well, at least they were following and they were once again on their way. He realized again how important it was for them to stay together, and he wondered if he had really meant what he had said back there, if he really would have continued on without them.

Thinking further, he realized that, in fact, he would have. He had done all he could do, and further discussion would have been pointless and a waste of time. With that realization, he felt better. At least he hadn't been phony.

The ledge that continued alongside the waterway was wide enough for easy traverse. It was indeed like a walkway, jagged on its outer edge but usually at least six feet wide. In this tunnel, visibility was better than previously, though he wasn't always certain where the light was coming from, perhaps partially buried beneath the increasing rubble he began to notice. As he took more careful interest in the area within his sight, he began to suspect that perhaps this section of the tunnels was older than the one they had recently left. He noticed the walls were pitted rather than merely slick and straight, and now and then there were chunks broken from the walls and torn from the edge of the platform. As he examined the first of these holes, he thought Nash's exuberant shooting spree might have been responsible for the damage. He dismissed that as unlikely as they encountered more and more damage, having occasionally to skirt boulder-sized chunks of the wall and ceiling partially blocking their pathway. What could have caused such damage, he wondered—an earthquake perhaps? No, that seemed unlikely. Earthquakes were known on the southern coast, but the ground would have been more buckled. Most of this damage seemed to have come from something monstrous, something that gouged chunks out of the ceilings and the walls in selected spots, leaving other surfaces untouched. Whatever had done such damage was more terrible even than their wonderful new weapon. Could it be that the Angle Beings were not the peaceful super beings he had come to assume? Did the Angle Beings have their conflicts, their wars with other super beings...beings like the Outhans?

When that awful idea occurred to him, Front hastily reminded himself how relatively primitive the armament of the Outhans was reported to be. Even with one weapon, such as their blue cylinder, and trying to be more objective than Nash seemed to be, they stood a chance of inflicting enough damage on the Outhans to at least intimidate them, if not drive them away. No, the Outhans could never have stood against the awesome power the Angle Beings must have commanded.

There seemed no answer to this new mystery about the Angle Beings. He only knew that whatever had caused this damage, it was beginning to cause his little troop considerable inconvenience. The way was now so cluttered the five of them were becoming strung out and almost separated in the returning gloom. Only Wonina, immediately behind him, seemed intent upon keeping close.

Nash with his stiff leg was next in line, but falling back. Front was concerned about Nash. With this new division within the group, Nash was now his staunchest ally. He felt even closer to Wonina, of course, but when it came to the encounter ahead of them, he would have to depend upon Nash. It was important that he look after Nash and maintain their good relationship. The other two—well, for the time being at least they were coming along. There was no doubt in his mind, however, that they were coming partially against their will and that their resistance would surface again. The resistance of the narrow, rubble strewn way, however, was making itself felt more immediately. Not only were the chunks of debris becoming almost impassable but the pathway itself suddenly stopped.

Front first thought the path might continue on, just beyond this cutoff. More careful examination revealed, however, the cutoff was probably the intended end of the pathway. It was back to the watery way for them.

While the others straggled in, Front examined his boat for damage. The boat-bark craft had proven itself amazingly durable.

When they had all gathered, he announced the obvious. "We'll have to continue on by boat. Is everyone all right?"

No one answered. The feeling of tension was still in the air.

"I think it best, however, that we eat before we continue."

Again, no one spoke. Instead, they arranged themselves in two obvious groups, and ate silently.

"Okay, back in the water." He tried to put some lightness in his voice, but they others merely responded to his orders mechanically.

He was examining his boat again, thinking how he was going to carry the weapon, when Nash volunteered, "Let me carry it, Front. I'm alone, and you and Wonina are in one boat together. I'll have more room."

Front wondered if there was a double message in what Nash was saying. But considering Nash's usual straightforwardness, he decided Nash meant only what he said.

"Okay, agreed. But how can we protect the weapon? It's been housed all these ages in an air-tight box. It fired, even after it was briefly wet, but I don't know about prolonged immersion in the water."

"It seems airtight to me, Front, but I have an idea," and he began removing his jacket.

"Hey," Front questioned with concern. "It's going to be cold in that water, remember?"

"I don't mind. We can't afford to take any chances with harming the weapon. And when I think what we're going to do to the Outhans, just having this baby near me warms me through and through."

That thought had just the opposite effect on Front, and he didn't look forward to once again entering the chilliness.

Nevertheless, after he repacked his food and again wound his tail of rope around him, and after checking to be sure the others were ready, he ordered a return to that painful cold.

He had a pleasant surprise when he and Wonina launched themselves—the water was surprisingly warm. He could hear the others behind him also voicing their relief at this discovery.

At least temporarily, the mood of the group seemed to have warmed with the water. As jokes echoed back and forth, it was like a holiday again, like surfing in Sebasa Bay. "At nighttime," someone added, and they sobered slightly.

But still, Front felt better about the group, even though as they flowed further along, and encountered even more rubble, the darkness eventually increased. But even so, but the warmth of the water now made that darkness seem less oppressive. His feelings about the group, and the fact that the dim but adequate light enabled him to see where he was going, was beginning to make the journey seem almost pleasant for Front. He had become used to partially carrying Wonina on his back, and the familiarity of her position was not only comforting, but, he soon discovered, coupled with the warm water, more stimulating than usual. With this new almost constant illumination, Front became concerned that the way she snuggled and occasionally caressed him might be obvious to those following—especially since the special warm spot between him and Wonina was now becoming positively hot.

He tried to calm himself by thinking of other things, but that calmness was further disturbed when Wonina laughed and whispered in his ear, "I really like riding my own personal sea serpent," and with her legs spread slightly, she reared playfully, moving her bottom against his. The effect was alarming, and he almost bucked her off in response.

She laughed, and clung to him even more tightly. Front wanted to look behind to see if Nash was observing all this. Wonina was so close upon him, however, he couldn't turn.

Front was almost relieved then when a new problem began to present itself. The warmer waters about them had, from the first, been almost sluggish. Now the current seemed to turning against them, and it became necessary for them, for the first time, to provide their own propulsion. In the beginning a small kick was all that was necessary, and then a constant kick, with more than just a guiding thrust of the arm was required, until eventually, it was necessary to begin a steady and increasingly tiring swim. Front guessed, through his growing exhaustion, that there must be another channel entering this one from somewhere up ahead. Then another very alarming thought occurred to him. Could it be that Nash's recent damage to the channel to the rear of them had caused even greater damage than he had thought, and now some underground cavern had opened up and was sucking back all the water? I should have been paying more attention, he chastised himself, giving this problem more thought as we went along, rather than allowing myself to be titillated by thoughts of Wonina's body.

Since the two of them in the boat made rigorous swimming difficult, he soon found it necessary to leave Wonina in the small craft while he swam alongside, holding on, tugging with one hand, and paddling ever harder with the other. His exhaustion was such that, when a new, brighter light appeared ahead, beneath the first large platform he had seen since discovering the weapon, he was not sure he would have strength enough to reach that promised safety.

As it turned out, Front was probably the only one so overly exhausted. His excessive concern with pulling Wonina's craft had made him far less efficient than the others. All five made the platform at about the same time, and scrambled up safely. There was no doubt, however, that the pull had been taxing for all. Everyone sprawled, panting and gasping on the new uneven and debris-strewn surface.

Only Wons seemed to have wind enough to gasp a comment, and Front could not help but catch the sarcasm of it. "And what now, leader?"

One thing at a time, Front cautioned himself. He could do nothing now about Wons' bitterness. The most important thing at the moment was to rest, and without his commanding it, the others certainly knew to do that. He would trust their bodies to rest, though their angry minds might want to do otherwise.

When he was somewhat more recovered, he began to examine the new platform. As was immediately obvious, this platform was far more damaged than the last. Even the light from below the platform seemed to be from a broken source, and the breaks in the light made the illumination less adequate. Remembering their discovery at the last platform, he peered hopefully into the depths, looking for another red glow, but there seemed to be nothing promising. The major portion of their platform, which he could barely make out in the distance, did not appear to be as wide as the one they had left. Since there was no side channel entering at this spot, Front reasoned there must have been something special about their former platform, something special that made it a place where Angle Beings thought it necessary to place their marvelous weapon.

For the first time, it occurred to Front to wonder if their new possession were indeed a weapon. Considering the awesome damage that had been done to this tunnel, by something obviously more powerful, their small blue tube was pitiful by comparison. Perhaps there had been a more peaceful use for their cylinder. He recalled the muffled clanging noise he had heard when he first opened the box. Was that an alarm of some kind? Was their "awesome weapon" actually only an emergency weapon—or even a tool?

Just another unsolvable mystery, he was forced to conclude as he rose to his feet. He spoke gently, so as not to appear to be issuing an order, "I recommend we see if we can walk to the main section of the platform before we stop to eat. How about it, do you have enough strength?"

The others grudgingly agreed, and once again, dragging their boats, they navigated around the strewn boulders and smaller debris. Wonina, as usual, kept close to him, and the others followed behind. When they finally made the broader center platform, Nash was limping more perceptibly, and he asked for Wonina to again examine his leg. After they had seated themselves and the others had begun eating, Wonina did as Nash asked.

"The wound seems to be closing, Nash, and there is still no infection. I'll give you a massage again after we eat. That should make you feel better."

Nash merely groaned in response, but allowed Wonina to begin eating her food. As Front watched Wonina and the others eating, he was reminded how low their provisions were getting. He ate sparingly, chewing slowly, trying to make each bite last as long as possible.

His slow chewing gave him ample time to reflect upon their new problem, but it also gave him time to glance across the circle and reflect upon how lovely Wonina appeared in this dim light, even with her hair damp and stringy and her rough, drab serpent-skin clinging about her body. That very clinging outer skin, in its own way, contributed to her attractive distractibility—it was far too revealing. And the way she casually, but obviously, returned his glances made it difficult to keep his eyes off her.

After they had all finished eating, and sprawled back upon their elbows, Front looked again at Wonina. Her smile was acceptance and promise such as he had never seen before. He suddenly decided he wanted to get away from the group, to think, he told himself, to plan—but he knew he wanted more than anything for Wonina to follow him.

"I'm going to walk ahead," he announced, rising. "I'd like to explore how far we can go in that direction."

"I'll go with you, Front," Wonina said, also quickly rising.

"But you were going to massage my leg," Nash complained.

"Oh, let them go, Nash," Wons slurred. "Maybe Fyva can take care of you now. Our leader wants to explore his new territory."

Fyva chuckled, but Nash merely groaned, it seemed to Front, in a more than usually pitiful manner. Front had the urge to turn and confront Wons' sarcasm, to demand an explanation, but on the other hand, he wasn't sure he wanted that explanation.

Without even waiting for Wonina, he turned and headed away from the lighted platform. Wonina hurried after him, and when they had rounded the first large boulder blocking them from the others, she took his hand in hers. They walked on silently, but when the way became a bit less difficult, she began playfully swinging their arms as they walked.

"I like walking," she commented, "especially after paddling so long." She then laughed gently," though being in the boat with you is certainly nice too."

He turned to her. "Being with you anyplace is nice."

She turned her head up to his, and it seemed so right that he should kiss her. He forgot about the others, even forgetting to wonder if the two of them were adequately hidden from view. Her soft mouth met his, open and accepting, and for now she was all that mattered.

Too soon, however, other thoughts intruded, and he pulled away and, without speaking, began to walk again.

She was quiet for a while, seemingly contented just to walk beside him, leaning her head on his shoulder.

"Let's talk about what's going to happen," she said abruptly.

"What's going to happen?" he almost laughed. He hoped and feared what she meant by that, but he didn't have the courage to be honest. "You mean what's going to happen up ahead? Haven't we worried that to death already?"

"No, Front, you know that's not what I mean," she chided quietly. He held his breath as she continued. "I mean the fact that we're going to have sex together."

What she had said, and the way she said it, seemed so natural, so uncomplicated, so clean—and Front was completely caught off guard. In his wildest imaginings he couldn't have hoped for any more desirable suggestion. It was so unlike anything all the other girls he had known would have said, girls who would have played coy, tempting and promising, and then been affronted and resistive when he finally gained the courage to make his move. Here was Wonina, the girl he desired more than any other, displaying more direct courage than he had ever hoped to have. He was completely stunned.

He started to make a joke of it, but realized that would've been unworthy of him—and certainly less than her courage deserved. He wanted to say something sophisticated, something to demonstrate he was in charge of himself and the situation. Even that was absurd, he realized—he *was not* in charge of the situation. He was not the leader in this situation. Wonina was leading him exactly where he wanted to be led, but he was afraid to follow.

The silence was growing uncomfortable. Finally he broke forth laughing. "God, Wonina, look what you've done to me," and he grabbed her and hugged her.

"What? What have I done to you?" she laughed uncertainly.

His frozen discomfort was thawing as he began to think aloud. "This...this isn't supposed to happen to me," he stuttered happily. "I'm the man. I'm supposed to be seducing you. I'm supposed to be making subtle hints, making you want me so much you can't resist, and here you come right out and announce we're going to have sex together. Suddenly, I don't know what to do." He laughed again, and made a small jump into the air. "I feel so stupid!" Then he enfolded her in his arms again. "And so good!"

This time her mouth opened further, and he seemed to be drawn into her. As he pushed his body against hers, she responded with a gentle thrusting of her pelvis. His hands wandered involuntarily down her back, lower and lower, gently encouraging that thrusting.

Abruptly he pulled away, leaving her gasping.

"Front, darling, why do you pull back?"

"Wonina, Wonina, I don't know what to do."

"Well, I know what I *want* to do," she said firmly. "I want to have sex with you. I want to make love to you." And she waited for his response.

He squirmed, trying again to think of something clever to say. But nothing clever, nothing he had ever said to any other girl, no subtle half-truth would do. He felt compelled to meet honesty with honesty, and, although he thought of himself as an honest person, he had never before been honest with a girl about sex.

"Wonina," he struggled to express himself, "when I came out here, I really didn't expect this to happen...I was glad you followed me. I thought maybe for the first time I'd be able to kiss you. I really didn't expect any more than that."

"But don't you want more than that, Front?"

"You know I do, Wonina, and I know it was wrong of me to think of being halfway about you. Somehow it seemed just kissing you wouldn't have been wrong—but having sex...." He hesitated again. He wanted to turn the responsibility back to her. He wanted to ask what she felt about abandoning Nash. He shook his head; that wasn't what he wanted either. Now that she had been so honest and open with him, the most important thing in the world had suddenly become that he be that honest and open with her. This hesitancy was his problem, not hers, and it was vital that she understand, that she not misinterpret his hesitancy, that she be completely assured that he did indeed desire her.

"Wonina, yes, I do want you. I do want to have sex with you, but I'm torn. What we must accomplish on this journey is also important to me. However it came about, I feel it's my responsibility now to hold the group together, and I'm afraid that every moment lately we're on the verge of flying apart. And here I am eagerly hoping to do something that just might be the very thing that will cause the final breakup."

She looked up at him, waiting expectantly.

"Wonina, what am I going to do?"

"I don't know, Front. What are *you* going to do?" She smiled, but there was no coyness in her smile.

"You're right," he shook in frustration. "It's not your problem, it's mine. Maybe all this is silly. Maybe I ought to just be a man and take you like we both want. What kind of a lover am I going to be if I have so much trouble making up my mind even to make the first move?

He tried to laugh off his frustration, but she answered seriously, "The kind of a lover I want—a man who's responsible, a man who's honest and willing to share with me his doubts and concerns. Your being what you are now, and showing it, makes you all the more desirable to me."

That was too much for him. He had to pull her close and crush her to him. "Oh, Wonina, you're tearing me apart. No...no, that's not right. I'm tearing myself apart," and he pushed her away again and did again his little dance of frustration.

Not knowing what else to do, he took her hand and began walking further along the platform. She walked silently beside him. He walked and waited, wanting her to speak, wanting her to say more, to somehow lift the burden of decision from him. He wanted to know about her and Nash. He wanted her to tell him about that relationship, even about how far they had gone together...but then he felt disgusted with himself. That relationship is none of my business! What she's done with anyone else is not important. The fact is that she's with me now and she's honest with me, and that makes whatever might have happened in the past irrelevant!

When she finally spoke, and brought up that very subject herself, he interrupted her. "I don't want to hear about you and Nash. Whatever you were and whatever you've done with him is fine by me."

"But I want to talk about it, Front. You seem to be trying to take all the responsibility for this on yourself. I know what I've been doing. I know

I've been, stimulating you, and I half knew what I wanted when I got up and followed you. I'm just as responsible as you are. And I'm also feeling guilty about Nash. I've never done anything like this before."

Front started to ask if that meant she had never had sex before, but he stopped himself, and he was proud of himself for stopping.

She answered his question anyway. "I'm not saying that I haven't had sex before, but Nash and I were promised a long time ago. What was between us had come to be expected by everyone else. But things have been different lately. Even before the trip, we really weren't getting along too well. Even if you hadn't come along, I don't think Nash and I would've lasted much longer together. I think I've been maintaining our relationship more for appearances, more because the families seemed to expect it, than because I really wanted it. When I began feeling about you the way I've come to feel, I knew I had to have you. I knew it was right for me to give myself to you, to feel what I've always wanted to feel with someone, and haven't felt with Nash...but still I'm feeling guilty."

They continued walking, and he found himself, still holding her hand, drawing somewhat apart so as to see all of her. She was lovely, lovelier than ever, but he began to realize his feelings toward her were changing. That desire, which he realized was akin to lust, had coveted her gentle curving body and its soft warm places. Those feelings were still there, but there was a growing feeling of what he had to term admiration and respect. This beautiful person was no longer just the object of his lust, she was much more.

Suddenly he laughed aloud. "You know what I've just been doing? I've been telling myself how wonderful you are, how I could no longer treat you as a sexual object. I'll bet if I think this way long enough, I'll be able to talk myself out of desiring you. I'll make you into a beautiful statue or something so noble I won't be able to touch you."

"You'd better not!" she half growled, half purred.

"When you make noises like that," he laughed, "I don't think It'd be possible."

"But I do understand," she became serious again. "This should be so simple. We're just two human beings, who want to be with one another, who want to enjoy and give pleasure to one another. Why must it be so complicated?"

"You're right," he answered. "Why don't I just carry you off to the rocks over there and have my way with you?" He chuckled, and peered at her sideways, trying to imitate a leer.

She stopped and faced him. "Yes, why don't you?" she asked simply.

"Yes, why don't I," he asked himself—and then he did.

They found a spot a little further on, back against the wall, where the ground was relatively dry, and they felt safe from being seen, but where there was still enough light to see one another.

He wanted to undress her, and she let him, saying, "I wish I could put out these lights."

"Well, I don't," he protested. "You've been taunting me with that lovely body of yours forever, and now I want to see every inch of it. Don't you realize what you did to me when you came to tuck me in that first night in the cave, and you were nude? Oh, you torturer."

"My poor baby," she soothed, coyly.

But now she was available to him, he held himself back. He didn't want to rush. Ha felt a new tenderness come over him. He wanted to care for her. Carefully, after thoroughly wringing out her undergarments, he sponged her as dry as he could, and he allowed her to do the same for him. The air was moist and, now they were drier, even warmer than the water. The stone floor was cold, however, and he inverted their clothes and spread them carefully on the floor. They lay together, and though he still wanted to prolong the gentle anticipation, as he kissed her softly, her belly began to press and move against his. That movement was intoxicating, and the tender waiting could no longer be endured. That warm spot that had been growing forever hotter between them was finally bursting into flame, and their bodies were becoming one burning fire.

As he moved, gently at first, still trying to prolong the moment, he whispered, "I've wanted so long to be in you. It's so right, so good."

"Oh, I know, I know."

And there were no more questions and no more waiting between them.

The air around them seemed to have cooled as he lay by her side, gently caressing her, kissing her about the face and shoulders. Her body continued to generate heat, however, and he had only to return to her for all the warmth he ever needed. He knew he couldn't return so soon, however much he might want to, and he laughed gently and shared an amusing thought while waiting. "You know, I've never been seduced before by honesty."

"Front, was I really chasing you? Was I really all that obvious?"

"Not chasing, and not necessarily obvious, just persistently there. But as soon as you started being honest, it was out of my hands."

"I hadn't noticed your hands were out of anything," she chided coquettishly.

"I mean, as soon as you indicated you wanted me, what could I do? I couldn't back out then; I no longer had any excuse for being a coward. I couldn't tell myself you didn't want me anyway." He pulled her close again and began stroking and tickling her back and rear. "Oh, you wicked temptress. You knew I'd be a small babe in your hands, and you tormented and bedeviled me with this tantalizingly sensuous body."

"Front, stop teasing. What are you doing to me?"

"Pleasuring you, I hope," he whispered in her ear.

"Oh, you are, you are!"

Then her movement took over again. He was being led, but this time there was no doubt, and he followed willingly.

10

COUNCIL OF CONFRONTATION

The trouble started as soon as Front and Wonina returned to the group.

"Out there uncoiling your rope, boy?" Wons questioned snidely.

Belatedly Front realized how obvious the coiled rope he now carried in his hand must be. He hadn't thought to rewind it about his waist. He hadn't been thinking at all about alibiing their long absence as he and Wonina strolled casually back to the group.

Now there was no time to think of excuses. Nash was rising to one knee, and glaring at them. "Where have you two been?"

For a moment Front thought the scowling fellow was coming up fighting. Instead Nash sank back, his voice suddenly more plaintive than angry.

"You said you were going to massage my leg, Wonina."

Fyva then took up the attack. "I'd guess Wonina has already done her massaging for the night, Nash dear." With saccharine sweetness, she grinned at Front, "Did she get out all your kinks, Front darling?"

Front had been concerned all along about the probable consequences of acting on his desire for Wonina. He assumed he would have to eventually confront Nash's anger. Wons and Fyva's indirect attack, however, was unexpected, and it left him confused and uncertain of how to respond. His first inclination was to defend himself, claiming his wanting to be with Wonina was only natural. But then he became annoyed—why should he have to justify his behavior? He started to lash out, telling them to mind their own business, when Wons changed course.

"But enough of this pettiness, this is Nash's affair, not ours."

Nash looked up again, and might have said something, but Wons gave him no time. "We have more important things to be concerned about now. It's obviously time we started heading back where we should have headed in the first place."

Fyva quickly followed up on Wons' new tack. Her tone was forgiving and conciliatory. "Front, I know you did what you thought was best, but you'll have to admit with the current now turning against us, and the effort it takes to swim, we've already come to that barrier you spoke of. I know you'll understand that we have to hold you to your promise. It's time we turned back and move with the current toward the Angle Being city."

Front's mind reeled; they were moving too fast for him. He started formulating a counter plan—they hadn't explored enough of the way ahead to know if it would continue to be an arduous swim. But then that's what he was supposed to have been doing when he went off with Wonina. As he glanced at Fyva, he feared what she would do with that argument. Her jaw was set, and she was wearing her most, I'm-going-to-be-logical smile. He then looked at Wons, who was lounging back with a smile of supercilious patience on his face. Anger then boiled up in Front. He was about to raise his hand and point accusingly at his two smug attackers, when he also glanced at Nash. The anger suddenly oozed out of him. His Anger would seemed inappropriate in the presence of the one person here who probably had a right to be angry. But Nash was not angry, and Nash was not attacking him—Nash was merely sitting there, looking bewildered and hurt.

Desperately he turned to Wonina, but then he realized her long silence was an unstated proclamation of her helplessness. The pained look on her face suggested she wanted to go to Nash, to comfort him, perhaps to ask for his forgiveness, but she was frozen, looking now to him and then to Nash, hopelessly indecisive.

As he looked again at each of them, none of them spoke further. Were these his people, he wondered—two enemies, a pitiful victim, and one helpless lover? Were these the people to whom he had talked so self-right-eously about his noble purpose? Were those the same people he was now wanting to outwit and bend to his way? Were these his friends, his companions in distress, or merely objects to be manipulated to win his point? This wouldn't do at all, he realized. To attack, to defend, even to try to order a group of friends and fellow human beings, seemed inappropriate and somehow ultimately doomed to failure. He drew a deep breath and let it out slowly. Could he have been wrong in giving in to his feelings with Wonina? But then, how could that which had seemed so right be wrong? He allowed himself a momentary escape into the memory of that cleansing experience of honesty with Wonina, when he had trusted her to accept and care for him, in spite of all his doubts and hesitation. He shook his head in dismay. No, if I can't have that honesty, nothing else is worth having, he realized.

He looked again at Fyva's set face, and then at Wons' sarcastic smile, and suddenly he felt very tired. No, he no longer wanted to force or manipulate those people into anything. If we're not all in this together, all working for the same thing, our chances of succeeding aren't worth a damn anyway. If the others can't or won't accept me and Wonina for what we are and what we've done, it's probably best that they go their own way and do whatever they think is right.

While he stood pondering, still no one had spoken, and he began to wonder at this. They were obviously waiting for him to say something. He realized they were still giving him the power, by their waiting, to lead

them, a power he had already abandoned. Maybe they didn't know what
to do either, he thought sadly.

As the moments dragged on, he realized he was probably right, and so
he finally said it. "People, I honestly don't know what's best to do, and I
suspect you don't know either."

Both Fyva and Wons started to speak at once, but then lapsed into
silence. So he continued speaking. "I do know one thing, however. The
fact that Wonina and I have just had sex together has nothing whatsoever
to do with what we must decide here."

Wons and Fyva, his former accusers, looked away, seemingly embarrassed by Front's sudden frankness. Nash, now that the obvious truth had
been spoken, finally gathered together his outrage, and cried out his pain.

"You bitch! You filthy bitch!" But even Nash's anger sputtered quickly
into silence.

Wonina had looked as shocked as the others, and for a moment Front
thought that the very person who had taught him honesty would now
attack him for being honest. Instead, her momentary look of betrayal
changed slowly to one of understanding.

She turned back to Nash. "Forgive me, Nash. I'm truly sorry I've hurt
you. You're the last person I'd have wanted to hurt. But Nash, you should
also be the last person to be surprised by this. You know we haven't been
right for each other for a long time now."

Nash tried to rekindle his anger, "But how could you do it like this, and
with everybody knowing?"

"Would it've been better to be secretive, Nash, to lie about what everyone suspected?" Wonina countered gently. She then looked more sternly
at Fyva. "I don't like being secretive. I don't like feeling ashamed of being
what I am." She paused and then smiled at Front. "And I'm not ashamed."
Her smile broadened. "I'm not ashamed—I'm proud! Proud that I love
Front and that I finally had the courage to admit it to him, to myself, and
now to all of you."

A burden was lifted from Front. He had that clean feeling again. He was suddenly so relieved he wasn't even annoyed when Wons interrupted the silence to complain.

"Well, this is all very lovely, but it has nothing to do with what we've been talking about."

Front stopped him. "You're wrong, Wons. It has everything to do with what we've talked about. We've been trying to decide what's best for the group, and even more important to decide what's best for the Sebasans. But we've been trying to make a decision without knowing all the facts. People have been advising what should be done without saying that they really believe. No, no, that's not the way to put it. *I've* been trying to advise the group, but until you know why I want to do what I want to do, you can't fully judge the worth of my advice. And I'm tired of trying to figure out what everyone else is really thinking. I'm not apologizing for it, but let me publicly state now—and I don't mean to hurt you, Nash—what I've been thinking most of the time we've been on this trip is how much I'd like to make love to Wonina. If you were putting your faith in me as your leader, depending on me to make good decisions, you certainly needed to have known that."

There was a small chuckle from the group. Even Nash managed to smile. Front took that as his cue to continue revealing himself.

"And let me admit something else. After I'd stalked off so grandly earlier today, having made my big speech, just when I should've been carefully planning how we were going to proceed, I was primarily concerned with having looked a fool for forgetting to bring my pack along."

Wons volunteered his surprise. "No! I didn't even realize you'd left it."

"That's just my point, Wons. Because I didn't know what you were thinking, and I didn't have the courage to ask because I was trying to maintain my pose as leader, I really couldn't be an effective leader."

Fyva nodded her head in understanding, but her impatient expression suggested she wanted to change the subject.

Front didn't let her. "I want to do something now—something I've never done before, and something I'm not even sure is worth doing. In fact, it might even cause more trouble. I only know it seems like the right thing for me to do." He looked about briefly, and when he apparently had their full attention again, he plowed on, "I've been harboring a lot of feelings, a lot of questions, a lot of doubts about all of you during this trip, and now that I've been courageous enough to start opening up, I want to clear up all those doubts; I want to clear up all these feelings that've been getting in my way. After this, whether I'm leading or following, I really think I'll be more effective for this group."

He saw Wons pull back from the others. Nash moved forward, as if readying himself to rise, and Fyva seemed to pull in upon herself, getting somehow smaller.

"Wonina, why don't you and I sit down," he gestured. "I feel as though I'm some kind of spider about to pounce on the others."

Front sensed that the other three relaxed slightly, but he knew they were still on guard.

Even as she followed his suggestion and seated herself, Wonina was another who was not yet with him. "Front, do you really believe you should...."

"Please, Wonina. No, I don't know if I should do this. I just know I want to do it." He looked them over again and settled on Wons. "And I want to start with you."

Front could see Wons was trying to smile his usual supercilious smile, but this time it didn't quite come off.

"Wons, I've always admired you."

Now Wons was a bit more able to smile.

"I've always looked up to you as someone more educated and maybe, although I wouldn't admit it, even more intelligent than I. I came on this trip, not just to be with Wonina, but also to be with you. I frankly thought you were a little off the deep end with your Angle Beings, but I had enough faith in you, enough faith that if you believed in them there must be something to them. But frankly, Wons, when you pulled your pouting act up on Mount Stareye, I thought you were...." He stopped himself. "No, no, that's not what I want to say." He saw that Wons, who had grown quite comfortable, even smug after the opening comments, had again drawn away from him. "It's not important what I thought you were. What's important is I didn't like the way it affected me when you behaved that way. I...well, I lost faith in you. For a while, I didn't even like you. For a while, it seemed your only response to everything was to sneer at it. I didn't start liking you again until you fell in the water, trying to grab hold of the rope to save me back there in the first cave."

Wons seemed to relax a little again.

"I think what really hurt the most, though, Wons, was just a moment ago when you started making those rotten remarks about what Wonina and I had been doing."

"Well, perhaps I was overdoing it, Front, but...."

"Please, Wons, don't interrupt. I don't want you to defend yourself. I'm not saying you were wrong in feeling the way you were feeling, even in doing what you did. I only want you to know I was annoyed and hurt."

"You deserved to be hurt," Nash interrupted, quietly but bitterly. "And I really don't want to hear any more of this garbage!"

"I'm sorry, Nash," Front cut him off. "If you don't want to hear it, then I don't want you to hear it, but I'm going to say it anyway. And if you don't want to listen, then it's all right with me if you go off somewhere else where you won't be able to hear."

Wonina looked concerned and leaned slightly away from Front.

Nash said nothing, but didn't move, so Front continued.

"Then if you're not going to leave, Nash, let me say what I have to say to you. Before this trip, I really didn't know you very well. I know I was envious of you. I figured you must be a nice guy if Wonina cared for you, but that's about all I knew. In spite of my envy, I was coming to like you during the first part of the trip. You were the one willing to take the chances. You could get things done. When you took over on top of Mount

Stareye, I was grateful. It wasn't until we started down the hill and you started pushing people around that I...well, I have to admit it, I got frightened of you. I began to dislike you, in fact. It wasn't until the moment, when we were trapped in the side cave, and you were ranting and raving about Fyva and Wons, and you went so far as to say you'd rather trust the Outhans, it wasn't until you finally realized you were being stupid, that I finally realized I liked you after all."

Nash had his head down, and Front couldn't read his expression. "I'm still not sure about you, Nash. The truth is, though, I have to depend upon you. I'm depending on you to be the most useful when we actually have to fight the Outhans, but at the same time, I'm afraid to depend upon you. That temper of yours might get in the way. I realize now, it wasn't out of fear of your feelings, or even out of fear of you that I was holding back from Wonina, but out of fear of losing you as a part of the group when we attack the Outhans. Well, I guess I'll have to face that fear now, and trust you."

He turned to Fyva, who seemed now to have unfolded a bit, the grim set of her jaw loosening and her eyes once again taking on that alertness they always had in the presence of something new.

Front laughed. "Fyva, you're doing right now what I most admire in you, and what makes you so important to the group. I think more than anything else, you'd want learn something new, particularly if there's a profit in it."

Fyva smiled in apparent agreement.

"And therein lies my problem with you, Fyva. I'm not sure I can trust you when you're like that."

She stopped smiling.

"When you do things, or when you make suggestions for the group, I always wonder whether they're really for the group or because you're plotting some new way to satisfy your curiosity, or even acquire something new to add to your list of trophies. I'm somewhat ashamed to admit this, but I actually thought you let that rope go on purpose, and allowed me to get washed away in the channel just so the group would have to come after me."

"Front," Wonina hushed disapprovingly.

"I'm not accusing her, Wonina. I don't even want her to answer me. I don't really want to know if I was right about that rope. The point is, Fyva, you're so smooth with your words that even though I often appreciate how effective you are in helping the group with your words, I still I have a problem in trusting you."

Front hesitated before turning to Wonina. Perhaps what he had to say next was the biggest risk of all. He didn't want to lose the companionship and cooperation of anyone in the group, but Wonina was obviously his most cherished companion. Still, he tried to reassure himself, you ought to know by now you can trust her to accept you, even the part of you that doesn't entirely trust her.

"And Wonina," he began, and then he was surprised that she looked shocked, and he noticed that she even edged away from him again. "Wonina, it scares me that you're pulling away from me right now...but I guess I'll have to accept that. It's more important for me right now to be honest and open with you than to be close to you—and I do have some concerns about you. I guess I have two concerns. First, I really do believe you love me, but I wonder how much of your love for me is based on the fact that, at least temporarily, I seem to be the one who's leading the group. It bothered me how you seemed to cow tow to Nash, when he took charge so forcefully, even though you seemed to disapprove of what he was doing. I don't want you to love me just because you think I'm strong, and just because you're dependent upon me. And second, it seems to me you're always protecting everybody else...No, I take that back. It's not that you're always doing it, it's that you seem to do it just when I really want to be angry at somebody. That's when you stop me. Maybe I should be stopped at those times, but then maybe I shouldn't. Next time I'd appreciate it if you'd let me make my own decision whether it's wise to get angry."

For a few moments he remained silent, and so did the others, as if they were waiting for him to say more. It finally occurred to him there was one other person to talk about.

"Now let me talk about me. I think, in a number of ways, I've already told you some of the things I don't like about myself, but let me sum it up. The main thing I haven't liked about myself is that, although I've always been honest, I haven't always been open with you. I've been holding back all these thoughts and feelings about you, and there was nothing you could do about what those thoughts were doing to me because I didn't have the courage to tell you about them. Well, from now on, I'm going to tell you everything. The hell with protecting you! If you can't take me as I am, then you don't deserve me."

Again there was silence in the group, but this time Front had no more to say. He waited, expecting almost anything, but he was surprised that it was Wons who finally spoke.

The smile was still supercilious, but it seemed no longer so insincere. "I feel kind of strange, Front. Somehow I think I ought to be angry at you. You said some things I didn't like hearing, but on the other hand, I didn't really hear one thing that surprised me. Maybe I'm not angry because, whether I like it or not, you confirmed what I've been suspecting about myself all along."

He smiled more broadly, a different kind of smile now.

"I do sort of feel like a big brother whose little brother has suddenly outgrown him." Then he fell silent again, with a bemused look on his face.

Front then noticed that Fyva was leaning forward, seemingly eager to have her turn. He turned fully to her, and she started immediately.

"Front, I really admire you for what you've just done...and damn you," she laughed, "you hit me right on the head! I'd been sitting here trying to figure out how you did it. I thought I had everything going the way I wanted, and then suddenly you were in charge again. Someday you're going to have to teach me how you pulled this off." She became serious again. "But I don't see how you can believe that I actually let that rope go on purpose. The rope was slippery. You had just told us to let the rope out further...."

Front held up his hand and started to interrupt her.

"I know, I know," she hurried on. "You don't want me to defend myself. I learn fast, remember? Let me see now—it was so smooth the way you did it...oh, yes, what I'm really trying to say is that it's important to me that you come to trust me again. That's it—I don't like the feeling of not being trusted by you."

She smiled and settled back, seemingly satisfied with herself.

Front then turned to the remaining two. "Wonina, Nash, I'd feel better if you'd also share what you're feeling."

Wonina seemed to be waiting for Nash to speak, but after a moment more, she went ahead. "I guess I'm a little hurt, Front, that you'd find any fault in me whatsoever... I guess I can learn to live with that though, particularly since everybody knows that I am something of a mother hen, always looking after everybody else. I guess that's just me, and I'm not sure I'm going to change it, even for you. And I don't think I'm defending myself—well maybe a little when I say that everybody also knows I can be pretty tough and nondependent when I want to be."

She gave Front a small defiant look, but then smiled.

Her smile again changed to concern as she turned to Nash. "But most of my feelings right now have to do with you, Nash. You haven't said a thing for so long, and it's not like you to remain so silent. I'd rather see you angry and being a tyrant than like this. My mind tells me that I really don't have to be guilty about what I've done, but the more hurt you look, the guiltier I get."

Nash looked up slowly. "I'm okay, honey."

Obviously no one believed him, so after a moment he continued, "It's just that my leg's hurting, that's all."

Wonina looked to the others for help, and Fyva then tried to bring him out. "I think it's important, Nash, that all of us speak, even you. I agree with Front. All of these confusing feelings that've been going on have been interfering with our being logical about things. What do you say, Nash, let us know how you're feeling."

"But I'm okay, Fyva. I understood what everyone's been saying, so let's get on with planning what we're going to do now. I tell you, I'm all right."

Both Wonina and Fyva were obviously dissatisfied, and started to continue their pushing, but Front stopped them.

"Nash, I'm also concerned that you haven't spoken, but I want to trust your judgment. If at any time you have anything else you'd like to say to me, I want to hear it." He turned back to the others. "However, I'm not sure this is the right time for us to continue planning. For one, I'm pretty exhausted. I think after a good night's sleep, I'll be much better able to make effective decisions about what we should be doing ...No, let me put it another way," he laughed. "I'll be able to make *my contribution* to the group's decision."

The others seemed also to feel the discussion had ended. No one, however, was ready to get up to prepare themselves for sleeping, and the group was apparently about to drift into small talk when Front noticed that Nash had turned away and was about to rise.

"Nash," Wonina asked quickly, "are you going some place?"

"Oh, I just thought I'd take a walk. I'd sort of like to be by myself for a while."

Nash then removed the serpent-skin jacket from the tube that had been nestled by his side. Front felt the whole group stiffening, and he wondered whether he should move to take the weapon away from Nash. He checked himself, however. He had just finished saying he wanted to trust Nash's judgment, and he guessed it was necessary to risk that trust. He settled back slightly, as Nash began slowly moving away from the group.

Fyva had her own reason for not trusting, however, "Nash, I wish you wouldn't take the weapon with you," and she rose to follow him. "There's something I've noticed I've been meaning to mention."

Nash turned back toward the group just as Fyva reached him and placed her hands over his.

"Nash, please don't fire the weapon again. I've noticed something. I'm afraid the power might be giving out."

Nash's face became enraged. "Take your hands off me!" and he jerked the weapon back from her. The nozzle slammed against his arm, and the dreadful thundering flash was followed by Nash's scream of outraged pain.

11

THE PEOPLE AND THE WAY ARE ONE

Nash was down, clutching his left shoulder, his face contorted in pain, his one scream of agony mingling with the thunder that echoed and faded down the cavernous channel. There was a grating sound, and Front glanced overhead where a gaping hole seared the ceiling, and suddenly a boulder sized chunk broke off and seemed to fall lazily to the floor.

Before that chunk ceased bouncing, Wonina was by Nash's side. For a moment it looked as though the wound might not be serious. There was no blood oozing between Nash's clutching fingers. As Wonina pried those fingers away, however, Front could see why. A bite-sized scoop had been neatly carved from the meaty muscle of Nash's shoulder and the blackened wound was cleanly cauterized.

"Quick, water!" Wonina demanded. "The flesh is still cooking. We need to cool it off."

Front, who was kneeling beside the edge of the channel, hastily cupped his hands and began scooping up the needed coolant.

When the water splashed on the wound, Nash finally allowed himself a complaint. "Damn, that stings!"

"What do you expect, you dolt?" Wonina both soothed and chastised. "If you go around lighting yourself with a match stick, you're going to burn."

"But the water's stinging me," he insisted.

"Use the water in your flask, Front," Wonina directed. "It should be cleaner."

Quickly uncapping his flask, Front began pouring more water onto the gaping wound. This time Nash seemed to get some relief from the dousing.

Wonina, who had unbuttoned her outer jacket and torn away a piece of what was left of her undergarment, was busy with the cloth, sponging and cleaning the wound. She seemed completely unaware of her revealing exposure.

In spite of his pain, Nash was not so unaware. He looked from Wonina to Front and managed a partial grin. "With only one good arm," he half groaned, half laughed, "she's probably too much for me to handle anyway."

With his good hand, he clutched Front's arm and squeezed. After a moment as a spasm of pain passed, Nash looked again at Front and shook his head. "You were really right about me always acting without thinking. I've got about as much brains as a pile of goat turds." He clutched Front's arm even more forcefully. "I'm sorry, Front. I've really screwed things up now."

Front tried to think of something reassuring to say, but the longer he thought about their dilemma, the less reassuring he felt. The stream was working against them, they were now burdened with a wounded man who might not even be able to float with the stream, much less swim against it, and if Fyva was right, their one weapon might be almost spent. Nash saved him the trouble of finding the right words. He shook his head again and laughed, and this time the laugh was no longer so bitter and self-accusatory.

"Funny thing—this pain in my arm is fierce, but you know it's almost better than the pain I was feeling inside when I wanted to walk away from the group. It's like, in my dumb way, I had to do something stupid, something to cause myself a different kind of pain in order to get rid of the pain inside I couldn't deal with."

Front was startled. It was hard for him to imagine such words coming from Nash. He realized suddenly he didn't understand this fellow after all, and he could begin to understand now why Wonina had remained engaged to him for so long.

Nash turned back to Wonina. "Cover yourself, girl," he said paternally. "I'm already on fire, don't make it worse."

"Oh, hush up. It's not like you hadn't seen it before."

Front felt a brief return of his old envy, before he realized the absurdity of it. Nash was acknowledging what they both already knew, that he had once possessed what now belonged to Front. The feeling that she should never have been anyone else's was old fashioned and irrational—but still very strong.

As he looked again at Wonina, admiring her doing what she did best, caring for another person, he could see how absolutely wrong it was for him to want to hold her back from giving of herself. She shouldn't, she can't belong just to me. I shouldn't try to possess her to keep her just for myself. In fact, he began to realize, I don't even want to possess her. If I owned her, there wouldn't be as much joy in her giving herself to me. It wouldn't be a gift, it would be an obligation.

Fyva pulled him out of his philosophical musing. She had taken up the weapon, and now she called him aside, obviously trying to get out of Nash's hearing.

"I'm afraid I was right, Front," she reported with concern. "When we first got the weapon, you remember these dots, every one of them was red. And now look here. After we started making the thing fire, I noticed, but I didn't think anything of it, that one after another the dots started turning blue. And now look."

Front followed her pointing finger to one remaining red dot. He then tried to count back, to remember how many times the weapon had been used.

"I've already figured it out," Fyva said, shaking her head. "It works out just right—seven times and seven blue spots. The weapon will only fire one more time."

Front didn't want to believe what she was telling him, but as usual Fyva's logic was hard to refute. He added this last revelation to his already pessimistic assessment of their chances of reaching Sebasa and achieving their purpose, and then he looked at Fyva again, expecting a firm set of her jaw announcing, "I told you so."

Instead she put her hand on his shoulder and said solicitously, "Don't worry, Front, we're not beaten yet. One shot from a weapon like this is more than we had before."

"But look at the facts logically," Front started to give the argument he had expected from her.

"You know I will, Front—but not right now. I believe you've already said we're too tired to think about our situation logically. Tomorrow we'll decide what to do."

To his total surprise, she embraced him and kissed him gently on the cheek, then left to offer her comfort to Nash. As his mind continued, unbidden, to count off all the factors working against them, a totally illogical feeling of comfort and reassurance spread through him. It wasn't logical, but he was enjoying a warm feeling of hope that was replacing the logical despair.

Allowing himself to feel hope also opened him up to the other feelings in his body. He became aware of the thirst that all the drama had created in him. He shook and then set aside his now empty flask and then went back to the edge of the channel. Cupping his hands, he first splashed his face and then gulped down a hasty swallow.

He gagged, and spewed out the rest. Brackish, he thought with disgust—wait a minute! Brackish?" He slapped himself on the forehead. "Of course! Of course, that's why I had hope in spite of the odds against us!"

His surprised bellow gained the others' attention. "The water's brackish," he shouted happily.

The others were puzzled, and Wonina was as usual concerned.

"Okay," Fyva shrugged. "So now we've got water problems. But get hold of yourself, Front."

"No....no problems, that is," he stopped and laughed again. "It's so obvious. If my mind hadn't been on other things....He suddenly felt embarrassed. "After all, I'm supposed to be the seaman. The water's brackish, it's salt water. That means the ocean. That means the tide. The tide's been coming in. That's why we were having so much trouble swimming against it. Now all we have to do is wait for the tide to go out, and we can just roll right into Sebasa, like children riding the surf."

The others finally understood what he was saying, and some of the heaviness in the group seemed to lift.

Front took a deep breath, and letting it out slowly he sat down with relief—and he also realized, with exhaustion. He should certainly sleep soundly tonight, he sighed, as he watched Wonina begin preparing her and Nash's sleeping bags. When he finally joined in the preparation, Front was again amused at the arrangement that almost seemed to happen by itself. This time, Nash was in the center, sided and attended to by both girls. He was pleased to note that Wons was again a part of the group, having placed his sack close up to Fyva's. In fact, his own sleeping bag was the only one a bit apart from the others, slightly separated from the engaged and concerned Wonina. It seemed all right, however. He didn't really feel apart from the group, and he didn't feel that Wonina's attention to Nash in any way detracted from what she was to him. She was Wonina, doing what she did best, and he was glad to realize that he wouldn't want her any other way. It was a pleasant feeling with which to fall asleep.

He woke groggily, wondering at first where he was and then what had awakened him. He listened to the constant murmuring of the water as it echoed down the channel before he realized it must have been Nash's groaning that woke him. He heard Wonina's whisper.

"Front, get me some water. I think he's feverish."

Hastily Front reached for his flask, and then he realized that he hadn't filled it because the water was brackish. Extracting himself from his sack, he quickly moved to the edge of the stream. He tasted the water and discovered with relief, it was no longer brackish, and it also cooler. The current had obviously reversed itself and was now moving in the direction of the sea. Considering its rate, he calculated it was well on its way to low tide. When they awoke in the morning, the tide would probably have turned against them again, and they would have to wait another three to six hours till flood tide to be able to recommence their journey.

Oh, well, all the more time for us to plan and for Nash to recover. That last thought brought a returning twitch of concern. He hurried to give Wonina his flask and then, moving quietly so as not to disturb the sleepers, he gathered all the others' flasks. He returned to the edge of the water to fill them, against the time when the channel would once again be brackish.

Time for one more task, he realized. It was just possible, although the partially destroyed light below their platform gave no hint of it, that there might yet be another weapon stored beneath them. Perhaps the red light bordering the glass case had been extinguished, but the weapon's cabinet might still be intact. They certainly could use another fully loaded weapon against the Outhans.

Having finished filling the flasks, he remained squatting at the edge of the channel, watching the bubbling water pushing toward the home he so longed to regain. Alone now with his memories, and away from the necessity of arguing his case against the others, and also feeling considerably more settled in his mind regarding Wonina, he began for the first time to think more clearly about the Outhans. His clearer thoughts were not reassuring. Even with more than one weapon, it seemed to him the Outhans would be formidable adversaries. He tried to remember the details of that dreadful view he had seen from high on Mount Stareye—twenty ships, he estimated, maybe more. The first shock had perhaps exaggerated the number, but twenty ships, or ten ships, or even five ships, how could one weapon, pitifully spent, even register on those seemingly unfeeling creatures? The friendly water running before him began to feel like an inevitable current dragging him toward a fate he might be wiser to avoid. He let his eyes follow the rushing water downstream to where the channel narrowed and the light faded. Somewhere beyond that distance, he imagined the bright town and the sparkling blue green waters of Sebasa, and though he tried to blot out the image, he pictured a black turbulent cloud churning overhead—and descending. Beneath that ominously descending darkness was a small dwelling, packed in among other small houses along a narrow street where his mother and his sister were waiting, agonizing over their latest loss, Front, staring hopelessly at the descending cloud above them.

Wise or unwise, Front realized it was inevitable that he would return home, and it was not the current before him that was the driving force.

When he woke again, Front found it more difficult than usual to force himself out of his sack. His many trials were now taking their toll. His stiffness and muscular pain, however, immediately reminded him of Nash, but he could see that Wonina was already attending their injured companion. He also heard Nash's protests.

"I'm all right, Wonina, I told you, stop fussing over me."

Front was again impressed with Nash's resilience—or his stubbornness. Nash made a point of standing up and walking about, trying to stretch himself. He hobbled slightly, from the old wound in his leg, and he was obviously reluctant to raise the newly wounded arm too high.

"Any more weapons you'd like me to test?" he joked weakly.

The others laughed, obviously more to humor Nash than out of amusement.

They ate silently, and Front noticed the others were in need of no caution about rationing their food. Both he and Wonina insisted, however, that Nash force down enough food to give him more strength. He also noticed that Wonina was covertly adding some of her rations to Nash's. Without spoken encouragement from Front, the others set about rearranging their gear and preparing themselves for the journey.

"We have time to talk," he informed them. "The tide's switched again, and I estimate it will be about three hours before we can move with the current."

They seemed in no hurry to sit themselves in their customary circle, however. It was obvious the others remembered that most of their circular sessions had been decidedly unpleasant. Beginning another such council was not something to be joyfully anticipated.

"Here's how I see things," he began, as the others finally seated themselves and shifted restlessly about. "I'm not sure how manipulative I was being at the time, but it seems to me we did agree earlier that our ultimate goal was to do whatever was best for Sebasa."

"You weren't manipulating, Front," Fyva assured him. "I for one want to think that's what we all believe."

Front looked at the others, and waited for further comment. Their silence seemed to indicate agreement.

"We talked about two alternatives then, and I want to look at the pros and cons of both of those alternatives to see how your thinking might've changed. We were either to head directly for Sebasa, to see what we could do with what we had available to us, or to search for further help in the other direction, in the place of power of the Angle Beings."

Fyva interrupted again. "I think the latter's no longer a reasonable alternative, Front. It seems to me we're heading in the right direction."

Wonina and Nash nodded their heads, but Wons' head remained steady, his expression unusually blank and unreadable. "Nevertheless, let's hear what Front has to say," he requested.

Front continued, "Frankly, I don't know how to weigh all the factors. The main thing I was worried about, the current's going against us, no longer seems to be a problem. We have only to choose our times and go with the tide as it heads out again."

He hesitated before mentioning his next item of concern, and Nash took the burden away from him. "And our powerful weapon, thanks to my stupidity, is no longer so powerful."

Fyva was apparently going to say something to lessen Nash's guilt, but this time it was Wonina who was firm.

"Let him say it. It needs to be said. We both overheard you and Front whispering about what's happened to the weapon."

"We know there's only one more time we can use it, and we know my childish stupidity is at fault," Nash continued.

"There's no way you could have known," Fyva said, still trying to say something reassuring.

"No, there's no way I could have known, but at least I could have thought about it for a while before I acted like a child—a goat-child at that!"

Nash's boyish glumness made him look almost a caricature of his self-accusation. It was hard not to laugh, and Wonina leaned over and gently poked him on his good shoulder.

"Maybe next time, honey. Even a goat-child can finally grow up."

Fyva took up her reassuring again. "Nevertheless, there's one good shot left in that weapon. I can't help but feel if we all use our heads we'll be able to put that shot where it'll really make a difference. I don't know about the rest of you, but I'm tired of talking and ready to start moving."

The others shifted and were about to rise, but noticing that Front was not yet moving, they settled back again.

"Are you sure that all of you have had a chance to say everything you to say?" He looked at each in turn, and settled finally on Wons.

Wons still looked enigmatic, and said nothing.

"Well, I suppose we could begin walking. The way is rough, and there are many obstacles, but it's passable. Wonina and I went almost all the way last night in that direction."

Wons guffawed, "I would've thought," he began, then suddenly sobered, and looked at Nash, and then quickly looked away. "I mean...I think...that is, I agree with Fyva, it's time to get under way." He was obviously embarrassed, as he hastily gathered together his equipment.

Front's concern about where Wons stood in the group washed away in a flood of relief. If his reason for it hadn't been so obvious, he would have rushed over and hugged the fellow. For Wons to have passed up such an opening, such an opportunity for sarcasm, was a noble feat of self restraint. From his quick glance at the others, he knew they were likewise aware of what Wons had sacrificed. Even Nash was smiling.

Front then remembered his other chore for the morning, and the new levity in the group carried over into his announcement. "Before we go, it's time for my usual solitary dip."

The others looked puzzled.

"From the look of the destruction on this platform, it might be futile, but it's just possible I might find another weapon down below."

He expected at least Wonina to protest, but instead she gathered the rope and began tying it about his waist.

He had to guess where the center of the platform might be. The light from below was diffused, and the beginning and ending of the damaged platform was undeterminable. He finally settled on his best guess, where the visibility was best although still was poor.

When he entered the water, he also had to fight against the incoming though somewhat sluggish tide. As much by feel as by sight, he worked his way down the inward sloping wall beneath the platform, and then hastily, but almost blindly, he followed the sudden cut inward. The back wall was now a murky gray. He was about to give up, when he finally encountered, by working downward with the current, what he suspected might be the ruptured edge of the cabinet he sought. It was necessary to return to the surface for air, however, before he could investigate.

The others waited patiently while he got his breath. He didn't even bother to say anything, but saved his breath for a second dive. This time he was able to come more directly to his goal, but his disappointment was equally swift. He had to be careful not to cut himself on the jagged glass, but his groping search assured him there was nothing remaining in that shattered container. Hastily he tried searching in front of the open box, on the floor of the channel. He encountered something in the gloom, but it was obviously much too large to be the slender cylinder he sought.

Nevertheless, he explored, considering the possibility that something else might be of value. The object his hands encountered was oblong, about as thick as his own body, smooth as glass, with none of the usual slime that accumulated on the walls of the channel. The surface was sharply angled, and at one end there was a smooth round opening. Cautiously, he risked reaching into that opening, and quickly his fingers encountered a mass of convolutions and jutting shapes, some rigid, some flexible, and all equally uncoated with slime.

Front then tried moving the whole object, but its weight far exceeded its size. He thought he felt a slight displacement of the object, but it might have been his imagination; the object could well be fixed to the bottom. At any rate, his air was rapidly being exhausted, and perhaps it was that or the gloom left by the damaged light above him, but Front suddenly felt oppressed by the object beneath him and by the gaping, torn cabinet almost within reach of the object. Suddenly the whole enclosure seemed alien, and yet strangely familiar. He had been in this strange subterranean world for so long it no longer felt new to him, but this particular place at this particular time both attracted and repelled him. As his need for air increased, he felt further and further out of time and out of place, and he knew his frantic surge to the surface was not entirely motivated by his need for air.

The others obviously felt no need to ask questions. His expression must have been explanation enough. They pulled him in and allowed him time to regain his breath. He then stood and let Wonina recoil the rope about him.

Again they commenced their journey. Front led, dragging his boat. Wonina followed, assisting Nash. Fyva and Wons trailed, side by side, waking silently and dragging the other three boats, carefully avoiding the increasing number of jagged boulders that partially blocked their pathway.

When Front reached the place that had been the end of the previous evening's journey, it suddenly came to him that he experienced this boulder nook as a place of celebration. Shyly he glanced back at Wonina. He was disappointed that she seemed not to be aware of the significance of the spot they were passing. All of her attention was fixed on Nash.

Perhaps I'm being overly sentimental, Front chided himself—but he was aware of a dull hurt that lingered on.

Soon after that, the way became impassable; a great gouge had been cut from the path and even from the back wall. They seated themselves to wait for the tidal change, and Front's small hurt was somewhat mollified when Wonina left Nash and sat beside him. Still, no one talked while they waited and while Front checked the current several more times. Eventually, he could tell by his inability to judge the direction of the current that the flood tide was upon them, and they could begin going forward with a minimum of effort.

Whatever lingering doubt Front might have had about Wons' new attitude was further assuaged when Wons, who had now become the weapon bearer, removed his jacket to carefully enfold the blue cylinder. Just as carefully, he affixed the wrapped package to the lashings of his boat, along with his staff. It was further reassuring to see that Wons' handling of the weapon was no longer so reverential, merely cautious.

"We know the water doesn't seem to bother it, at least Nash knows it, but just in case, it'll ride out of the water here," he commented, patting the jacket covered weapon.

Front sliced a small section of rope and unbraided it so as to rejoin the four smaller sections. Then, in spite of Nash's protests, he tied one end to Nash's boat and gave the other end to Wonina.

"It's just in case, Nash. Don't be so touchy."

As if in defiance, Nash pulled out of their assisting hands and jumped into the water without their further help. He clambered successfully, but with obvious pain, into his boat.

Fortunately the current had now begun moving with them, and it wasn't necessary to actually pull Nash. His stiff leg and one functioning arm made his navigation rather awkward, but he managed more or less alone.

The greatly diminished light at this end of the platform soon faded altogether, and they were again headed into that familiar unlimited subterranean vastness, that dark sea without shores. This time, to Front's pleasure, it was for a while a salty sea, warm and no longer uninviting. He could almost imagine himself nighttime fishing on a moonless Sebasa Bay.

He was beginning to remember, however, that even nighttime fishing could get mighty old, as the "night" wore on and the endless channel moved ever onward in the endless darkness. In fact, he was feeling more and more alone, until Wonina shifted her weight and leaned forward to whisper in his ear.

"I love you, Front."

A groan of relief, and a degree of doubt he didn't know he felt, escaped from his throat. Gratefully, he squeezed her encircling arm between his cheek and shoulder.

Still the night wore on, and he caught himself having difficulty in realizing it was not in fact night, that above them, beyond the tower of stone that was the mountain range up back from Sebasa, there was sunlight and a land of sparkling silver threads of water, tumbling down mountainsides to a sun drenched, red roofed, whitewashed town. The joy at that image faded, as he further imagined dark thorny bodies crawling through those streets, leaving behind a smear of offal trailing from their insectival forms.

The prolonged darkness was apparently bothering Wonina as well, or perhaps it was that Nash had let out an involuntary moan. She called back, "Nash, are you all right?"

After a pause, Nash half grumbled, half groaned his reassurance.

"Fyva, Wons. Are you still there?" she called to the others.

"Here," they checked off their presence.

The sounds of those voices were much closer behind them than Front had imagined, and it was reassuring to feel their closeness.

It wasn't long after that he called again for a count of voices in the darkness, and then he made the count off a regular ritual.

In time he began to sense a change in the current of the water, and the echoes off the walls seemed to reverberate differently. Finally he realized there was something ahead. He veered slightly and slipped past a boulder that rose sharply out of the darkness. He called back his warning, just before he narrowly avoided another such boulder. These were the first obstacles they had encountered in the stream itself, and he could only imagine what damage there must be in the darkened ceilings and walls about them. He shuddered. He wasn't sure why, but something about this even more terrible damage brought to mind the ominous object he had encountered beneath the last platform.

He had trouble banishing that image from his mind, but he was aided by his and Wonina's having to dodge more and more frequently these islands of stone in their sea of darkness, shifting their weight back and forth, always keeping one hand out in front of them to fend off a sudden jolt and a jagged stone edge.

"Everybody okay?" Wonina called out after every obstacle.

"Still here...Here...Here"

On they went, the force of the tide continuing to rush them against the up jutting boulders. Front was beginning to be concerned about this ever increasing speed as the jolts were coming even more frequently, and he could hear Nash groan with each new bump. They jerked around another sharp bend, and even though there was no lessening of speed, he was relieved at least to see a glimmer of light ahead. The waterway was less cluttered here, and the light brightened their way even further, but then the returning gray light brought with it a scene of destruction that he almost wished he couldn't see. There were, in fact, no longer recognizable sides to their channel, and, in places, seemingly no longer a ceiling—only massive wounds, dark empty holes leading to glimpses of even more cataclysmic destruction.

The dim light seemed to be rising from a great distance, over mountain like boulders, fading out of sight. Front knew the height of those boulders could be no more than ten or twelve feet, but in the dim visibility, all was exaggerated, and it was as though they were sailing through a sea of volcanic islands whose ominous shadowy peaks threatened a return of the awesome eruptions that must, so long ago, have caused the chaos about them.

His fanciful imaginings were becoming quite disturbing to Front, all the more disturbing when he and Wonina were so frequently separated from the others as sharp turns thrust boulders between the members of the group.

He was so relieved to be allowed escape from his fearful fantasy world, when they were suddenly thrust out of their twisting pathway onto a calmer, wider channel, that he was momentarily unconcerned by what he actually saw. They had run head on into what seemed to be a solid wall.

A small portion of an obviously broken light was just beneath the surface, at the foot of that wall, allowing him a reasonable view of the barrier. Front's brief moment of relief quickly faded as he hastily examined the wall. He could see where the current gurgled into crevices at numerous spots along that barrier, but none of those crevices was large enough to admit them.

They were soon bumping impotently on the wall, and Front began looking desperately for some indication that there was an alternate route.

Fyva maneuvered herself ahead, and to the left of them, and moved toward the brighter than usual light. This new light was so near the surface she was able to reach down and finally make her own firsthand exploration. She left her boat and scrambled up the tumbled embankment to a flat slab of rock just large enough for her to lie down and lean over to continue her examination.

Wonina pulled Nash closer to them, and then Front could see that Wons was the only one who had done something that seemed practical. He had back paddled along the wall, and soon he shouted back his discovery of a ledge broad enough for them to pull themselves from the water. There was even a stony pathway, he informed them, leading forward into the darkness. Front and Wonina struggled against the current, dragging Nash behind them, and made their way to Wons. Wons then assisted them out of the water, and Front was particularly pleased at how gently he handled Nash.

They dragged themselves and their boats across the gaping crevices that cut through Wons' barely passable pathway until they found themselves about six feet above Fyva's perch.

"Darn it," she voiced her consternation. "I still can't figure out what these things are. They seem almost solid. I thought at least there would be some kind of fire inside them, but this one's almost like a piece of solid light. I'd so like to have a chunk of this to take back." But obviously her prying blade had been unsuccessful.

She put away her blade, as Front called for a lunch break. He guessed that it was past the time to eat, and his weakened body went along with that guess.

As they ate, Front further examined the wall that blocked their way. He had no doubt that the barrier was not meant to be there. It consisted of a tumble of great boulders that had fallen from the heights above them. The barrier, however, extended upward into that darkness, and he had no way of determining its ultimate height. He was not eager to begin scaling into that darkness either. Their only recourse seemed to be the black hole into which Wons' pathway would lead them.

"Are you going to be able to make it, Nash?" he asked.

"Yes," was all Nash answered.

Once again Front led the way. This time they were forced to go in single file, with Fyva the last to leave her tantalizing light. At first Front nourished the illusion that perhaps this was a planned pathway, but the awkwardly placed, the cruelly jutting rocks, and the ever narrowing slits through which they had to squeeze soon squelched that illusion. They were going some place, however, and in spite of their difficulty, rather rapidly, even though there was a slight incline to the path.

In time it dawned on Front to wonder why they were still able to see their way. Surely all the turns they had made should have blotted out the light from that single beacon behind them. He then realized that the glow, though dim, was obviously colorful.

He looked back and was startled to see they were apparently being followed by one of the giant serpents. The whole idea was so absurd that the fearful feelings that should have accompanied such a discovery didn't have time to develop before he figured out that it was Fyva's swamp serpent skin, the numerous jewel like nodules glowing in the dark, their phosphorescence having apparently been stimulated by their long proximity to the light near which Fyva had tied her boat. They seemed he was encountering the ghost of his murdered swamp serpent after all, but apparently the ghost had joined their side. It was a silly but somehow reassuring image—just our little band of weary travelers with our friend the serpent god watching over us.

The serpent god's fiery eyes were rapidly closing, however, as the too briefly stimulated light soon faded—and then the narrow darkness closed in upon them. An outcropping of jagged boulders menaced their blind eyes and drastically slowed their progress. Front fumbled on, now stooping, now crawling. He recommenced the ritual of calling the roll, and occasionally the results were briefly heart sinking, as someone failed to answer immediately. Then they moved on. There seemed nothing more to do but crawl and climb and fend off, and turn and twist, and bruise and scrape, and suffer and force their way onward.

Front's fearful imagination began to haunt him again as he felt sideways against the wall where a wall should have been and when, for the hundredth time, his hand slipped into nothingness. He frequently encountered narrow crevices that would clutch at his wrist. Too often, now, he was yanking his hand away, as he pictured claw-like, thorny hands grabbing his, as larger than life Outhan monsters reached out to draw him into their gaping mouths. For the hundredth time, he called for the roll of voices. He waited again for the reassuring voices that seemed each time never to come.

At that moment his outstretched hand reached for the floor—and also passed into emptiness. He thudded his chest against the rough rock flooring, stretching his arm into empty space, and his mind lurched fearfully to the prospect that those behind him would not answer because they had already fallen into such an emptiness.

The pain in his chest was relieved, and he could breathe again, when all four voices finally answered his call.

"Hold up," he called back. "There seems to be a hole in the floor ahead of me."

When the scraping of four other bodies had stopped, he hung his head over the side into the hole. He was fairly certain that down below he could hear the rush of the stream from which they had departed, seemingly years ago. He realized now they must have been on a constantly upward sloping climb. The stream, which had held so many terrors for him, seemed to be calling a welcome message with its gurgling voice, "Come home from your darkened tomb above me."

He didn't even pause to consider the dangers as he began to uncoil the rope from about his waist. Hurriedly he thrust one end behind him.

"Pass that back to Wons," he demanded.

"What are you going to do?" Wonina asked fearfully.

"Don't even ask. Just do as I say."

Nash intercepted the rope, however, and tied it about his own waist.

"But you'll be dragged and hurt, Nash," Wonina protested.

"That's about the only worthwhile thing I can do with this battered body of mine," he laughed, and then called ahead, "Good luck, Front."

Looping the other end about his own waist, Front reached back in the dark to grasp Wonina briefly. Then he bent himself, legs downward, over the edge. It was risky, but the only thing he could think to do was to slip over and quickly re-grasp the rope. He realized belatedly he had had forgotten to warn Nash to expect a sudden jerk, but Nash must have been thinking more clearly than he was. The rope snapped taut after only a brief moment of slipping.

Now at least I know I'm right side up, or at least I assume I am. The darkness was so disorienting his only clue was the upward stretching rope.

"Let me out some rope," he called up, and began trying to ease himself down by grasping blindly for the jutting rocks about him. He encountered one brief ledge before he gratefully felt his feet touch the water. Still dangling, he swished his feet back and forth and discovered the channel here seemed to be quite wide.

"All the way," he called up, and soon after he splashed into the dark water.

Pulling himself even more line, he swam back and forth, and then called out, and heard his voice echoing gratifyingly into the distance.

He shouted upward, "All right, now pull up the rope and then lower my boat."

After retrieving and securing his boat, he shouted again, "Wonina, you come next."

He held his breath as he heard her banging and scraping above him, and he finally remembered to breathe only when she plunged into the water beside him and scrambled over to clutch him convulsively.

"You next!" he could hear Wons urging Nash. Eventually, he was even relieved enough to laugh when he heard Fyva protesting, "Be careful of my snake!"

Wons was last to lower himself hand over hand down the rope. Fortunately, he had discovered a jutting rock over which he was able to the loop the rope end.

After several tries, Front was able to flip the loop from it rock, and they were soon again on their watery way. It wasn't long, however, before they noticed that the current was slowing. The tide was turning. Still, even though they now had to propel themselves again, it was a relief to see from the occasional light the passed that for the time being there was at least a clear way ahead of them. Even the islands of boulders that had been impeding the channel were no longer there, although they occasionally encountered obstacles beneath the surface. Fearfully, Front remembered another time when the water seemed to have risen higher than they had expected, and it had turned out that the ceiling was sloping to the water, blocking their way. His echoing voice gave no indication that such was happening again. Still, he was profoundly relieved when another light ahead revealed that, whatever sloping there might be in the ceiling, there was no sloping evident in the uneven, pockmarked roof above them.

Returning light, however, brought to Front's dismay another jumble of boulders burying the waterway. By this time, though, they had a more immediate problem. The tide had fully reversed, and Front found himself in the familiar race against the current to reach the safety of what now seemed to be a receding ledge.

Moreover, he not only had himself and Wonina, but Nash to pull against the current. He worked his way over to the side as far as possible, and only against that eddying current was he able to eventually reach the promised ledge. He had to rest much longer than usual.

"Before we go on," Front finally recovered himself enough to direct, "we need more food in us. Let's eat."

As he opened his pack, the pitiful amount of food still remaining added to his concern and discouragement. He thought of the ghostly companion that had lighted their way through the dark, snake like cave, and he mourned, less for the murder of their friend the serpent than for its delicious and nourishing meat, which must now be rotting and reeking far to the rear.

They ate slowly, and since they needed even more time to recover, Front's mind returned to speculating on what might have caused the horrendous damage around them. He had become used to assuming it must have been a gigantic struggle between the Angle Beings and some mythical adversary that had caused this damage, and he put a question to Wons.

"You must be able to guess more about this than any of us, Wons. What do you think, was it really a war between the Angle Beings and some other beings that led to all this destruction?"

From Wons' long hesitation, Front thought he might now be reluctant to talk about his fallen heroes, but when Wons finally began, his voice contained an echo of his former tutorial tone. "I've been thinking about what Emanuel speaks of as the 'Mutanos.' Let me say right off, you can't really depend upon what this book says. You realize, of course, that Emanuel didn't write this himself. My guess is someone must have written it all down much later, maybe someone who didn't himself even compose the poems. Perhaps they were oral legends passed on from generation to generation. At any rate, all I can do is sort of guess what might've happened, putting pieces together from here and there in the book.

"The Angle Beings, in spite of what I might have said a long time ago," he grinned, "don't really seem to be quite human. There's something both superhuman and other than human about them. Maybe they weren't even of flesh, but something harder, metal maybe, and that's why they become known as 'Angle' Beings. On the other hand, the Mutanos seemed at first to be talked of as children, sometimes as the 'first children.' Emanuel speaks with fondness of them, and then with a growing concern, and then with an almost sad bitterness, a resignation regarding what he was going to have to do to them. Maybe that led to the war that caused all this destruction.

"Then there were other people who are talked about later in the book, children who are obviously humans, like us, but maybe different kinds of children, children who are being sent or carried to different places, apparently by the Angle Beings. It's all very confusing. At times it seems like they're one big family, at other times it's a great impersonal businesslike army. I also get the silly picture that the children were being carried places on giant birds, giant black, angular birds."

"Hey!" Front interrupted. "That sounds like the emblems painted on the sides of the Outhan boats. You remember, great black bugs, or birds maybe, too squarish to be able to fly, it seemed, but obviously aloft and carrying in their beaks their colored worms...."

"Or swamp serpents!" Fyva broke in excitedly, and then caught herself. "But I always thought about those emblems as just stylized representations. Surely nothing alive could be square like that."

"And your innocent swamp serpent didn't have great and vicious looking teeth," Front added, "or the evil cast to the eyes described by the sailors."

"Never mind about the worms and the bugs," Nash demanded. "Are you suggesting that the Mutanos and the Outhans are the same?"

"There's nothing I read that makes me confident of such a guess," Wons answered. "On the other hand, there's nothing I read that refutes such an assumption either."

"Well, whoever they used to be," Nash said with sudden sadness, then seemed to sag, "they're with us now. I just hope they're not as destructive as they were back then."

For once, Nash's tone in speaking of the Outhans was not belligerent. In fact, it pained Front to feel in Nash's tone bordering on resignation and defeat. The mood of depression emanating from Nash, and echoing from the traumatically wounded walls about them began to close in on Front as well. He glanced about, and the others were also sagging. He wanted to say something heartening, but nothing came forth.

Wonina seemed particularly troubled. "I'm undoubtedly old fashion, but I always thought that God brought us from the heavens."

"Well, my uncle the Chaplin wouldn't argue with that...but there are those who argue that the 'god' that managed all that was a being who occupied all space, and no space, who resided in Heaven and beneath the earth, a god called Computer."

Wonina seemed to shudder, and sink into herself. The other were likewise withdrawn.

When Wons spoke again, for a moment Front thought that the old sarcastic Wons had returned.

"Oh grow up! I get tired of you people making the Outhans to be something other than human. I've heard nothing to indicate they are that much different from you and me. In fact, the more I hear about them, the less impressed I become. Any people that wastes time painting mythical monsters on boats is probably a bunch of ignorant savages, no matter how powerful they might have been in the past. I don't know about the rest of you, but I'm too smart and too civilized to scare myself with monster tales. Frankly, I think we're all too smart not to be able to find a way to handle anything they can throw at us!"

Nash brightened instantly. "You bet your holy book we can!" he shouted.

"And it's not a holy book, damn you!" laughed Wons.

Somehow the situation seemed suddenly less hopeless, and Front began looking around for new openings in the wall behind them. This time the next entranceway into their new darkness was much smaller and required a great deal more squeezing. But, although there was no guarantee the hole they chose would lead anyplace, no one grumbled as they followed Front into his hole.

The recharged ghostly companion lighted the way only briefly this time, not having been sufficiently stimulated by close enough proximity to a light. That brief lighting showed nothing new, only the threat of more turns and twists, more scraped knees and bumped heads. Still they dragged themselves onward, and Front was even more careful to check the way for sudden drops.

Their brief meal had given them barely enough energy to endure the first hour on their new torture trail. Front was growing weaker as well as gradually more discouraged, when he began to experience what felt like a buzzing in his ear. As the buzzing continued, it almost sounded as though he could occasionally distinguish audible words. He halted their progress, and listened. The very walls seemed to vibrate with a constant hissing hum that now seemed to be saying something—something ominous and forbidding, but unclear and therefore all the more foreboding.

Onward they crawled and squirmed and grew weaker and more disheartened. Now the buzzing had become a chattering muffled rasp, so disturbing that, when a bright flash ahead broke the gloom, Front forgot to be encouraged and relieved by the return of light. It seemed that the air about them was changing, growing warmer. No, not warmer, but filled with the smell of smoke, the smell of something burning. The flashes of light, becoming more frequent, were red and flickering. Something was burning, and the return of light to the gloom, which should have been a sign of hope, carried with it a chard odor and a feeling of disgust, disgust so overwhelming as to bring Front near to retching. That revolting odor was all the more distressing since it seemed vaguely familiar and yet his mind was unwilling to interpret the familiar smell.

Now the source of the noise became more certain. Ahead of them, growing even louder, as they moved forward, the rumbling became a chant, and the chant became clearly audible, a blasphemous chant in an unknown tongue, pouring down an evil and continuous curse from above "Killaputa! Killaputa! Killaputa! Killaputa...."

12

HE LEADS WHO BLEEDS

Wonina crowded up behind him in the narrow passageway. "My God, Front, what's happening?"

"I don't know," he hissed, unable to keep a tone of disgust out of his voice, and he pushed her back, more roughly than he had intended. "Some kind of chant. Let's move on—but don't crowd me."

The chanting grew louder and the stench more oppressive.

Front was now able to rise from his knees and move forward in a crouch. The flickering red lights came more frequently as the pathway widened and began to divide at a large boulder. As the others crouched behind him, Front crept cautiously around the boulder. He was already imagining an enormous camp of savages encircling a dancing pit of fire where dreadful sacrificial rituals were being performed. But, he knew better than that, and he was not surprised when he finally rounded the boulder to see a great chamber. Across a stretch of water, was a circular platform, its surface here and there pockmarked with puddles of water, reflecting flickering firelight and smoke that oozed from small cracks in a circular ceiling high above them—they had returned home to the Commons.

But of course, it was the Commons as Front had never before seen it. They were obviously still underground, and a quick scan of the chamber revealed no apparent way out—but to his immediate relief, there was also no way in for those fearsome chanters who still bellowed somewhere above them.

Most of the fiery light that flickered over them came from tiny cracks clustering at the center of the ceiling. And yes, overhead there were the familiar circle with radiating lines from its center, the pattern that marked the Commons and the pattern he had come to expect to be at the centers of the Angle Beings structure. But directly beneath those circle in the ceiling was something he hadn't seen before, something that needed closer inspection before he could even begin to name it.

They had come out of their passageway in the back wall and were standing on a ledge of rocks, about a foot above the water. To his right Front could see their old friend, the channel, issuing from that same wall and spreading into the broad plain of water surrounding the platform. He stared forward, trying to study even from this distance the strange assemblage rising out of the flat surface in the very center of the platform.

"Looks like a derrick to me," Fyva whispered. "Like they use to load the boats that carry fish and skins up the coast. And that square box at the bottom, we've seen something like that before. Come on," she urged, "let's paddle over there so we can get a closer look."

As the others were preparing to launch themselves, Front was still familiarizing himself with the chamber. He estimated the height of the ceiling and compared that with the height of the dock he assumed lay outside of this chamber. Surely the Angle Beings wouldn't have constructed the floor of this chamber beneath the surface of the surrounding water. To test his assumption, he stepped forward into the dark water—and sank only up to his knees. The floor of the pond was barely a foot and a half below the surface, but even that great a depth surprised him.

As they waded out toward the center, Front whispered his puzzlement, "I don't understand this. Why did the Angle Beings build below water level? At high tide, the water must rise over to this rock ledge behind us."

"Maybe they were fish," Nash joked, apparently trying to dispel his nervousness, as he frequently glanced overhead.

"Or maybe there wasn't any water then," Wonina added, with more seriousness.

"Don't be silly, look at the water marks on the wall. There's always been water here...Or had there been? Front looked about the chamber with renewed awe—just how old are the works of the Angle Beings?

The assemblage in front of them showed no evidence of advanced age, however. They went first to the center box, still whispering as they discussed the shiny contraption. Then it occurred to Front to wonder why they were whispering. After all, the droning chant from the Commons would surely override their normal voices. Still, as the flickering light, the smoke, and the stench oozed from above, whispering still seemed more appropriate.

They examined a latticework of what appeared to be of dark gray metal. When Front felt its glassy smooth surface, it suddenly reminded him of that dark object he had encountered underwater at the last weapons box. He shuddered slightly, but continued his examination.

"It's obviously a small rising container," Fyva said confidently.

"A person stands in the middle of that circular container, protected by the vertical guard rails, and rises up and...."

"And the person bumps his head," Wonina laughed nervously, and then quickly put her hand over her mouth.

"No," Fyva continued, "then the crisscross latticework underneath the platform expands and pushes the platform up to the ceiling and stops before anyone's head is bumped."

Looking up, Front noticed that at center of the overhead circle were the familiar crisscrossing cracks. "I suspect," he suggested, "when the pointed top of the container hits the circle, the whole thing cracks open upward."

Nash looked puzzled and annoyed. "Hell of a complicated way of getting out of here. Why didn't they just build a staircase?"

It was a while before Fyva risked a guess. "Maybe there used to be something on the Commons above, something you had to get into by going straight up through a narrow chamber...Or just as likely, maybe there was something resting on this platform and held in place by what I called a rising container. That thing must have long, tall, and pointed. But who knows why the Angle Beings did things. It's a waste of time to wonder why. Let's just study what we can see here. Maybe we can make some use of it."

Fyva's practical approach won out, for want of other alternatives, and she continued her speculation. "The box here must have been the power source."

"Which just about makes this whole thing useless," Wons interjected, as he explored around the sides of the box, and even beneath water the box stood in. "I've been looking-for some kind of switch, like on the weapon, but there's nothing, no way of turning this thing on and no way of getting inside it. Here are the metal bolts again."

Fyva was undaunted. "There has to be a way. I'm sure about this being the power source. Notice how this lever-like arm extends from the latticework at the bottom of the platform and enters the box here. Can't you see, if you push down on this arm," and she was trying unsuccessfully to do just that, "because of the way the other parts interact, the platform should rise up rapidly."

Front studied the complicated structure, and although his mechanical logic had not yet caught up with his intuition, it did appear that Fyva was right.

They all continued their tactile exploration of the box, groping and touching and pushing, and then doing it all over again, until even Fyva was becoming frustrated.

More and more often now, they glanced at the light flickering from the ceiling and the seeping smoke that light illuminated. Wonina finally gagged. "What is that awful smell? You don't suppose they're burning people...." and she gasped in horror at her own half spoken thought.

"Shit!" bellowed Fyva.

They were all startled, as much by the crude language Fyva had used as by the obviousness of her revelation. Fyva could talk about anything, but she never cursed, she always used just the proper words, and shit is the proper word, Front realized.

Nash obviously agreed. "You're right, damn it, you're right. Those filthy bastards have shit all over the Commons." And though he was apparently trying to be angry, he broke out laughing.

"What I meant to say," Fyva regained her composure, "was that they've apparently been performing some kind of primitive ritual. They've spread their offal around the Commons, and that's what's burning and smelling so."

Front was greatly relieved to agree with Fyva. He had not wanted to think about the possibility that the smell might have come from burning human flesh. The overwhelming stench suddenly became much more bearable. Not pleasant, but bearable.

His temporary relief was quickly blotted out, however, by a sudden silence descending from above. They all stared upward, and stood achingly still. Front had to fight off the fear that they had been discovered and that the Outhans would ooze down upon them like the reeking odor of their burning offal.

The silence was finally broken by a booming voice that, though muffled, echoed harshly through the hollow chamber.

"Now hear the Chief! Now hear the Chief!"

There was another pause before a quieter, higher, but more piercing and even more audible voice broke the stillness.

"Puta fears the Firstborn!"

The chant of "killaputa" was shouted ritualistically, just once, and then ceased immediately.

"Vile Puta so fears the Firstborn, he will not answer our challenge. The betrayer hovers fearfully even now in his lair and will not rise to answer us, even though we defile and desecrate his temple."

"What say the Firstborn?" roared the first booming voice, and the answer came instantly, as a great chorus of voices shouted in unison, "Shipisoz! Shipisoz! Shipisoz!"

This new chant also ceased abruptly.

"Puta must be destroyed forever. Our honor cannot be cleansed until our oath is fulfilled...."

Again the chant, "Killaputa! Killaputa! Killaputa!"

"Bring forth the leader of the Newborn!"

From behind them, overhead, they could hear a brief scuffle, and their eyes followed the noise of footsteps across the Commons, leading to the center circles.

The stentorian voice again echoed through the chamber. "I give you this one last chance. Command your false priest to perform the ritual that will bring forth Puta!"

A new, angry, and very familiar voice broke forth from above. "I don't perform rituals, you savage!"

"Uncle?" asked the startled Wons.

Nash put his hand to Wons' mouth to quiet him.

There was another brief scuffle above and then the sound of blows.

The Outhan chieftain spoke again. "I grow weary of your lies and delays. Puta must be brought forth. Bring me the Newborn child!"

The five beneath the Commons looked at each other uneasily, and Wons was now obviously agitated.

Another voice shouted from above, "Not my daughter! No! Oh God, no!"

"Father?...My God, they've got my little sister!" Wons shouted before Nash could clamp his hand over the fellow's mouth again.

"Daddy! Daddy! They're hurting me," came a small pitiful voice from above.

There was scuffling again, before the commanding voice rang out, once more bringing them all to silence.

"The child will not be hurt...yet" He paused an agonizing moment, "We the Firstborn, know the importance you place on Newborn children.

I give you until the moon centers the sky. If Puta is not called forth, the smoke of this child's flesh will be sent down to declare the cowardice of your god."

There were cries of horror above them. They could hear angry voices coming even from the distant perimeter of the Commons.

Wons was also struggling and shouting frantically, "They're going to burn my sister! We've got to do something!" He broke away from Nash and churned through the waist deep water to scramble up the latticework toward the raised circular shelf.

Front reached him before he could scale to the top, which would nowhere nearly reached the ceiling anyway. He tried both threats and soothing to calm his agitated friend. "We'll find a way, Wons, we'll find a way," he repeated. "Hold your voice down, please, hold your voice down!"

Fyva also climbed up to join in the struggle, and it was her calm voice that finally overcame Wons' desperation. "We'll not let it happen, Wons. But we've got to plan, we've got to plan."

By the time they had half dragged, half carried Wons back to the dry rocks, the chanting from above had ominously ceased. But when they finally arranged themselves in their circle, their own silence was even more ominous.

What plan? Front worried helplessly. They had come all this way with vague hopes and fanciful illusions about the power contained in a slender, almost spent cylinder. Now, with the horde of Outhans spread like a mountain of offal above them, their pitiful inadequacy crushed down upon him. He looked about the silent circle. Nash was angry but slumped forward, unmoving. Fyva was lost in thought. Wons had lapsed into dejected immobility. He looked finally at Wonina, wondering fearfully, when it came right down to it, if he would even be able to protect the person most precious to him.

At that moment, however, Wonina didn't look in need of protection. Her jaw was set, and her eyes were flashing angrily.

"All right," she demanded, her voice rising alarmingly to the ceiling above. "What are we going to do?"

Fyva broke from her reverie. "I still believe there's a way we can get that contraption to work."

"And then what?" Front spread his hands. "There's obviously a huge bonfire overhead. Whoever went up would be burned along with...." He stopped himself before he expressed that awful thought.

"We can blast our way out," shouted Nash. "Use the tube. Shoot through the floor, right where that chief's voice is coming from."

"And perhaps hit someone we don't want to hit," Front cautioned.

"But we've got to do something, Front," Wons' voice rose almost to a shriek.

"Calm yourself, Wons," Wonina's tone had now lost some of its stern edge. "We'll find a way. Now calm yourself." She then turned on Front, "And you. We'll get nowhere if you instantly find something wrong with every suggestion anyone makes."

Front felt chastised and wanted to protest, but Wonina's voice softened and took away some of the sting. "Let's just think," she continued. "However wild the idea might be, let's get it out. But don't criticize, Front, not yet anyway."

"What she says makes sense." Fyva was attracted, as ever, to a logical idea.

Front had to agree the idea had merit. But when the silence fell again, he continued thinking his pessimistic thoughts. What could they possibly do with what little they had available to them? He began sinking further into his feeling of hopelessness, and he looked again at Wonina for help. She smiled, and he drew a deep breath and tried to will away some of his hopelessness. He let his eyes roam about the chamber, looking for something to stimulate his imagination. He reexamined the circular enclosed pond, its flat surface broken only by their partially submerged platform and the structure in its middle. He studied the far wall, beyond which he knew stretched the Bay of Sebasa, and the he looked above them where he knew there was floor of the Commons, hitherto a place of peaceful work or joyful celebration. He pictured in his mind the annual carnivals he had known from childhood, the gay Sebasans dancing to the sound of traditional music, the concentric circles that somehow superstitiously were never tread upon except...and then he recalled his weird dream of many nights ago—and, in spite of himself, he smiled. A small laugh left his lips as the beginnings of an idea flashed across his mind.

Wonina asked encouragingly, "Yes, Front? Say it. Don't hold back."

He started to dismiss the thought, but she persisted. "Anything will do for a starter. Let's have it."

"Well," he made a face. "I know this is absurd, but this all seems like a dream I had...."

They waited.

"I was standing on a platform, in the middle of a circle, dressed in what appeared to be the swamp-serpent's skin, but also like a regal robe. And people were bowing down to me. Well, anyway...." and he hesitated again.

Fyva looked interested. "Go on, go on."

"Well, perhaps one of us could dress up in the swamp-serpent's skin and, if you really believe we can get that contraption to work, Fyva, he could rise up through the hole with the weapon, and then...Well, I don't know what then, but do something...."

He fell silent, and the others seemed merely to stare into space. "I told you it was a silly idea," he finished lamely.

"No...No," Fyva said, in measured tones. "It has possibilities. That way, you could get a shot at their chief for sure," she said more eagerly. "Or at least threaten to, if they didn't leave."

"And I'm the one to do it!" Wons said firmly, rising to his feet. "It will work, it's got to work!"

"Wait a minute, hold on," Front protested. "It was just a wild idea. Wonina said we should begin suggesting ideas. This isn't a finished plan."

Wons sat down abruptly. "Then let's make it a finished plan. Only hurry! We have no idea when the moon will be directly overhead. We've got to do something now!"

Again Front drew a deep breath. "Okay. Okay. Just calm yourselves. I frankly think my plan is stupid, but if you want, we'll think it through before we go on to something else."

Fyva was suddenly excited. "I have an idea. I know how we can get that container to rise up." She plowed on, without waiting to be asked. "We'll take the rope and strap two of the boats on either side of the lever, near the box. Then we'll pile stones in each of the boats. If that's not enough, two of us will sit in each pile of rocks and a third person can jump on the lever from the box. That's got to be enough power to force the cage up through the opening."

"Maybe so," Front agreed reluctantly, "but you'd still be right in the middle of their bonfire."

"It's a risk we'll have to take," Wonina said firmly. "Besides, the top of the cage would probably scatter the fire anyway."

"But then what?"

"If the fire's too hot," Wons insisted, "I could still get off a quick shot, and then you could lower me down again."

"But we don't know if we can even get it up, much less get it back down. Again."

"There's a way, Front, there is a way," Wonina said with conviction.

"And even if the fire gets scattered, and you don't have to shoot right away, and you have tried to say something, how do you know that your costume will mean enough to the Outhans to make them want to stop and listen?"

"You said yourself that the Outhans' great black bird seemed to be fighting the swamp serpent."

"Yes, but what's that got to do with anything?"

"In their primitive religion, the swamp-serpent is obviously Puta!" Wons pronounced with conviction.

Front tried to disagree, but Fyva was also convinced. "That's it. That's it. They think the great god swamp-serpent lives inside the Commons, and they want the Chaplain to pray for it rise up so they can kill it. It must represent some kind of evil force in their religion, and their oath is that they're sworn to kill that evil. Like 'Killapuda. Killaputa.' You heard them."

"But you don't know any of this," Front raised his arm in exasperation. This time they all just glared at him, and he sat back down and merely shook his head. They waited, apparently leaving the next move up to him.

He made one last stand. "Very well. *If* we can get that contraption working, and *if* we can make the serpent-skin to look halfway believable and menacing, then I'll be the one that goes up."

"No! Me, me," Wons shouted, and his expression was one of pleading. "It's got to be me, Front. It's my sister and my father up there...."

"Wons, it was my stupid suggestion. I couldn't let anyone else be killed because I couldn't keep my mouth shut."

"Please, Front, please...." Wons was desperate. He had risen to one knee and he was clenching his hands before him.

The sight of his tall friend, obviously begging, was painful for Front to see, and he was torn, wanting to say "yes" and wanting to say "no." But he was saved from deciding immediately, however, by a new thought. Who was he to give permission anyway? He started to voice this new idea, when he looked about the circle again. All were staring at him, waiting expectantly. He had the fleeting feeling of a return to his dream, to that moment of worshipful expectancy as his followers knelt at his feet. The absurd memory brought him a moment of brief relief, until he looked again at his waiting friends. Then the crushing sense of responsibility re-descended. They wanted him to decide, they wanted him to send somebody to what he believed was certain death, and their conviction and confidence in his foolish plan was forcing him toward that decision. He didn't want this responsibility! But as he looked again at their faces, he didn't want to dash the hope that somehow, inadvertently, he had planted there.

Caught in between conflicting needs, he wasn't ready to decide. He stalled, trying to put off the final decision. "Let's take it again, step by step," he said cautiously. "First, can the costume be made to look alive, and fierce enough?"

"I can do it! I can do it," Wonina shouted almost happily.

Tension broke in the group. They all started talking at once. Front realized, belatedly, that they had taken his attempt at stalling as approval of their demand for action. His need for temporary relief made him delay in disabusing their misunderstanding, and the longer he delayed, the easier it was for him to ignore that his indecisiveness was in fact spawning a decision.

Fyva untied and unfurled her prize possession. Some of the glow had vanished from the jeweled nodules, but Front had to admit it was still impressive, even awesome.

"Look, the neck hole is plenty big for Wons to slip his own head through," Wonina was busy planning. "Fyva and I can bind up the tears along the back easily enough. Then we'll just fold up the rest of the skin to fit Wons' height."

"But what about the mouth?" Front asked weakly. "It's hardly fierce enough to look like something evil."

"I could pry out its teeth," Nash suggested, "and we could stick jagged slivers of rocks up through the openings. The slant of the jaw is certainly frightening enough."

"Cut holes for my arms, Wonina, and maybe use some of the extra skin to tie on flaps and disguise my arms."

"Right...it'll be easy."

Wonina, Fyva, and Nash then launched themselves busily into preparing the costume, and Front could think of nothing to do that would add to their creation. He got up and walked to the edge of the water, wanting to be alone with his thoughts, trying to determine if he was doing the right thing by allowing them to go on with a plan in which he had so little confidence.

After she had worked a while with Wonina, Fyva joined Front and tugged at his arm. "Let's go out to the platform. I want to check it out again."

She was insistent, so he followed dutifully.

The first thing she looked at was the slender arm entering the slot down the side of the box. They peered once again into the box, but could see nothing beyond a brief continuation of the arm.

"It should move; I don't think it could be frozen, no matter how old it is. Feel the metal that goes into the box. It's slicker than any grease could make."

When they both tried pushing down on the arm—as before, nothing happened.

"Let's you and me tie boats on either side," Fyva directed, dragging him back to the bank to retrieve the rope and boats.

Fyva's plan was straightforward and Front had to admit likely to work, if her speculation about the purpose of the arm was correct. Moreover, as the labor of carrying stones back and forth from the bank and placing them in the two boats soon became so exhausting that he was glad to be relieved of the necessity of thinking—and worrying. Returning once again to the bank, he was startled to see a great swamp-serpent rising sinuously before him. His tiredness was such by now that for a moment he forgot to remember that inside that dead skin was his friend Wons, preparing for what kind of fate, he hesitated to think.

Still the effect was, at least in this dim light, rather convincing.

"It's great. It's great," he heard Fyva whisper excitedly. "Seeing you from this distance I almost want to run myself."

"Or throw spears at you," Front added, under his breath.

"Okay," Fyva urged. "Stop playing costume monster and help us carry stones."

The other three joined in the labor enthusiastically, and soon the two boats were filled to overflowing—but still the container had not budged.

"Wonina, let's sit on top of the rocks and see what happens."

The men helped the girls settle themselves on top of the two piles of rocks, and they all looked up at the container.

"I think it moved slightly. Did you feel it, Wonina?"

"It seemed like it. Yes, it seemed like it. You fellows push down!"

They did as they were told, and Front could indeed feel a slight give to the arm. He looked up to see the top or the platform cage ease another fraction of an inch toward the center of the circle at the top of the ceiling.

"We've done it! We've done it!" Fyva almost shouted, and then hushed and looked fearfully above. "We've done it," she whispered again. "Get your costume, Wons. Let's be ready to go when we hear they're all gathered up there again."

Their frantic effort to force the sluggish machinery into motion had temporarily pushed from Front's mind the ultimate purpose of their efforts. His doubt about the wisdom of their plan was not far below the surface, however, and even as Wons sloshed quickly to the bank to fetch his costume and the blue cylinder, Front was again trying to think of ways to stall the plan.

Suddenly the long ominous silence above them was broken. The deep voice intoned, "Now hear the Chief! Now hear the Chief!"

Wons covered the remaining distance to the platform in a dash. The girls leapt off their rock piles and assisted in his frantic effort to swallow himself in the serpent-skin. Front had no time for further doubts as he was called on to help Wons begin his ascent to the container. He climbed most of the way with Wons and shoved him onto the perch.

The girls had already remounted to their rock-filled saddles and were bouncing their weight up and down. "Come back down, Front! Help me shove on the bar!" Nash called.

As Front reached them to add his weight to the effort, he looked back to see the top of the container was now rising, slowly at first, and then with increasing speed, until it was thrusting against the crisscrossed circle above Wons' head. Wons was looking up expectantly, peering at the circle in the ceiling through the slits in the serpent's partially opened jaw. Overhead the chant of "Killaputa! Killaputa! hillaputa!" began slowly building to a crescendo.

"Hurry!" Wons shouted down, but the girl's efforts at bouncing on the rocks seemed to be having little further effect on thrusting the platform upward.

The chant broke, and the chief's piercing voice demanded, "Well, Priest, have you cast your spells? Will you bring forth Puta?"

"Can't you understand," shouted a hoarse voice. "There is no Puta. I have no spells. Please, for God's sake, let the child go."

Again Wons screamed for more effort, his voice now breaking with agitation. As Front pushed even more fiercely on the crossbar, he could see that Wons had taken out his dagger and was trying to pry between the slits in the circle above him.

"It seems to be cemented together. Someone help me slice it open! Hurry!"

Front responded to the call by rushing to climb the latticework.

"Bring forth the Newborn child," came the menacing command from above. There were pleading cries and angry protests from overhead, and then the slow, building cadence of the chant drowned all else.

Wons was now stabbing at the circle above him in his furor. Out of the corner of his eye, Front saw Nash leaping from a cross-arm above the boats to stomp down on the lever bar.

Suddenly Front felt a lurch, and the latticework on which he was climbing shuddered and began closing on him. He shoved himself away from those pinching cross-arms and dropped to the shallow water below.

Scrambling to his feet again, Front looked up to see, for the first time in an age of days, the black sky suddenly appear between cracks in the central circle. Fire was licking through those cracks, as with increasing speed, the container pressed upward. But he could also see that Wons was having difficulty catching his balance. The container shuddered again and shot upward into the night, and to his horror, Front could see the slender blue cylinder, their power and their hope, slip from beneath Wons' arm and tumble toward the black water.

Frantically, Front scrambled to retrieve the tube. Overhead he could sense the sudden silence that greeted Wons' bursting forth into the fiery night. He groped fearfully into the murky water and was rewarded quickly with the feel of the tube beneath his fingers. Clutching it to him, he glanced up, preparing to re-climb to the container. He heard Wons' voice, a bit shaky at first, becoming gradually firm, deep, and commanding.

"Now hear this, Mutanos!" The words seemed to burst like a curse from the leering slit of the serpent's mouth. "Now hear the words of Emanuel!"

"Puta! Puta!" There were shouts from scattered points about the Commons. "Puta has come!"

A small chorus of "Killaputa" stirred, but Wons hushed the beginning chant with his threatening tone. "You shall defile no more, Firstborn! Release my child! Release my people!"

The now shrill voice of the chief pierced the night. "A spear! A spear! Give me a spear!"

Front could see Wons turning toward the voice, and then several objects clanged against the metal bars of the container. Other objects then whizzed by overhead. Something thudded against and careened off the skull of the snake, and Wons had to steady himself.

Just as Wons started to speak again, there was another thudding sound and he buckled slightly. Front felt suddenly sick as he saw the shaft of a spear vibrating between the folds of serpent-skin enshrouding Wons' body. He continued climbing the tower, thinking the worst, and already blaming himself, when Wons' voice rose again, even louder and more commanding than before. "Cease your childish attacks, children. Hear my curse! If by sunrise you have not taken to your ships, returning to your homes, I will come forth again and bring blue thunder down upon you. Now hear this!"

Front then heard a shaky voice whisper from within the serpent-skin. "Down, take me down!"

"Down!" Front shouted to the girls, and he saw them leaping from their stone baskets and saw Nash pulling forth his dagger to begin hacking away at the ropes. There was another lurch, as one of the boats fell away, and to keep from being sliced by the closing latticework, Front jumped backward into space and tumbled again into the water below.

13

No Need to Lead

Wonina was trying to climb to Wons. Pulling himself from the shallow water, Front grabbed and pulled her back down. He shoved the blue tube into her hands, before scrambling himself back up the tower.

If Wons is dead, it's my fault, he thought despairingly. How could I ever allow such a stupid plan?

Wons was slumped against one of the eight vertical bars of the container, and Front was relieved to hear that at least his friend was moaning. The next thing he noticed, however, was the end of the vicious spear thrusting outward from the snake skin near the middle of Wons' body.

Wons had grasped the spear shaft, and now he was cursing.

"Don't touch it, Front!" he groaned. "I had a hell of a time getting this long thing through that hole up there. Just don't touch it again!"

Wons continued to steady his newly grown appendage as Front guided him inch by inch from the container and down the outside of the tower. When they reached the watery floor, Wons wanted to try walking, but the others insisted on carrying him back to the bank.

"Easy. Easy," cautioned Wonina, again and again. "Let's take him higher up on the dry ledge."

When they had at last settled Wons on his side, Front blurted out, "My God, I'm sorry, Wons!"

"Not now, Front," Wonina, ordered impatiently.

Drawing out her knife, she hastily sliced the serpent skin away from the spear shaft.

"Sorry about that, Fyva," she called over her shoulder.

"You can slice the damn thing to shreds for all I care," Fyva said bitterly. "Why did I ever insist on bringing it?" she berated herself.

Wonina then cut through Wons' jacket and undergarment and exposed the wound. There was not as much blood as Front expected, but the hole was larger than the shaft.

Wons, gritting his teeth and grimacing with pain, managed a small laugh, "Going in wasn't so bad. It was the wiggling around that hurt."

"Good," said Wonina.

Good! thought Front, startled and horrified at Wonina's seeming callousness. "Wonina, can't you see he's badly hurt?"

"Shut up, Front," she said brusquely.

With her knife, she shaved what appeared to be feathers off the end of the shaft.

"Quickly., Front, give me your undershirt."

Still horrified, Front nevertheless complied.

Wonina ripped off two wads of the cloth and then shredded the rest into bands, tying the ends together. The remainder, she folded and formed into a large wrap-around bandage.

"Okay, Wons, let go of the shaft. I've got to do some more quick wiggling."

Wons seemed to understand what she planned to do, so he let go with obvious reluctance.

"Hold your breath, Wons," she commanded, and grasping the bloody point of the spear that protruded from Wons' back, she eased the long shaft the rest of way through Wons' body.

Moving quickly, before much more blood could spurt out, Wonina pressed the wads of shredded cloth against the two open wounds and then directed Nash to pin them against Wons' body with the makeshift bandage and bindings.

"Okay, I need all of you now. Help me remove the skull from his head and peel the skin off him. Then, we'll get him inside his sleeping sack. We've got to keep him warm."

Wons, the ordeal of the spear removal finally over, seemed to have used up his last remaining strength. He groaned and dangled limply in their arms as they did their best to ease him into his sack.

Feeling helpless and miserable, Front stood up and backed away. He watched briefly while Wonina held Wons' head on her lap and helped him sip water from his flask.

He saw that Fyva had gathered the torn snakeskin and seemed about to toss it into the water, but he heard Wonina calling angrily.

"Don't be a fool, Fyva. We could still need that."

With obvious disgust, Fyva hurled the skin back down on the bank. Fyva's a kindred spirit in misery, Front realized, but he wanted to be alone. He waded out toward the tower, and the sight of that contraption finally reminded him to consider what must be going on overhead. Now that he remembered to listen, what he heard was not what he expected. Rain, he realized. It was beginning to rain—one of the late summer storms had suddenly moved in from the ocean. As he thought back over the events following Wons' injury, he realized his mind had also registered what was happening on the Commons—shouting, seeming confusion, a stampede of footsteps in all directions, and then he remembered the rain had been going on quietly for some time. Drops were falling through the many crevices in the ceiling, and the great fire above them was obviously burning less brightly.

Now he began to worry that perhaps the Outhans, being certain that something was beneath the Commons, would be redoubling their efforts to enter his sanctuary. He remembered he had heard some pounding and scratching from above, but it hadn't continued very long.

In the slowly fading light, he was reexamining the circle in the ceiling when he felt Fyva at his side. Her presence reminded him of Wons, and the guilt returned.

"It was a stupid plan, Fyva. Why did I ever suggest it? Why did I go along with it?"

"It wasn't the plan, Front, it was the planning. We shouldn't have been so hasty in forcing things along. We should've thought it through more carefully."

Before they could continue their self-recriminations, Wonina called them back. "The rain's coming in on Wons. We need to carry him to a higher and drier place."

Front trudged back reluctantly. Returning to Wons was like returning to proof of his stupidity.

After they had settled Wons beside some sheltering boulders, across from where they had originally entered the circular chamber, Wonina turned to Front and Fyva. Some of the hard edge was off her voice, but she still addressed them firmly, "It'd be more helpful if you two would stop sharing your guilt and start sharing your brains. What are we going to do now?"

Front felt his ears burning, and his stomach knotted in anger. He looked at Fyva, expecting a similar response from her, but he saw a smile begin to spread from the corners of her mouth. That puzzled him, and he drew a deep breath and let it out slowly. The anger faded somewhat, and he began to realize Wonina was right. No matter how wrong he had been in allowing the plan to be carried out, that was behind them now and he must force himself to think about the future.

Front wanted to pull the group together away from Wons, but Wons objected. In spite of the group's protest, he insisted upon being propped up and included in the discussion. The rain was now coming down in torrents, and the clatter was so loud and the light so dim, it was necessary to draw into a tight circle about Wons to be able to hear and see one another.

"All right, Wons, you're getting your way, but don't do much talking," Wonina cautioned.

"You're playing mother again, Wonina. I tell you I'm all right."

"Yes, I guess you are. The shaft seems to have missed any organs or bones, but still, if you get excited or start lecturing us, you're going to open those wounds again."

All this talk about wounds was heightening Front's guilt. "I'm sorry, Wons. All this is my fault. I should've told you, no. It was a stupid plan."

"Yes, you did say that, didn't you," Wons grimaced.

"I said it, but I didn't say it strongly enough. I was supposed to be the leader. I should've told you, no, and meant it."

Wons propped himself up a bit more. He was grinning again. "Emanuel says:

'To lead is not just to tell. It's not what you say.

It's what you give of yourself that leads the way.'"

Nash groaned, and then laughed. "It's been a long time since we've heard from Emanuel, and I still don't understand him."

"And neither do I," added Front. "It seems you gave everything of yourself, Wons. What was I supposed to be giving?"

"Trust," answered Wonina quietly.

Trust? thought Front. What does she mean by that? He stared at Wonina, but she said nothing further.

Somewhat annoyed, he started up again. "Okay, I should've trusted my own judgment and gone along with my feeling that the plan was stupid."

"Maybe you did or didn't trust your own judgment, Front," Wonina stated more strongly. "But, the real problem was, you didn't trust us. I don't know why you didn't have more faith in your own plan, perhaps because it seemed unreal to you, having come from a dream. But we all liked the plan. Instead of trusting our judgment, trusting our opinions, all the time we were working, you were dragging your feet, or dragging your mind, when you should've been using your mind to improve the plan."

He stared again at Wonina, having trouble believing that she was the one saying all this.

Then Nash added, "And who are you to say it didn't work?"

Wons took it up. "As far as I'm concerned, it worked, at least part way. I couldn't see all that was going on up there, but at least I saw my sister break away from her guards and run to my father and uncle. And we haven't heard any more of that damn chanting, have we?"

It dawned on Front that, in all their frantic rush to care for Wons, no one had bothered to ask Wons what he had seen above. The questions poured forth now, and Wonina had to keep cautioning Wons to not overexert himself. Wons insisted on describing what he had seen, and all but Front were soon totally involved in listening.

With half a mind Front heard the answers to the eager questions; with the other half of his mind, he pondered what he had just been told. Could it be true he didn't trust his friends? He thought back, remembering when he had been the one to take all the risks. Was it true that he had always been the most qualified to take those risks? Or was it because he distrusted anyone else but himself? Was he in fact the leader of the group, or just someone who needed to play expert over those he secretly believed to be less qualified? It was not only a rather sobering line of thought it was also a lonely one. What kind of leader was he, and what kind of leader did he want to be—a remote expert or one among peers?

The questions to Wons seemed to have abated, so Front asked his own different kind of question. "Wons, did Emanuel have anything to say about trust?"

The others looked surprised.

"I thought we were already off that," Wons eventually responded. "But as a matter of fact, I do remember one thing Emanuel said. 'If I have not the trust of the people, I am not the leader of the people, and if I do not trust the people, why do I wish to lead the people?'"

"Why do I wish to lead the people?" Front echoed aloud, gazing upward toward the drizzling ceiling. Shaking his head, he turned toward the group. "And do I trust you?" He looked carefully at each person. "No, I guess in some ways I don't," he answered himself. "But I'm beginning to realize I don't like the responsibility of thinking I can do it all myself."

He looked again at each one of them and back again at the ceiling before returning to them. "But I still want to lead. I want to lead because I think we all want the same thing, and I need you to get us there. And sometimes, maybe even most of the time, I think you need me to get us there."

He paused, but no one seemed to disagree.

"So now I've got to learn to trust more," he added firmly. "Okay, here goes—I've got another plan."

The others leaned forward, and suddenly he felt the return of discomfort.

"Now wait a minute," he laughed nervously. "I said I've got a plan, not a solution."

"We heard you," Wonina said seriously. "You said you were going to trust us, remember? We heard you."

He flushed and grimaced. "Right...Anyway, it's not a new plan, just a return to the old one. But this time, with the better preparation we should've had the first time. Wons has already set the stage. He threatened that if the Outhans didn't clear out, they'd have to pay. Nash has already suggested the best use of our weapon would be to blast the Outhan leader. Everything seems to revolve around and maybe depend upon that leader, and they just might be disorganized enough to bolt if we could destroy him. Now my guess is they're going to be really waiting for us at dawn, so here's what I suggest. Let's carve up the two remaining boats and stuff them inside the serpent skin, filling out its bulk and leaving only enough room for one of us to squeeze inside with the blue cylinder sticking out a hole. At least two layers of that boat-bark is sure to stop any spear."

He paused and waited for their responses.

"I don't see why not," commented Wonina. "Even if the Outhans are sitting on top of the hole waiting for you, that container pops up with such force they'd all be tumbled off long enough for you to see whether you have a chance to hit the leader."

Fyva added, "I think we've mastered that expanding-folding derrick contraption now. We'd be ready to yank it back down again at your signal."

Front turned to the two men. "Nash? Wons?"

"I'm all for it," commented Nash.

"It's a great trip," quipped Wons. "I'm all ready to go again."

The others laughed, but Front continued seriously. "And that brings us to the next question. And here's where I have to learn to trust," he added. "Who's going to be the one to go up?"

They all looked at one another.

Nash started to speak, but then glanced down at his near useless arm.

"Well," said Wonina slowly. "I could be the one...."

Front felt a slight sickish feeling in his stomach as Wonina continued. "Or so could Fyva for that matter."

"Yes," Fyva added. "We're both strong for our sizes, you know."

"But," Wonina took it up again, "the serpent skin, stuffed with bark is going to be more awkward than heavy. I hate to admit it, Front, but it'll probably take someone stronger than we are to handle it...I think you have to be the one, darling."

Front sagged with relief. "I hope you people realize how much trust that took," he groaned.

"Yes," was their reply.

Drawing in another breath, and steadying himself, Front looked again at the sprinkling ceiling.

"I've been trying to figure out from the tides and from the position of the moon that Wons described, and I'm not sure, but my guess is it must be a little after midnight. That means we've got to get the new work done and be all set to go in about five hours from now. I'll carve up the boat-bark."

"And I'll bind up the serpent skin," Wonina volunteered.

"Come on, Nash," Fyva said rising. "Let's re-lash other two boats to that contraption out there, and put even more stones back in. This time we should be able to balance it just right so only a little bit of pressure will be needed to shoot Front up through the roof."

"And I'll get some sleep," concluded Wons, to a full chorus of agreement from all the others.

Fyva was right. The lever arm had now loosened enough so that even without the girls sitting on top of the rocks, and with Front inside his serpent skin fortress within the container, Nash had merely to lean on the lever to begin the smooth thrust of the container upward. They were ready for their promised return to the surface.

Front left the serpent skin in the container and cautiously eased himself down into the now even greater gloom on the platform below. He and the others groped their way back to where they had left Wons. Wonina reported that, much to her relief, their wounded friend was sleeping naturally and deeply.

The height of the storm was hitting the coast, and the thunder that had reverberated in the distance now seemed to be shaking the very Commons. Flashes of lightning illuminated, for brief seconds, the cavernous Commons basement, and as Front stretched himself out in his bag, as close to Wonina as possible, he could see, at intervals, his serpent skin armor awaiting only its tender innards before it was set into motion at dawn.

He shuddered, and snuggled even closer to Wonina. She returned his need for closeness, clinging to him as they both listened to the thunder echoing and fading down the distant, stoned-up channel. Wonina now felt so good in his arms that he was annoyed to find himself thinking back over their recent encounter. He pulled away, just enough to be able to look her in the face as lightning flashed again.

"You feel the same. You look the same. But I'm not sure you're the same person."

"What do you mean?" she asked, surprise in her voice.

"You were pretty rough on me in our little group discussion, remember?"

"You deserved it," she countered.

"No doubt, but it's going to take me a while to sort through how I feel about you."

She waited.

"I mean, I always pictured the girl I was going to love as someone who knew and kept telling me how wonderful I am. You, more than anyone else, seem to be the first one to see my faults. I'm going to have to think about this new development."

She kissed him, and he heard, for he could no longer see her smile, "I trust completely," she emphasized the word 'trust,' "that in your wonderful wisdom, you'll be able to figure it all out just right." She snuggled again into his arms, and promptly settled herself for sleep—and he realized, without much further thought, she was right.

He awakened to a graying light and to Fyva, who was shaking him gently. She had apparently either willed herself awake, or stayed awake to be sure they didn't miss the dawn. "I should've set a watch," he whispered.

"Trust me," she patted his cheek, "and you won't have to think of everything yourself."

"Not you too," he grinned, and allowed her to help him up.

There was no more food, so they didn't have to waste time eating. All but Wons, who was awake but too stiff to move this morning, gathered around to give Front an unnecessary boost up the tower to his perch. There was barely enough room in the container for him to raise the awkward overstuffed serpent off the floor of the small platform, so that he could squeeze and wiggle his way into the monster's inner recesses. Wonina, who had followed him up, shoved the blue cylinder through its prepared hole. The tube poked against the middle of his chest, and he maneuvered to get it around his arm and under his shoulder. He made sure, through his peephole between the serpent's teeth, that Wonina was out of the way before he placed his hand around the red circle that he hoped would release doom on the chief of the Outhans.

"Be careful, darling," Wonina cautioned unnecessarily, before climbing back down to the floor below.

Overhead, now that he was closer to the ceiling, Front could hear the shuffle of footsteps, and that made him squirm urgently to make final adjustments to his costume. As the gray chamber became lighter, announcing the coming dawn, he had expected a renewal of the hated chanting. Instead, he heard only those muffled footsteps. Nor had the probably soaked logs above them been relighted, for which Front was certainly thankful. He had resigned himself to an assault by a barrage of spears, but at least there would be no attacking fire to add to his peril. He tested his ability to shuffle his armored fortress around quickly, to the right and to the left, and then he made a full pirouette. He would have to be able to quickly spot the chief before the protruding Outhan spears halted him within the vertical bars of the container.

With one last turn, he sighed—he was as ready as he was ever going to be, and then he pointed himself at the spot Wons indicated the chief had been the night before.

Before he called down his readiness, he asked himself one more time, is this really the best plan? They said last night I was needed to lead the group, but do I really need to do this? He knew he was just stalling for time, however. He glanced down below, and through his limited vision, he could see that a shaft of light was breaking through a crack in the ceiling and sparkling on the water below. It was as though a larger power had announced the time had come.

"Up!" he commanded.

This time, their chariot of the god Puta responded instantly. He broke into the light, and even from within his snakeskin encasement, that light was temporarily blinding. He steadied his awkward, towering form and looked hurriedly below for his intended victim, but the chief was not where Front had expected. Quickly, he shifted his body to take in a wider view, thinking to find, as Wons had described, the row on row of black clad Outhans, launching their row on row of deadly spears. His eyes finally encountered, further back than his first glance, a circle of people who seemed to roll back briefly, and then lean forward, a circle of multi-colored clad people, from whom now arose a mighty gasp.

Frantically Front shuffled his awkward snakehead upward to peer seaward.

Nothing!...then more nothing! Meaning, there were no black uniformed Outhans on the Commons, nor were there any black Outhan ships at sea. There were only the pleasant Sebasan clothing colors he had known all his life. As far as he could see in all directions, there was nothing but a whole town of brightly dressed awestruck Sebasans, come to gawk at the monstrous serpent god that had reappeared in their midst.

*   *   *

The five of them sprawled, in their now familiar circle, on the sun drenched Commons. Even though there was a hint of coming fall in the air, they were hot, basking there. Ever since their return from interment, however, hot or not, they all seemed to spend more time in the sun. Front, casually stroking Wonina's hand, had been looking out to sea, the calm blue green Bay of Sebasa stretching westward until it met the ever present wall of dark turbulence. He looked back toward the circle in the center of the Commons. Their metal container was now propped up, well above the hole, guaranteeing access to the chamber below. A fence had been erected, and the children of the town had been sternly warned to stay away, but Front knew it wouldn't be long before the town would have to find a better way of securing that entrance. Those curious children would eventually overcome their fear and have to prove to themselves that there was no serpent god lurking below.

He smiled, and though he had described the scene hundreds of times before, he couldn't help reminiscing. "You should've seen their faces. I felt, at any moment, they were going to fall down on their knees and start worshipping me. I started to get so embarrassed, I almost ruptured myself trying to get out of that costume. Then, when they saw who I was,

I think it was my mother who shouted, 'It's my Front! It's my Front!' and they all started shouting and rushing toward me. Then I really got embarrassed. They started acting like I was some great hero, and I kept shouting down, 'No, no, it was Wons, it was Wons.' It took me the longest time to get them to realize that all of you were down below."

"All I could think of," laughed Wonina, "was how in the world did the Outhans know your name, and why were you giving us away, telling them we were down below."

Wons, who was sitting up straight with his legs crossed underneath him and leaning on his cane, added to their happy reminiscence. "But I set them straight at the Officer's Council," he stated pompously. "I explained to them how I'd already taken all the risks and just wanted Front to have the glory."

"You did not," Fyva bumped him gently. "Everybody knows you gave Front most of the credit, and if I do say so myself, I haven't heard a more logical and modest description of our whole adventure given by anybody."

"Just as I was saying, being modest, I wanted Front to have all the credit."

They groaned.

"And," he continued, "I don't even take credit for the Council's decision to appoint Front leader of the Defense Forces."

"And that's another thing," Front interrupted and became serious. "That was ridiculous. What do I know about defense? What do I know about being a leader of soldiers?"

"What does any Sebasan know about being a leader of soldiers, or even being a soldier?" commented Fyva. "But I agree with the Council. You are the best choice."

"Fyva, for the first time in your life, you're being illogical. Anyway, I'm not even sure we need a Defense Force. Wons, didn't your uncle say he thought the Outhans were gone for good?"

"It's all speculation. They had to piece their theory together from snatches of conversation that lots of different people heard from different Outhans. The Outhans didn't talk too much among themselves you know,

and their leader seemed to only make speeches. Nash may have been right
all along. My uncle is beginning to think the Outhans aren't quite
human—more like a subhuman species. Only their leader, who seemed to
have been the guiding force behind the expedition, was more like us. He
was taller, slimmer, and had less hair on his body. Anyway, when he tossed
his spear right through me, and I didn't even budge...at least they said I
didn't budge," he laughed, "I know damn well I budged. Anyway, the
Outhans must have thought that Puta was in fact invulnerable and that
their leader had lied to them. My uncle described they were like a wave of
ants rolling toward their ships. Their leader tried to stop them, but was
pretty thoroughly trampled. They carried him away with them, but Uncle
said that, from the looks of him, he wasn't going to live."

"So there," Front concluded. "With no leader, I doubt that a primitive
group of humans would ever consider returning to the spot where the
mythical monster they'd feared all through their history had proven to be
real and invulnerable."

"Nevertheless," Fyva persisted, "a Defense Force is necessary. We can't
base the security of our town on theoretical speculation."

"Okay, so it's necessary, but there're lots of older men in the town
with a lot more authority and wisdom. Why should I be the one chosen
the leader?"

There was a long pause before Fyva spoke again. "I can't really speak for
the Council, Front, but I've been giving that question some thought, and
I think the way you're behaving right now is the answer."

Front raised his eyes questioningly.

"The fact is, at least it seems to me, you don't *need* to lead, and that's
why you make the best leader."

"I don't understand."

"Think back. Each of us took over leadership of the group at one
time or another, but each of us had our own, sometimes hidden reasons,
for leading. You were the one, more than anyone else, who wanted to

lead primarily to accomplish what the group had set out to do—drive out the Outhans."

"Wait a minute. I remember, and with a great deal of pain I might add, our discussion about my not trusting the group. What kind of a leader was that?"

"A growing leader," Fyva concluded, a slightly smug smile on her face.

Front responded lamely, "Well anyway, I really don't want to lead a Defense Force."

"I guess that's the kind of problem leaders have to deal with," Wons smiled. "But defense leader or not, don't forget you promised to lead us back through the channel to the Angle Beings' city."

"Hold on...Hold on," Front said firmly. "I distinctly remember only promising that we'd go back there after we dealt with the Outhans. I didn't say *I'd* lead us. And anyway, Fyva just told me, I don't need to lead."

Wons, already straight from his stiffness, seemed to straighten even more. He went smoothly into his best oratorical voice. "Emanuel said, 'I do not need to lead the people. I am the people, and when I become myself, the people are born with me.

When Wons' voice stopped rumbling, there was a silence that seemed to stretch for an awkward duration. Front, finally realizing that no one else was going to say anything, expressed his puzzlement, "Does Emanuel mean born as in 'being born,' or borne as in 'borne along?' And speaking of being born, what did the chief mean about the 'Firstborn' and all that?"

"How should I know?" Wons smiled. "But now that you've become leader again," and then he glanced pointedly at the waiting entrance in the center of the Commons, "I'm confident you'll lead us to the answer of all such questions."

The Way to Lead

A Manual on Leadership
(Emanuel, Leader of the Ship?)

This book is primarily intended as entertainment—a novel that doesn't entertain doesn't succeed as a novel. But the book is also intended to enlighten, and as I told you in the Introduction, the concept about which I wish you to become more enlightened is leadership. More specifically, I have attempted to write a novel based upon the leadership theories and concepts taught in leadership training workshops conducted for many years at Miami-Dade Community College. My expectation is, if you experience these theories and concepts through the medium of fiction, the ideas and skills will be more understandable and alive, and thus more easily retained and applied.

Leadership is a central experience in the human endeavor. It is one of the primary ways we go about accomplishing the tasks of surviving and fulfilling our destinies as human beings. This is not to say that leadership is the only way to achieve these ends; rather, it is my belief that leadership is one of the more effective ways of achieving many of our desired ends. Certainly some tasks do not require leadership. Some tasks are more effectively accomplished by individuals working alone. Moreover, it might sometimes be more efficient to direct or even to force people to follow rather than to lead them. It must be admitted that dictators are sometimes very efficient, at least in the short run. But for those tasks that cannot be done efficiently or effectively alone, it is my belief that the use of leadership, rather than dictatorship, has fewer bad side effects.

This brief manual on leadership will focus on one way of understanding an aspect of leadership, the Blake-Mouton Managerial Grid. The novel was specifically created to represent this theory, and in this manual, examples from the novel will be used to illustrate the theory. In addition, several other leadership related issues are discussed and illustrated by events in the novel, issues such as task group dynamics, uses of leadership power, and the philosophy and psychology of leadership. Additionally, you will be offered the opportunity to apply the concepts illustrated in this manual to examine your own style of leadership.

A Forewarning. Notice my word choice when I said I believe leadership is usually a better way than dictatorship of achieving task goals, that leadership is usually more effective if not always more efficient. Words like better and more suggests someone is making a decision that something is good or bad. Be forewarned, the study of *leadership is value loaded.* As much as social scientists would like to be objective, it is still true that most of the theorizing and research about how people behave is overtly or covertly based in the belief systems, the cultures, the philosophies, or the theologies of the theorizers. I certainly don't pretend to be an exception to this rule. Let me say, before I go further, that *none* of the theories or concepts presented here is value free, and that, particularly, my interpretations of these theories are based upon my own value system.

Since, however, one of my values is the belief that I should not impose my values on others, I usually try to clarify my values before presenting an idea—so the listener can more clearly hear and be able to avoid my value judgments. Briefly then, I consider myself to be a Humanist, a concept that was best expressed by the original Humanist, Protagorus, who said, "Man is the measure of all things." Thus I tend to understand what is good as that which is good for the individual, and what is good for a group of individuals as that which is the best possible good for all individuals in the group. Obviously, such a philosophy is not always easy to apply, particularly since the standard by which all things are to be measured is not yet understood. What is this "man" (or woman) by which all else is to be measured? Nor is it usually possible to know what is best for any one individual, particularly in leading groups of individuals, since using a standard to determine what is best for everyone is usually a guarantee that no one will receive what is best.

Nevertheless, I have chosen the philosophy of Humanism as a useful, though admittedly general guide for the way I will view and evaluate the world, so be forewarned that my views on leadership are glimpsed through this humanistic filter. In the meantime, my task as a social scientist and as a Humanist is to use the precepts of the sciences to continually redefine and refine what is human so that I may have a more useful standard by which to guide my theories and my actions.

In my opinion, then, *humanistic leaders,* and of course for me the best kind of leaders, are those who are aware of and concerned about fulfilling their own humanness and who are also striving to enable others under their leadership to fulfill their humanness. Goals the humanistic leader chooses to promote are thus humanistic goals, and the methods of achieving those goals are also compatible with being human. Obviously then, for the humanistic leader, ends do not justify means if those means are harmful to individuals.

*   *   *

ASSESSING YOUR LEADERSHIP STYLE
A Brief Leadership Style Questionnaire

Before you read further, respond to the following questions. This abbreviated scale is constructed after the fashion of a Blake-Mouton self-assessment scale (Blake and Mouton, 1964), and is designed to give you some notion of your preferred style of leadership. You will be able to score and interpret your scores after reading this manual.

Directions: Rank order how you would most likely behave in each of the following situations. Place a "1" by *your most likely behavior*, a "2" by your next most likely behavior, etc., until you have placed a "5" by your least likely behavior. Place a number (1 through 5) by every choice, and do not repeat a number; there should be no ties.

I   When Nash and Wons were moving toward actual physical fighting, had I been leader of the group I would have:

_____a. Intervened firmly to insist that open conflict should not occur. Such personal conflict between group members would interfere with the primary purpose of the group and should be suppressed early.

_____b. Maintained a position of strict neutrality, so as to avoid the appearance of taking sides, with the expectation that the conflict would pass over and I would still be seen as an unbiased leader.

_____c. Intervened immediately to smooth over the excessive feelings. The combatants should be reminded that they need each other in order to achieve the group goal.

_____d. Allowed the conflict to go only so far, to allow Nash and Wons to ventilate a little, but then intervened to help each see that he would have to give in a little for the good of the group.

_____e. Intervened to encourage the combatants to get all their feelings out in the open. I would trust that, despite their anger toward each other, they were both concerned for the group goal and that airing their differences should free them to use their energies better in the group.

II   When the group was trying to decide whether to return to
      Sebasa or to go on to the Angle Being City, if I had been the
      leader, I would have:

      _____a. Emphasized that the group's primary responsibil-
      ity was to defend Sebasa, and they had to be making head-
      way toward that goal, quietly and efficiently. I would make
      it clear to them that they should be willing to work toward
      the same goal.

      _____b. Realized that the group was probably already
      overtaxed, that although we had to get to Sebasa, I would
      probably have to explain, persuade, and nudge the people
      into wanting to do what had to be done.

      _____c. Worked with the group until I was sure I had
      clearly stated my opinion and that I had heard all of
      theirs. Ultimately, the responsibility for the results of
      our decision would weigh on all of us, and I would have
      assumed they had both the wisdom and capacity to bear
      that responsibility.

      _____d. Continued working with the people, allowing
      them time and encouraging them to work through all
      those feelings that were hindering their being an effective
      team. My responsibility would have been to maintain a
      workable group atmosphere; then they would be better
      able to make and support the best group decision.

      _____e. Reminded the group that it was understood that
      the group's primary purpose was to aid Sebasa, and then
      expect them to remain loyal to this established commitment.

III. When the group was planning how best to encounter the
      Outhans, had I been the leader, I would have:

      _____a. Reminded the group what we had agreed to do
      and let them come up with their best plan.

_____b. Encouraged them in their struggle to create their plan and then given them my support and faith that they would be able to make the plan work.

_____c. Called for and encouraged ideas from everyone but insisted that the final plan be one I agreed with as the best we could possibly do.

_____d. Articulated the plan that would be acceptable to the others so that most would feel they were a part of the planning and would thus give their full support to the plan.

_____e. Assumed full responsibility for recommending and carrying through on the plan that I knew would give us the best chance of reaching the group's goal.

*   *   *

THE LEADERSHIP WORKSHOP

The workshop upon which this fantasy novel is based is an experiential workshop, which means that the participants experience various simulations of real life situations so that they might behave as they would typically behave when called upon to lead. Then they are given numerous leadership theories to enable them to analyze their behavior. Based on this analysis, they develop strategies to further develop their leadership skills.

The challenges encountered by the characters in the novel generally follow the order of the sessions in the workshop. As did the Sebasa group, the participants first get to know each other and begin bonding as a working team. During this initial trust building session, the participants are taught the skill of feedback, an essential tool for leadership development. As with the characters in the novel, however, the participants don't risk giving significant feedback until later sessions.

In the workshop, the participants form teams to construct boats from four-by-eight foot corrugated cardboard sheets. These boats must stay afloat while transporting one team member in a race in the College pool against the other teams' boats. This of course parallels the Sebasans' terrifying trip down the subterranean channel.

Next, the workshop participants are given complex social and political dilemmas to which they must provide solutions upon which all members must agree. One such issue is: If your child's life can only be saved by expensive technology, and you have exhausted your own funds, should public funds be used to save your child, even though those limited funds might be used instead to prevent numerous other children from ever becoming as sick as your child? In light of such dilemmas, what should be the government's policy on the distribution of public healthcare funds?

The Sebasans also had numerous debates over life threatening issues, and employed or failed to employ the group management skills that will be described in this manual to effectively resolve their dilemmas.

Then the participants are involved in a leadership power struggle, in a simulation called the Peabody Power Game. The structure of the game gives each of the competing teams equal power but limits the communication between teams, though they must reach a solution to their common challenge that is acceptable to all teams. The Sebasans faced such a challenge when they were split, with two members trapped in each of the two side channels, and only Wonina could communicate between each subgroup. The Sebasans had to share power and reach consensus on a solution or they would die.

There are other skills taught in the workshop but these are those most clearly illustrated in the novel. Effective use of all of these leadership skills, however, requires increased self-awareness and enhanced interpersonal skills. I hope that reading this novel and text will provide you all of these benefits.

*   *   *

DEFINING TERMS:
Who Leads, Who Follows Where?

The term "leadership" can be defined so generally as to cover every act of guiding another individual, or even oneself, or so narrowly as to include only specifically assigned leadership roles, such as the chairperson, the foreperson, or the president. In this book, and in the workshops I facilitate, I define leadership somewhere between these two extremes. *Leadership is the talent, skill, and practice of influencing or enabling others to do whatever is necessary to accomplish the common goal of a group.* This definition implies that Leadership is partially an innate talent with which the individual must come equipped and partially a learned skill that can be acquired and sharpened. Above all, this definition implies that leadership is behavior. *A person does not lead who does not act.*

Leadership, as herein defined, is concerned with the achievement of some kind of goal. Unless the group is trying to accomplish something, there is at that moment no need for leadership, and the concept or the person of the leader is at that moment superfluous.

The kind of leadership with which this book is concerned is primarily the leadership of small groups. In larger groups or organizations, where there is limited interaction between the leader and most other individuals in the group, it might be that other kinds of leadership styles and behaviors can better explain effective leadership. However, even the leader of a nation usually works with a small group of advisors or cabinet members, so all the skills described in this manual are relevant to such leaders.

Finally, the definition given above emphasizes that leadership can only take place if there is in fact a common goal within the group, embraced by both the leader and the group members. People who do not want to go where the leader wants them to go might be forced to go, but they the are not being *led.*

This book also promotes the concept of ***participatory leadership:*** *i.e. the leader enables and encourages a task participant to assume leadership* *when that person's skills make him/her the most effective member to lead the group.* Thus, though there may be a nominal leader in a group, at any given time any group member might be the leader of the group. Participatory leadership encourages an atmosphere that promotes the sharing of the leadership role.

This sharing of leadership also means, to a certain extent, the sharing of power. This might be seen as a risk. Since it is understood that all individuals in a group are not alike, this means that a participatory leader may have values and interpretations of the group's goal that vary from the leader's values and interpretations. The Humanistic concept of leadership sees this as a risk worth taking. These differences of opinions, these varying interpretations of what should be done, along with the mutual sharing of power, though it might lead to conflict, is also an opportunity that might lead to greater creativity and ultimately to more effective solutions to group problems.

Participatory leadership, or any lessening of firm leadership control, also increases the possibility of individuals' subverting the goal of the group. Although individuals within a group could have given their overt allegiance to what appears to be a common group goal, those same individuals will usually have covert goals, or hidden agendas that they might be attempting to carry out within the group. *Hidden agendas are covert goals striven for by individuals in the group, goals that are usually different from the overt goals of the group.* Athos and Coffey (1968) suggested a simple way of describing the dynamics of an organization that might make the concept of hidden agenda more easily understood. Athos and Coffey suggest that there are three systems operating in the working of any group—the required system, the personal system, and the emergent system. *The required system is those goals and guidelines handed down by persons in position of real or nominal power.* The owner of the company or perhaps the president of a large organization is an examples of real power. An appointed or an elected committee chairman acting on the behest of a CEO might be an example of nominal power.

The required system and its real power usually reside outside the group. Whatever goals or guidelines are recommended by these power agencies outside the group must, in reality or in appearance, be attended to. But no group of people always does everything that someone outside the group tells them to do. Even in the most oppressive dictatorial authoritarian circumstance (a concentration camp or a prison for instance) individuals within the group are creative enough to also find ways of meeting some of their personal needs. Thus, in addition to the required system operating in the group, the personal system is also operating. *The personal system is the behavior of individuals who, in the process of achieving the goals set by the required system, are also working to achieve their own goals.* The interaction between the required and the personal systems results in what actually takes place in the group, the emergent system. Seldom do the powers-that-be get *exactly* what they want when they assign a goal to a group. The eventual variation in what was originally intended by the required system is the result of the influence of the personal system. *It is the interaction of the required system and the personal system that is* **the emergent system.**

A hidden agenda is a covert expression of the personal system, a goal that a group member is usually reluctant to reveal to the required system or to those who might be loyal to the required system. Hidden agendas are probably always operating as the group goes about trying to achieve some goal, but hidden agendas are not necessarily disruptive, since they are part of what motivates people to exert themselves in a group. *The creative task of leadership is to recognize and satisfy the hidden agendas of members of the group in ways that lead toward the accomplishment of the group goal.*

In the novel, *To Lead the Way,* and particularly in the chapter, "Who Leads Who Follows Where," the group goal is at first only loosely defined, and a number of hidden agendas are beginning to be apparent. Ostensibly the group is on a holiday, primarily to take advantage of a lull in the seasonal work schedule in Sebasa. Secondarily, the group is curious about what might be on the summit of Mount Stareye. Nash also has a second-ary goal, which is initially only of passing interest to the others. However, it is certainly not a hidden agenda. He has been led by Wons to believe they might discover some ancient weapon to combat the impending threat of the Outhans. Wons, on the other hand, has a genuine hidden agenda, one that he denies when asked. The Angle Beings have become an obses-sion for Wons, and his primary goal is the affirmation of his quasi-reli-gious convictions regarding the Angle Beings.

Fyva's acquisitiveness, both for knowledge and for objects, is another hidden agenda that surfaces later in the action. From the very first, Front's hidden agendas are apparent to the reader. He desires to become a closer member of the group, and he particularly desires to become closer to Wonina. Thus, though it appears that Wons is leading the group toward a common goal, in actuality, there is no common goal. A sociologist might describe these five people as an aggregate rather than a group. *An aggregate is a gathering of people in one geographical location or social situation who are not psychodynamically operating toward the attainment of a common goal.* Of course, on a geographic and a social level, the young Sebasans are a task group. They are heading toward the common geographic goal of the mountaintop. They are interacting socially, but in terms of achieving some kind of group goal, they are an aggregate, not a group. *The leadership tasks in the group at this stage of its development should have been to focus on the articulation of a common group goal and, if necessary, to surface hidden agen-das that might have been subverting this process.* As will be seen, the kind of leadership style that Wons displayed at that time was not up to tackling such tasks.

*   *   *

The Blake-mouton Managerial Grid

Robert Blake and Jane Mouton (1964) developed a clever and convenient way of categorizing the various styles of behavior used by individuals to influence others to achieve a common goal. Blake and Mouton used their Managerial Grid theory primarily as a means of understanding the motives and categorizing the philosophies and typical behaviors of industrial managers. Having operationally defined various managerial styles, they were then able to demonstrate the relative effectiveness of the styles and combinations of styles. They were also able to support their own theory of how managers *should* behave.

While Blake and Mouton developed their theory to understand industrial management or "corporate leadership," the Blake-Mouton Managerial Grid has been used by others, and will be used in this book, as a general descriptive leadership theory, a convenient way of organizing our thinking about the concept of leadership as it applies in many less formal situations. Thus, in the following discussion, I will use the term "leader" rather than manager.

Blake and Mouton reasoned that there are two factors operating as a group goes about trying to achieve some goal, two kinds of interests or motivations that determine what will actually happen in the group. There are the **production concerns** *and behaviors and there are the* **person concerns** *and behaviors.* The production factors and the person factors, roughly equivalent to Athos and Coffey's required system and personal system, are valued by a leader to varying degrees. Some leaders are primarily concerned with getting the tasks done. Other leaders are primarily concerned with doing what is right for the individuals within the group. Blake and Mouton devised a graphic way of describing the interaction of those two factors, and this graph or grid leads to the categorizing of five different leadership styles (see Figure 1). On their Leadership Style Grid, moving from left to right along the horizontal axis, is the production dimension.

Position 1 on the Production axis represents a minimal concern for the completion of the group goal. At the other end of that horizontal axis, Position 9 represents maximum concern for the achievement of the goal.

Position 1 on the vertical axis represents minimal concern for people, and Position 9 on the vertical axis represents maximum concern for people.

Blake and Mouton then use the numbers that correspond to the four corners of the graph and the point within the very center of the graph as labels for five leadership styles. For example, the person employing the 1/1 leadership style is, by definition, a leader with very little concern for production and also very little concern for people. The person using the 9/1 leadership style is concerned primarily with production and not at all with people.

In the novel, I used each of the five characters to represent each of these Blake-Mouton leadership styles. These leadership styles are not intended by Blake and Mouton to represent personality types, and even in a novel, I don't think believable characters can be created from such absolute styles. These styles are intended as descriptive extremes. No one is actually a 9/9 leader or a 1/1 leader, and no fictional character could be believable if so depicted. A story with such characters would be too allegorical, and the reader could not easily identify with the characters. Nevertheless, I have done my best to highlight, through the characters' actions, the salient aspects of these five leadership styles, and then I've attempted to make the characters more real by allowing them to grow, to experiment with different styles, and thus to become more effective in their leadership. It was also my intention to show by the characters' growth that experimenting with one's leadership style and achieving more flexibility across styles is possible and desirable.

As the story proceeded in the novel, Wons, when he was using the 1/1 style, was primarily concerned with his own agenda and had minimal concern for either task or people. Nash, as a leader who was inclined to use the 9/1 leadership style was concerned primarily with task and very little with people. Wonina, using the 1/9 style was overwhelmingly concerned

Figure 1

The Leadership Styles of the Five Characters in the Novel

As Found in the Blake-Mouton Managerial Grid

	1	2	3	4	5	6	7	8	9
9	1/9 Wonina								9/9 Front
8									
7									
6					5/5				
5					Fyva				
4									
3									
2									
1	1/1 Wons								9/1 Nash

Concern for People

Concern for Task

for people and willing to let the task wait. Fyva, using the 5/5 style, was concerned somewhat with the task and somewhat with the people, but willing to compromise both. Front, using the 9/9 style, had total allegiance to the task and also total allegiance to the people.

Similarly, the purpose of our leadership-training workshop at the College is for individuals to become aware of their current styles so they may then meaningfully experiment with change and growth. Blake and Mouton obviously believe that some styles are more effective than others. However, they allow that under certain circumstances even the less than 9/9 styles have their usefulness. I attempted to show in the novel both the effectiveness and the ineffectiveness in each of these five styles. As the sequence of events allows for each of the five individuals to assume leadership during a part of the journey, that leader exercises effective use of a particular leadership style. Then when that leader begins to fail, the ineffective aspects of that leadership style are demonstrated. At that point, the ineffective leader gives way to another leader with another leadership style who can be more effective in the new circumstance.

*   *   *

WONS, THE 1/1 LEADERSHIP STYLE:
We Work Up, The Words Come Down

1/1 leaders are unlikely to achieve group goals by their leadership efforts. If the group goal is achieved, it is because things take their course while the leader stands back and hopes. 1/1 leaders are not particularly committed to the goals of the group, and they make the assumption that the people in the group aren't either, so the people will probably only put up resistance if leadership pressure is exerted. The hallmark of the 1/1 leader is the avoidance of conflict, and the primary tool used to avoid conflict is dependence upon outside authority. The 1/1 leader goes by the book, not necessarily to achieve the group goal, but rather to avoid the blame that will be incurred if the goal is not achieved. Wons is used to depict a 1/1 leader, not necessarily because he was indifferent to people or not committed to a goal, but because his goal, his hidden agenda, was not the group's goal. His adherence to "the book" does, more typically illustrates the 1/1 leadership style. Whenever there was a decision to be made, an issue to be resolved or illustrated, Wons referred to *The Words of Emanuel, Leader of the Ship*. As long as the group goal was somewhat ambiguous, but roughly centered around reaching the summit of Mount Stareye, and thus somehow related to "the book," Wons was able to use quotes from the book to lead the group. But when Wons was frustrated in the achievement of his own agenda, when he was disillusioned at discovering there was nothing on the summit of Mount Stareye to affirm his religious beliefs, his behavior illustrates another salient characteristic of the 1/1 leader. He took flight, psychologically. He withdrew from the people and from the task of the group into sulking and indifference, and he protected himself from further feeling and involvement by sarcasm and bickering. As such, he abandoned the responsibility he had been given, informally, by the group, and the result was temporary chaos in the group. This chaos left room for the emergence of a new leader and made the group ready for any kind of leadership style that could quell the chaos.

*   *   *

NASH, THE 9/1 LEADERSHIP STYLE:
You Must Build Boats

Out of conflict may occasionally come creative solutions. Out of chaos may also come a dictator. Most political revolutions seem to result in temporary committee rule that is not too effective and then in the eventual emergence of a tyrant. The people seem willing to struggle against one oppression, but when the chaos that generally accompanies committee rule continues, and the new struggle begins to seem interminable, they are likely to hail a new authoritarian ruler as a blessed relief from this turmoil. The 9/1 leadership style is not necessarily dictatorial, and the person who assumes that style is not necessarily a dictator, however, there are characteristics in common between the two concepts. 9/1 leaders have a clear perception of the goal of the group. Working from that clarity, they can give clear direction and firm orders to the group. 9/1 leaders, however, tend to be their own interpreters of the group's goal and to be indifferent to or scornful of other possible interpretations. 9/1 leaders, because of their devotion to production, tend to see the people who must work to achieve the production goal as means rather than ends, as tools to be managed, tools whose primary purpose is goal achievement. Personal systems and hidden agendas operating within the group are seen as resistances that cannot be tolerated. Uniqueness is seen as lack of uniformity, and individuals must be shaped to fit the task directed roles they should occupy within the group. 9/1 leaders, therefore, are frequently very efficient, and in one sense, very effective. They do get the job done. Sometimes, however, this is at the cost of passive or rebellious resistance and the eventual dissolution of the group.

Nash emerged from the "Council of Chaos" as the one person with a clear goal, to reach the Angle Beings' legendary weapon. He set forth forcefully to achieve his own goal, his own interpretation of what the group should be trying to accomplish, and the group sighed an almost unanimous sigh of relief. To be told what to do, even though it was not quite what they originally had in mind, felt much better than not being able to make up their own minds. Even Front, who doubted the practicality and wisdom of Nash's decision, kept his doubts to himself, preferring not to further arouse dissention and fearing a return of chaos.

Certainly Nash's 9/1 style was effective in preparing the group against Front's imagined attack by Outhans, as the team traversed the mysterious moss covered, mist filled terrain down the back of Mount Stareye. When

Front shared his concern with Nash, Nash barked his militaristic commands, and a reasonably defendable perimeter was quickly established. The 9/1 style is probably most appropriate under such "battlefront" conditions. Even the military, however, during peacetime, is experimenting with other less oppressive styles of leadership. The military's rationale for considering such a change is that a technological army must be made up of people who can do their own thinking. The military recognizes that a 9/1 style, as was intended, promotes conformity, but not creativity, not the kind of free thinking necessary for certain kinds of problem solving.

Nash's 9/1 style temporarily established a goal that the group was willing to follow, and his subsequent actions further diverted the group toward his own interpretation of the group's goal. Gradually, however, two things began to occur: (1) Not being willing to risk Nash's anger, the group volunteered fewer and fewer suggestions, and thus the resources of the group were diminished. As a result, basing his decision exclusively on his own input, Nash began to make errors in judgment. (2) Resistance began to grow in the group. Wons' foot dragging and sarcasm slowed progress and loosened the group's cohesiveness. Wonina, who had at first expressed her appreciation of Nash's strong leadership, began to complain about his abuse of the others. Front, typical of this stage in his leadership development, was beginning to doubt but not yet voicing his disagreement with Nash. Fyva was slowly emerging as the power behind the leadership, as she used her particular combination of logic and compromise to aid Nash. In this manner, however, though still supporting Nash, she was in fact gaining control over him, bending his leadership to her own ends.

Finally, resorting to the ultimate in an extreme 9/1 style, Nash used brute force to punish Wons' resistance and tossed him into the water. Front, then being primarily concerned with going to Wons' rescue, wasn't able to resist when he was about ready to resist. The group was then committed to the irresistible force of the water and to the seemingly fatal mistake brought on by Nash's 9/1 leadership style. The hapless Sebasans were cast over the falls, into the black hole, and trapped in the side caves, and leadership then passed from Nash to the one person best suited to heal the wounds in the group's intra-relationship, the wounds caused by Nash's oppressive behavior. Wonina now assumed leadership.

*   *   *

WONINA, A 1/9 LEADERSHIP STYLE:
We Must Stand Still Before We Can Move

The 1/9 leader is ostensibly concerned with the feelings and well being of the individuals within the group. The task, if it has any value for the 1/9 leader, is at least an excuse to keep the people together. However, if the 1/9 leader must choose between production and the people, the 1/9 leader chooses the people. Conflict within the group is seen by the 1/9 leader as dangerous and destructive to the group's solidarity and cohesiveness. Conflict must be met by avoidance and reduction of group tension. Good feelings and good morale are the goals of the 1/9 leader, and, if necessary, these must be purchased at the cost of neglecting production. The 1/9 leadership style is necessary, however, when the group reaches an impasse. Whereas the 9/1 leader attempts to force individuals to submerge their own needs as a way of breaking through an impasse, the 1/9 leader encourages the open expression of divergent needs so that they might be met. Then the group can return, if it so chooses, to the task. The 1/9 leader, however, allows the expression of those unmet individual needs in a controlling style that insists upon no open conflict, only conciliation. Without the use of a 1/9 style, in certain circumstances, conflict might indeed erupt that would be destructive to the group. Wonina felt, and probably rightly so, that the group must stand still, must recover from the traumatic ordeal it had just experienced, must mollify and control the intra-group bickering or it would not have the strength to go on.

It was also the other group members' confidence in Wonina's dependable concern for the individuals in the group that enabled them to trust her, on blind faith, when trust was all that could possibly save them from inevitable death. If they had failed to resolve the dilemma of their distrust when the two subgroups were trapped by the irresistible force of the oncoming water, the four trapped members would have died of exposure.

Out of her constant concern for the well being of the individuals in the group, Wonina also had the courage to risk considerable danger, and thus she was able to rescue and bring the group back together. Her rather maternal style also forced the group to eat, rest, and recover itself physically. Her 1/9 style, however, was unable to resolve the conflict in the group, only to temporarily suppress it—and all the while the group was going nowhere. Out of her fear for the safety of the group, Wonina could only counsel standing still, neither going forward nor backward, but it was becoming obvious and logical that a decision had to be made. Herein lies the great weakness of the 1/9 style. Underlying the overt concern for others and the belief that conflict is destructive to the group is the 1/9 leader's personal fear of conflict. The 1/9 leader must control conflict for fear of being personally engulfed by the emotions and the feared results of that conflict. Wonina's leadership finally broke down and the underlying fear emerged, to the surprise of the others who apparently were unaware of the chronic fights in Wonina's family. Wonina revealed that she has been constantly exposed to her parents' marital conflict, an exposure that has conditioned her to be fearful of conflict in her own life.

Fyva, seizing on the absolute logic that they could not forever stand still, was able to recommend a compromise that would enable the group to at least consider moving forward.

*   *   *

FYVA, A 5/5 LEADERSHIP STYLE:
Council of Compromise

5/5 leaders are primarily production oriented, but they recognize that the people's needs must also be met, at least to an extent. Unlike 1/1 leaders, who believe that production and the people are hopelessly out of their hands, or 9/1 leaders who act as though they must win all or all is lost, or 1/9 leaders who sacrifice production in order to satisfy the people, 5/5 leaders attempt to accomplish at least part of the goal by giving in partially to the people. 5/5 leaders, in compromising, also compromise the goal. 5/5 leaders believe compromise is necessary because they lack full confidence in the capacity and the commitment of the people. Thus the 5/5 style, although it is intended to achieve at least partial success in meeting the goal, is also an expression of an attempt to avoid what it is feared would be the destructive consequences of open confrontation among the group members. When Fyva assumed leadership, she didn't lead an open discussion of the alternatives, rather she carefully articulated her version of two alternatives, and then offered a compromise. She then sweetened her own choice of the alternatives by offering to sacrifice herself. Even though she might not have been the best choice for the task, she offered to allow herself to be dangled on a line into the dark opening in order to move the group a little more in the direction of her own version of the group goal. Front was swayed by this sacrifice, partially by Fyva's logic and partially because it was easier on him.

Later, however, when Front was himself dangling on the line, and the line was let go, Front wondered about Fyva's true intentions. Herein lies one of the problems of the 5/5 style. Sometimes compromise is difficult to differentiate from manipulation, and it can lead to distrust within the group.

Nevertheless, Fyva's style of offering selective alternatives did get the group moving again toward what was generally seen as the group goal. It was only when new events in the life of the group provided a clear-cut alternative, and two apparently opposing goals, that Fyva's 5/5 style ceased to be effective. When the weapon was discovered, and part of the group wanted to return to Sebasa immediately and the other part of the group wanted to continue seeking the Angle Beings, Fyva again tried offering alternatives and compromise, but her alternatives were now seen as more clearly biased. Open conflict then broke out. Rather than confronting the conflict, Fyva joined Wons in falling back on the 1/1 style behavior of sarcasm. Then Front, the potential 9/9 leader, finally risked those kinds of behaviors that would enable him to assume effective leadership of the group.

*   *   *

FRONT, THE 9/9 LEADERSHIP STYLE:

Council of Confrontation and Cohesion

9/9 leaders are fully committed to the task, but 9/9 leaders also have confidence in the commitments and capacities of those they lead. *Based on this confidence and respect for people, 9/9 leaders are willing to confront conflict within the group.* Conflict among people, in the process of working toward a common goal, is seen by 9/9 leaders as inevitable and also potentially constructive. Personal systems operating within the group are seen as potential sources of motivation, but usually only if these systems are openly recognized and ways are then found to satisfy those that contribute to the group goal.

Front, of course, did not begin as a 9/9 leader. Early in the novel he did show sensitivity to and an awareness of the interactions between the group members as well as a capacity to reflect upon his own needs and behaviors, all of which are necessary capacities in a 9/9 leader, but at first Front lacked the courage of his own beliefs. His commitment toward the goal of the group expressed itself in his willingness to work on behalf of whichever leader seemed to be effective at the moment, but he did not himself risk assuming the responsibility of leadership. His expertise as a boat builder made him valuable to Nash, and his expertise as a swimmer made him valuable to Fyva, but even while he was working for these leaders, he doubted the wisdom of their actions. Thus, he was not being totally true to himself nor was he actualizing his potential contribution to the group. Had he risked an earlier confrontation with Nash, they might have avoided the dangerous predicament in which they eventually found themselves by following Nash on his ill-fated boat trip.

Perhaps out of courage or perhaps out of disgust, Front finally assumed leadership when he initiated a discussion regarding the ultimate goals of the group. His style at this point might still be best characterized as a 5/5 style, since he did not ask for, or perhaps even trust the capacity of the group at that moment to arrive at its own conclusions. Instead, he articulated a generalization that seemed to tie together the two conflicting goals of the group. The ultimate goal of the group, he suggested, was doing what is right for Sebasa, and thus he recommended they discuss effective strategies for achieving this ultimate goal.

First, Front risked offering his own opinions as to what would be the most effective strategy, but then he called for discussion. By this act, he finally attempted a 9/9 approach to leading the group. This 9/9 intervention failed, however, and Front then fell back upon a series of interventions that eventually led to the group's following his leadership.

*   *   *

THE FALLBACK ORDER:
Fall Back Forward

As I stated, Blake-Mouton's leadership styles should not be confused with personality types. Any person may use any or all of the leadership styles in leading a group toward achieving its goals. Each of the leadership styles can be effective under certain conditions, and an effective leader uses each style when appropriate. The leadership construct that approaches more closely a personality construct might be the back up or "fallback order."

Employed by a leader in confronting the diverse challenges of leadership, the **fallback order** *is the sequence of leadership styles habitually used by a person when that person is leading a group.* Each of the characters in the novel was depicted as having a dominant or primary leadership style, but when that leadership style became ineffective, the character then fell back upon another of the five possible leadership styles.

In order to command immediate action, both Wonina and Fyva, after showing concern for the group's needs or by attempting compromise frequently fell back to a 9/1 style of demanding group compliance.

Nash fell back to a 1/1 style when his primary 9/1 style failed. So did Wonina and Fyva when their secondary styles failed. Wonina broke down crying, thus giving up any attempt at leadership. Fyva fell back into non-constructive 1/1 bickering. Wons, during his initial term of leadership, showed only the 1/1 Style, in two versions, reliance on the outside source of authority of Emanuel and then sulking and sarcastic flight or withdrawal.

Individuals with any primary leadership style can use any combination of the other styles to make up their typical fallback order. Moreover, under certain circumstances, one person may completely change his or her fallback order.

In their research with 716 managers in what they considered to be a representative industry, Blake and Mouton found that the most typical managerial fallback order is 5/5, 9/9, 9/1, 1/9, 1/1. However, as the maturity, education, and effectiveness of the managers increased, the fallback became 9/9, 5/5/ 9/1, 1/9, 1/1. The most effective managers had a 9/9, 9/1, 5/5, 1/9, 1/1 fallback order. Thus, Blake and Mouton argue that the most effective managers operate from a 9/9 philosophical base and react first in leadership situations with a 9/9 behavioral style. When encountering resistance to their leadership, these effective 9/9 managers will next fall back on a 9/1 style.

Industrial management is only one form of leadership, however, and the power invested in the industrial manager's position as well as the high value placed on production in industry probably accounts for the effectiveness of the manager's falling back first to the demand (9/1) style. In industry, the greater resistance that sometimes results from the early use of the 9/1 style can be suppressed, and the continuance of the work group can be assured by the power of the manager to fire current group members and hire new ones, thereby creating a fresh working group not yet ready to resist the 9/1 style.

In more general leadership situations, and particularly from a more humanistic orientation in which the individual is not considered to be "exchangeable" as a means of achieving the group goal, another fallback order is recommended. The rationale for this all-purpose "ideal fallback order" is as follows: Believing in the value of the group goal and also in the worth, integrity, and commitment of the group members, the ideal leader prefers to approach the leadership situation in a 9/9 leadership style. In the face of continual resistance, such leaders then fall back sequentially to a 5/5, 1/9, 9/1 and finally to a 1/1 leadership style.

Jay Hall of Teleometrics International, a management consulting firm that creates and uses psychometric instruments for assessing and teaching management effectiveness, also recommends the above fallback order as ideal for conflict management (Hall 1973.) Hall believes that the 9/9, 5/5, 1/9, 9/1, 1/1 fallback order, in the face of conflict, has the beneficial long-range consequences of maintaining trust, openness, and belief in the positive intent of the group members.

This ideal conflict management fallback order, which is also seen as a Humanistic fallback order, was represented in two places in the novel, in Chapter Two by Wons' quotes from "The Book," and by Front when he opened discussion on the group's goal. In Chapter Two, Wons recited the liturgy according to Emanuel, describing how Emanuel stood before the people and shared his heart, etc., and each time the people continue their conflict, Emanuel fell back, in the ideal fallback order, until he eventually walked away—and the group followed. The ideal fallback order uses only the effective characteristics of each leadership style, and the ideal fallback order is seen as proceeding from a basic 9/9 philosophical and attitudinal position. Thus, when 9/9 leaders have tried open discussion in confronting conflict, and the group is still unwilling or unable to reach a decision, 9/9 leaders then fall back to a 5/5 style. Recognizing and respecting that there are genuine differences in the needs of group members, it is necessary to temporarily sacrifice some aspect of the group goal in order at least to get on with the work. The 9/9 leader's compromise of the group's goal is not so drastic, however, that it will be impossible to ultimately achieve the full goal. If a 5/5 style fails, 9/9 leaders then fall back to a 1/9 style, recognizing that there are times when group tension or conflict is so great that, if not lessened, it will result in the breakup of the group. Unlike the less effective primary 1/9 leader, the 9/9 leader in falling back to a 1/9 style is not concerned with mollifying group feelings but rather with clarifying group feelings. Thus, 9/9 leaders in falling back to a 1/9 style, insist upon the surfacing of tensions, having enough faith in the strength of the group members to believe that, when given the opportunity, they will be able to deal effectively even with their own negative feelings. In other words, confrontation is not negative as it was for Wonina, but positive as it was for Front (Con*front*ation).

Only when these first three styles in the ideal fallback order fail to achieve progress toward the group do 9/9 leaders fall back on the 9/1 style. They then *insist* that the group members honor their original commitments to the goal. Even in using this demanding 9/1 style, ideal 9/9 leaders behave in ways that will maintain respect for the members of the group, while also insisting on the group's respect for the leader's commitment to the previously agreed upon group goal. (For an assessment of this essential "Mutual Respect" component of your leadership, see Appendix

D.) Only when the 9/1 style fails do these ideal 9/9 leaders finally fall back to the 1/1 style. Even the 1/1 style, when used by an ideal 9/9 leader, is potentially constructive and is intended to achieve the group goal, not to avoid it or to avoid conflict with the people. 9/9 leaders, recognizing that the group is not at this time willing to act toward the achievement of the goal, state their belief that this is only the *current* attitude of the group. They publicly proclaim their unwillingness to participate in the ineffectiveness of the group and, declaring their own continued commitment to the group goal and their decision to work alone toward that goal, 9/9 leaders then withdraw from the group.

Front demonstrated this ideal 9/9 fallback order when he finally assumed leadership of the group. After opening the discussion on the group's ultimate goal (9/9) and finding that the group continued to bicker he offered the compromise of promising to return with the group to search for the Angle Beings after they had first gone to assist the Sebasans (5/5). When this compromise failed, Front fell back to an attempt at opening a discussion about the feelings that were dividing the group (1/9). When this 1/9 approach failed, Front reminded them of the strength he brought to the group, implying that they would be helpless without him, and attempted to use this as at threat to coerce the group toward the group goal (9/1). When this 9/1 style failed, Front restated his commitment to the ultimate group goal and announced his intention of going on alone (a constructive 1/1). He turned his back on the group, and only then did the group follow. Thus Front, as an ideal 9/9 leader, never abandoned his understanding and commitment to the group goal, nor was he disrespectful to the people in the group. At all times he left open the possibility that the group, when ready, would return to constructive action toward the group goal. Even his withdrawal from the group was an example of a positive 1/1 leadership style in which he was still attempting to move the group, despite its reluctance, toward Sebasa.

*   *   *

OTHER LEADERSHIP ISSUES
Group Process: Councils of Chaos, Coercion, Concern, Compromise, Confrontation, and Cohesion

Obviously leadership is not all that takes place as a group attempts to achieve a common goal. Other important kinds of behaviors are going on in the group as group members compliment and counter one another in the process of undertaking the group tasks. *It is the interaction of the leadership role and the numerous other roles assumed by individuals in the group that is described as* **group process.** Group process either results in the achievement of the group goal, or accounts for the group's failure to achieve its goal. To understand leadership and to become an effective leader, one must also understand and be able to make use of these dynamic interpersonal interactions among the group members. Throughout the novel, I attempted to illustrate group process, particularly in those chapters in which the group met as a "council" to discuss their situation. Although group process is going on any time people gather and work together toward some end, the process is most clearly seen in a small group problem solving discussions. In the novel I tried to show that, as leadership became more effective in the small group discussions, that is, as leadership proceeded from Wons' 1/1 leadership to Front's 9/9 leadership, more effective kinds of group process behavior also emerged. It is my belief that *Leadership is not effective unless complimented by effective group process.*

Different styles of leadership typically use different methods of managing group process. The ideal 9/9 leader develops and encourages an interpersonal atmosphere within the group that will enable individual members to assume the task roles that are the logical extensions of their personal interests in being in the group. The 5/5 leader might encourage the members to bargain to achieve a safe compromise that will enable most members to accomplish some of their goals. The 1/9 leader might encourage the development of an open group atmosphere, but primarily to please the group members and only secondarily to achieve the goal. The 9/1 leader, and perhaps the 1/1 leader, might attempt to impose a rigid system that demands that certain procedures must be followed regardless of the personal interest of individual group members.

In teaching and understanding group process, we rely upon a system of labels to indicate the functions involved in group process. It is a system that was developed by many other people. The system I will now describe, although frequently modified by others including myself, was originally developed by Morton Deutsch (1960).

In this system, there are two task functions and three categories of task behaviors that label behaviors used by problem solving group members in their attempt to accomplish the group goal.

I. **Task Functions:** In the most general sense, for a group to achieve its goals, the group members must engage in two activities: a) **defining the problem**, TFA, *engaging in those discussions that will enable the members to understand and clearly articulate what they are trying to accomplish as well as the difficulties they are likely to encounter along the way,* and b) **solving the problem**, TFB, *finding the best solution among the many possible solutions.* (The three-letter code following each label will be explained later.)

    The two Task Functions are approached in three general ways by the leader and other group members. These are the Task Functional Behaviors, the Maintenance Behaviors, and the Process Problem Behaviors.

II. **Task Functional Behaviors:** *The logical cognitive strategies used by members to define and solve the problem posed for the group are called Task Functional Behaviors.* Following are some typical task functional behaviors and examples of their use by the characters in the novel:

A. **Deciding How to Start,** DSF. Nash told the group, now here's what we're going to do. Fyva suggested several options. Front shared his opinions and asked for others' opinions. Wonina demanded that they eat first. And Wons quoted Emanuel.

B. **Exchanging Information and Opinion,** EIF. Even under Nash, when the group began boat building, the natural energy of the group resulted in a free exchange of possible suggestions on how to best to build their boats.

C. **Clarifying Ideas,** CIF. Fyva, although for the purpose of manipulating the group, made a point of explaining and elaborating her ideas to insure understanding by the group.

D. **Generating Alternatives,** GAF. In trying to improve their plan for confronting the Outhans, many group members quickly suggested possible variations in Front's original plan.

E. **Testing for Feasibility,** TFF. Several times Front doubted the feasibility of the group's plans. He only began testing for feasibility, however, when he began asking the group to think through the possible consequences of their plan to attack the Outhans.

F. **Challenging Tradition,** CTF. If the old ways always worked, there would be no problems to be solved. Even though the existence of the Angle Beings and of their magical weapon seemed unlikely to Front, Nash insisted that, under the circumstances, the traditional expectations should be ignored. Ultimately Nash's challenge to tradition led to the correct solution to the problem of the Outhans.

G. **Wrap-Up,** WUF. Wons attempted a "wrap-up," which is the establishing of consensus within the group. At the end of the novel he concluded that Front was going to eventually lead them on another adventure to discover the Angle Being city.

H. **Testing for Consensus,** RUF. After Wons' "wrap-up," we don't know if anyone tested for consensus, that is, determined the degree of acceptance of an idea or solution. Perhaps that's what would happen in a sequel to the novel.

III. Maintenance Behaviors: If group members were machines, they would not need to have their human needs attended to during the process of reaching a group solution to a problem. Even the most task oriented group, however, at times needs to back off from the task to allow for the humanness of its members, to allow the members to regroup and regain their energy, and to reestablish group cohesiveness. *This concern for the humanness of group members is termed* maintenance behaviors. Following are some examples from the novel of maintenance behaviors:

A. Leveling, LEM. The group that does not allow and encourage all members to participate is likely to be missing some of its potential resources. Nash's extreme 9/1 behavior, his threatening to abuse the others, stifled some of the potential contributions of his group members. Wonina, however, insisted several times that the members be heard, and eventually even Wons demonstrated this kind of "leveling" behavior.

B. **Blowing the Whistle,** BWM. Wonina was firm in pointing out that Front's and Fyva's indulging in self recrimination over Wons' injury was counter productive to the agreed upon purpose of the group. She was

"blowing the whistle," or calling their attention to
their deviation from the group's agreed upon purpose.

C. **Involvement, INM.** Front was concerned, during
the "council of confrontation," that Nash was no
longer a member of the group. He attempted to get
Nash's opinion. Although he failed at that time, he
was attempting the maintenance function of
"involvement," drawing out less involved members
to insure that all resources of the group are available
to the group.

D. **Protecting Others, POM.** Sometimes in the aggressive
pursuit of the group goal, less assertive members tend
to be brushed aside and even attacked. So as to assure
the eventual contribution of these members and the
cohesiveness of the group, such members must be protected at times. Wonina was usually quick to under-
take this role of protecting others.

IV. **Process Problems Behaviors.** *For the purpose of frustrating a
group that is moving in a direction other than that desired by a
particular member, or for the purpose of meeting one's own personal
needs, individual group members frequently involve employ behaviors that interfere with the group process. Such behaviors are
process* **problems behaviors.** The 9/1 leader might choose to
punish such behaviors. The 1/9 leader might choose to humor
people involved in such behavior so as to not raise conflict. The
1/1 leader, if anything, might attempt to use rules to overcome
such behavior. The 5/5 leader might ignore such behavior, so
long as too much of the group goal is not compromised. The
9/9 leader is more likely to confront such potentially nonfunc-
tional behavior in a direct manner by bringing attention to it
and reminding the offending member of the purpose of the

group. The 9/9 leader, however, is also alert to consider such behaviors as indications of tensions in the group that might require falling back to a 1/9 approach so as to eventually proceed more smoothly.

Following are examples of process problems behaviors:

A. Blocking, BLP. Nash, Fyva, and Wons engaged in blocking behavior when they purposely attacked one another, when Front was trying to bring the group to consensus of the group's ultimate goal. Blocking behavior is intended to interfere with another person's right or opportunity to express ideas or opinions. Frequently blocking takes the form of attacking the person rather than discussing the issue.

B. Early Quit, EQP. Wons wanted to effect an "early quit." He tried to shut off discussion of an issue before there was a chance for it to be thoroughly considered. He attempted to end Fyva's discussion of her plan to enter the black hole by turning to Front to suggest they work on Front's plan to make it back up the falls.

C. Flight, FLP. The 1/1 style, in its negative sense, is a flight style, and Wons frequently engaged in such flight behaviors as sulking, moodiness, moving himself physically apart from the group, and sarcastic retorts.

D. Topic Jumping, TJP. Wons also attempted "topic jumping," or drifting from one idea to another so as to avoid the group's reaching conclusions.

E. Con Man Tactics, CMP. It is not clear whether Fyva was using a "conman tactic" in her many attempts at offering compromise. At one time Front suspected that she had manipulated the group into the black hole by letting the rope slip, so the group would then have to come to Front's rescue. Later she denied it, but if her behavior was indeed an attempt to consciously or subconsciously steer the group in a given direction in a secretive manner without its full consent or knowledge, she was using a "con man" tactic.

F. **Uni-Decision,** UDP. Nash frequently made "uni-decisions," or decisions made by one or a small group of persons and imposed upon the group, when he forced the group along before dissent could develop.

Deviant or irrelevant behaviors, DBP, and **hidden agendas**, HAP, are also problem behaviors in a task group.

Process problem behaviors aren't always problems for a group, however. It depends on how well the leader manages them. All such behaviors indicate energy, an investment on the part of those employing in these behaviors. The leader's challenge is to get these members to invest in the group goal rather than just in their own goals.

I tried to demonstrate that under the task oriented but person respectful 9/9 leadership style, the councils in the novel became more productive, that more task and maintenance behaviors took place, and that there were fewer process problems behaviors. 9/9 leaders recognize that group process is not problem-free. *When diverse human beings attempt to reach a common goal, because of the diversity in human beings, conflict is inevitable.* Conflict usually begins as soon as a group begins. At each step along the way, as the group attempts to solve a problem, different opinions on how best to solve the problem will generate more conflict. 9/9 leaders reason that, since conflict is inevitable, it is efficient and effective to directly confront the conflict, whenever possible, trusting in the strength of the participants and in their valuing of the ultimate goal of the group. Effective 9/9 leaders actively participate in group process, even conflictual group process, rather than oppressively controlling group processes so as to avoid conflict.

*   *   *

USES AND ABUSES OF POWER:
Power Pulls Apart Together

In order for a group to accomplish its goals there must be motivation. Ideally the motivation will come from each individual's commitment to the group goal, from his or her desire to see that goal achieved. Typically, however, not all individuals are fully invested in the group goal. Personal systems are operating that are indifferent to or even counter to the group goal. A leader must redirect these personal systems toward achieving the group goal. *The force that enables the leader to motivate others toward achieving the group goal is called* **leadership power,** henceforth simply called power.

The leader might have an effective leadership style as well as an understanding of and skill in directing group process, but to be most productive, the leader must also have power.

Power can be applied directly, as with a caress or a blow, but power is usually applied indirectly, as with a promise or a threat. Power is used to persuade, and the method of persuading is either rewarding or punishing.

Dictators use power, usually the power of punishment, threatened or administered. Followers are thus forced to accomplish the dictator's goals. Such punitive power is real, and it works. But the use of such power is a certain indication that *leadership,* as defined in this manual, is not taking place.

Only when a leader applies power directly, as in physical force, is the source of power within the leader. In all other cases, the power to lead is given to the leader from an outside source. The sources of power used by the leader, and others in the group when they assume leadership, can be categorized in the following ways:

1. **Legitimate Power.** *When the leader of a group is given authority by something or someone outside the group, a source of power that is also recognized by the members of the group, then the leader has* **legitimate power**. Legitimate power is also given to

the leader in the democratic process by the members of the group, saying in effect, by our election of you we recognize your right to direct us. Legitimate power thus rests in the office or position recognized by the group and not in the individual holding that office.

Money is obviously a source of power, and can be used to persuade. It is the control of money that is the source of the power. If the money is personal wealth, the power resides within the leader. If the control of money is conferred by outside authority, as from the board of directors, the power is legitimate power.

None of the five characters in the novel had legitimate power. During the adventure, there was never the formal recognition of anyone that would have made the leader's power legitimate. In the last scene, however, the others seemed about to bestow such power on the reluctant Front.

2.   **Charisma Power.** *Some individuals, because of their personalities or physical appearance are given the power to lead. Followers of such leaders project onto their leaders powers far greater than those that are actually possessed by their leaders. Such leaders are said to have* **charismatic power.** People who are fearful of the responsibility of leadership and in need of someone to lead them may attribute to the charismatic leader those strengths they believe will enable that person to successfully lead them. The projection is usually on to someone who stands out in some way. That leader's outstanding feature is made larger than life, this unrealistic perception is generalized to other aspects of the leaders, and the leader's weaknesses are discounted. The projectors then see only what they wish to see in their idealized leader. The charismatic leader uses this projected image as a source of power to direct others, for who could say no to such a godlike being?

In the beginning of the novel Wons had charismatic power. Front assumed that Wons should lead because Wons was a member of the class of leaders, since Wons' father was the town Steward. Wons was also tall, and research suggests (Stogdill, 1974) that one consistent finding about leaders is that they tend to be tall. This phenomenon is probably based upon the fact that, as children, our original leaders, our parents, are taller than we are, and thus we go through life expecting our leaders to be taller than we are. Wons also had the kind of stereotypical deep voice frequently associated with the fatherly leader. All of these characteristics made it easy for Front to project onto Wons the expectation that Wons would be the best leader, when in fact, being tall, deep voiced, or the son of a legitimate leader were only characteristics onto which Front projected his need for a leader. They were not characteristics that guaranteed good leadership.

3. **Expert power.** The wisdom of most groups allows the person who has the expertise to lead whenever that expertise is needed for the achievement of the group goal. *The power given to the expert to lead is called* **expert power.** An expert might also hold legitimate power, particularly when the group is set up to solve a task of a highly technical nature. But in most situations, experts should only be given power to lead temporarily, and only in the area of their expertise. There is the danger that experts will be given charismatic power, and will have expertise attributed to them beyond their area of expertise. Such has often been the case when it is assumed that scientists or doctors must also be good leaders.

    Effective leaders, however, are also experts; their area of expertise is people. But such people experts will wisely give way to experts in specific areas when such expertise is called for. Even when Nash was in charge of the group, and Nash was not a people expert, he gave way to Front's knowledge of boat building. Likewise Fyva was willing to let Front literally lead the group along the watery pathway and to bow to his expertise in swimming when swimming expertise was called for. And Front did not hesitate to allow Wonina to tend to Wons' wounds, realizing that Wonina was an expert in caring for people.

These are some sources of expert power: knowledge, intelligence, technical expertise and skills, group process skills, interpersonal skills, and intrapersonal skills such as self-awareness and emotional management.

Whatever the source of power, and whether applied directly or indirectly to reward or punish, power is being used when a person is trying to persuade others to act in some way. The working relationship one establishes with others often determines or is determined by the way one uses power. In trying to achieve a goal that requires involvement with other people, one can choose to relate coercively, to negotiate, or to collaborate. **Coercion** *is the use of reward or punishment in a manner that gives other people little choice but to choose the goals of the coercer.* **Negotiation** *is a give and take process that may involve a compromise of the negotiator's original goals.* **Collaboration** *proceeds from the assumption that it is possible to accomplish the goals of all involved if all work long enough and hard enough to arrive at the correct solution, and no one gives in to the temptation to coerce or to negotiate.*

In our leadership training workshops we use a learning exercise that is intended to make the workshop participants aware of their typical uses of power. The participants are placed in a situation of considerable ambiguity, where full direct communication is impossible, and the only sure way to win, against seemingly inevitable forces, is to risk trust and attempt collaboration. I tried to create a similar set of circumstances in *To Lead the Way, in* the chapter, "Power Pulls Apart Together." The power of the oncoming water had, literally, pulled or pushed the group apart, and distrust, particularly within Nash, was further destroying the group. Nash first wanted to coerce Wonina and the others into giving Front and him the tools to get out of their cul-de-sac. He then attempted negotiation, but Fyva and Wons weren't willing to trust either. Finally, even Nash realized that they were being destroyed by his distrust and vilification of the other members of the group, and he allowed Front to give the rope and their staffs to Wonina to be delivered to the other pair. Collaboration was only possible with trust, and trust means a lack of certainty—trust means risk taking. No one could win until trust was risked—and then everyone could win.

The results in such an idealized and very controlled situation is, of course, no proof that in real life everyone can or should be trusted. People may be more alike than they are different, but they can be significantly very different. At times people do have different needs, and it is wise to expect them to try to meet these needs, even if it means hurting others. Under extreme circumstances, trust is not always wise, and thus collaboration is difficult. Nevertheless, 9/9 leaders proceed from the assumption that the differences between people can be seen as less than originally believed, and pursuing a common goal can be seen as more productive. With persistent effort, and given time, 9/9 leaders assume that a common ground can be established. With risk taking, trust will be discovered to be possible, and the results of such risk taking will prove to have been worth working for.

The source of power available to the desperate pairs in their separate cul-de-sacs resided in the possession of all four staffs and both ropes. This is an example of legitimate power, in which the source of the power is unavailable to either trapped pair. In other words, the legitimate power resided outside the group. Each pair might use the part of that power they did possess to coerce, to negotiate, or to collaborate with the other pair. Since the partial power was balanced, coercion wasn't possible. Since neither pair had anything else of value to sacrifice, neither was negotiation. Since there was no trust, neither was collaboration. Front had to use whatever power he had to persuade Nash to trust the other pair. He tried the expert power of logic, but failed. Wonina's power was also expert, as well as charismatic; she had the expertise of being the only one able to communicate between the pairs, and she had her general trustworthiness to inspire trust. She also failed; her communication was too limited by the time and effort it took for her to travel between the two groups, and Nash was already losing trust in her love. It was the power of shame that finally persuaded Nash to trust, and to collaborate. Front forced Nash to face the enormity of his distrust, that he was even willing to trust the Outhans more than his friends. Power, even the power of shame, used in a collaborative way, can pull together that which has been pulled apart.

*   *   *

VALUE CONFLICT IN LEADERSHIP:
The Leader is Two is One, A Humanistic Resolution

Just as leadership theories are usually, and perhaps always, value based, certainly people who lead base their decisions on their values. The 9/9 leadership style makes the value assumption that people are basically competent, dependable, trustworthy, and more alike than different. Once the 9/9 leader has established that there is a common group goal, the assumption is also made by the 9/9 leader that differences in values among group members can contribute to a variety of possible solutions to the problem and need not necessarily be hindrances to the achievement of the group goal. Thus, 9/9 leaders confront rather than avoid value conflicts between group members, seeking creative resolutions to the conflicts that can also contribute to new approaches to the group task.

Even the most effective 9/9 leaders, however, are not free of their own internal value conflicts. Front is one such leader. Having clearly defined the group goal and committed himself to the achievement of that goal, Front found himself trying to achieve a group goal that seemed to be in conflict with a more immediate personal need. Thus, as the leader, Front was torn between two apparently conflicting desires—he wanted to do all he could to enable the group to get back to Sebasa to effectively confront the Outhans while at the same time, his biological and affectional need for Wonina was growing and being further stimulated by his forced closeness to her in the boat. He was torn between the belief that he should do his duty toward his people and his belief that he should "be a man" and respond to his biological needs. He was in a value conflict—the leader was two, and a leader divided against himself cannot be totally effective.

There were two reasons I chose to use the issue of sexual behavior as a way of illustrating this value conflict within the leader: sex behavior certainly makes a story more interesting, and I confess I wanted to capture the reader's interest, but more important, from as far back as David and Bathsheba to as recently as sex scandals in the White House and in Congress, sexual misconduct has been an issue in leadership. Sexual satisfaction is one of the needs, along with the need for more power and the need for material gain that a leader might attempt to satisfy through the misuse of leadership power.

My placing Front's need for Wonina in opposition to his need to be an effective leader, however, does not imply a belief there is anything wrong with sexual behavior. Indeed, as a humanist, I see the caring expression of ones sexuality as an unqualified good. Leaders who attempt to use their leadership role in order to satisfy personal needs may be guilty of abusing the power of leadership, but they should not be condemned merely because they have personal needs, even sexual needs. It is the abuse of power that is the "sin," not the indulgence in sexual behavior.

The abuse of power is a chronic problem in leadership. All systems of governance try to build in controls against abuse of power by the leader. Thomas Jefferson insisted that the Constitution should "bind the President down in chains." The Legislature and the Judiciary were conceived as a part of the system of checks and balances to control the Executive—but still, Presidents abuse their power.

When considering becoming involved with Wonina, Front's initial concern was that he would alienate Nash and lose Nash's support against the Outhans. There was no abuse of power involved in this conflict, rather a tradeoff between a low risk behavior that kept him in conflict with himself and a high-risk behavior that enabled him to be less self-denying and eventually more effective as a leader. There was one aspect of Front's relationship with Wonina, however, that might have been a typical example of abuse of leadership power. He worried that Wonina was only attracted to those in power, and that he might be taking advantage of this. Wonina assured him this wasn't so, but his concern is understandable. Followers do become enamored with the leadership role, generalizing the power associated with that role beyond its intended limits, seeing in the leader the power to care for all their needs, even their sexual needs.

Leaders who fail to recognize that it is the role and not they who are the objects of this attraction, or leaders who purposely take advantage of this attraction, are indeed abusing their leadership power.

In the novel, Wonina demonstrated she was not blinded by Front's role. She loved him, even though, as he complained, she was the one to always point out his faults. Thus Front had no need to worry about the motivation behind Wonina's love, and it would have been unwise and unnecessary for him to have denied his need for her. But people frequently do expect their leaders to be self-denying, to be more than human in their capacities to forgo their human needs. In addition to being unrealistic, such an expectation may also be dangerous. In trying to live up to such a demand, the leader is attempting not only to become more than human but also is in danger of become other than human. Such a leader is operating on an idealistic rather than on a realistic concept of what is human and is in danger of losing contact with the human needs of the people.

Just as 9/9 leaders respect the potential wisdom of those they lead, so also do they accept their own human limitations. 9/9 leaders do not need to be superhuman, since they believe there is ample strength in those they lead to do what must be done. A humanistic philosophy of leadership insists there is enough wisdom in our humanness that we can also allow our leaders to be human.

Nevertheless, the fact that Front gave in to his sexual urge and risked alienating one of his group members might still be seen by some, if not as abuse, at least as a failure in leadership. Certainly Front was concerned that he was compromising his leadership when he coveted Wonina, so he struggled to suppress his sexual needs. The result of that struggle, however, was a continual division within himself that was making him ineffective. His fascination and preoccupation with Wonina was such that he failed to realize what should have been obvious to any fisherman—he failed to recognize that the current going against them was a tidal current. He would have been provided with an argument against Fyva's counter plan had he been less divided and more alert. I am suggesting that leaders who fail to attend to their personal needs, at least to some degree, will cease to be effective leaders. I am further suggesting that, since leaders are human and have personal agendas, what constitutes an abuse of power is not primarily the use of power to achieve personal gain but the use of power in a manner that interferes with the group's achieving the common goal.

Since Front's denial of his sexual needs was also interfering with the group's achieving the common goal, he had to find the way of satisfying his sexual needs that would cause the least disruption of the group. After Wonina taught him the value of open and honest discussion of needs, Front settled on a way that he hoped would solve his dilemma. He chose what might be termed a 9/9 humanistic solution to the universal problem of conflict within the leader between duty and desire, between group needs and the individual needs of the leader. He chose to trust the good intentions and intelligence of the group members, he chose to trust they would allow him to be human. He tested his assumptions about the group's basic strength when he was honest about having been human, when he openly admitted that he and Wonina had just had sex together. The indirect attacks by Wons and Fyva were then undercut. The power of those indirect attacks to influence the group was weakened since the "sin" was publicly acknowledged.

Front and Wonina's sexual behavior could then be put into better perspective and found to be irrelevant to the primary group goal. Open discussion of one's needs makes it possible to determine if those needs are aligned with or opposed to the group needs, whereas secrecy about one's needs makes such a determination impossible. Without such openness, potentially additional motivation toward achieving the group goal could thus be lost to the group and resistance to the group effort might not be faced and resolved.

Seeing that the group was not destroyed by his revelation, and gaining more confidence in himself and in the group, Front then seized the opportunity to "fall back" into a 1/9 leadership role, from a 9/9 position. He directed the group into airing all of the potentially destructive tensions and resistances that were working against the group goal. He initiated a feedback session, (see Appendix B) which even Fyva admired, even to the extent of wishing to emulate Front. Then the leader who had been two had now become one, the leader who could lead the divided group into wholeness. When Front risked trusting the intelligence and wisdom of the group, and sharing his humanness, the divided group could heal itself.

Feedback, as used in leadership training, is a powerful tool in leadership development. When used by a trained, skillful, self aware and self-confident leader feedback is one of the most powerful tools available to the humanistic leader. **Feedback** *is a method for systemically providing information about a person's behavior that is available to that person in no other way.* Feedback is the gift of being shown ourselves as others see us. Feedback by the leader to subordinates helps the subordinates to improve their performance and contribute more effectively to the group goal. Even more important, feedback to the leader helps the leader grow. Leaders even more than subordinates are vulnerable to misinformation about their performance, as subordinates attempt to please and placate those whose have power to reward and punish them. If you really want to learn about yourself as a leader, make use of Appendix B.

*   *   *

A Psychology of 9/9 Leadership:
No Need to Lead When the People and the Way Are One

The Blake-Mouton Managerial Grid is based upon the assumption that if people are working together toward a common goal the goal will be achieved more effectively through an equal concern for the task and for the people. The style of leadership that is characterized by the greatest concern for both the people and the task is the 9/9 leadership style. Front, the character in the novel intended to depict the 9/9 leader, was the most reluctant to lead. He was the person who made the statement, "I have no need to lead." Fyva suggested that this was one of the factors that made Front the best leader. She reasoned that although all the others in their way were concerned with the group goal, they also needed to lead for reasons other than to reach the group goal. Wons had led to affirm his religious beliefs, Nash out of a need to overcome a feeling of social inferiority, Wonina out of a fear of conflict, and Fyva out of a need to acquire and to know. Only Front seemed to be leading primarily because of his identification with the group goal. This suggests that the best motivation for effective leadership is a close identification with the group goal. The 9/9 leader identifies with the people, and from that identification evolves an understanding and a oneness with the group goal. Thus it might be said that the 9/9 leader's high concern for production is merely another way of expressing a high degree of concern for people. As the heading above implies, the people and "the way" (or the goals of the people), are one, and effective leaders are not divided within themselves. It follows that in the 9/9 leadership style, the people, the way, and the leader are one.

And He Leads Who Bleeds. This close association between the leader, the people, and the task, although it gives the 9/9 leader great purpose, also makes such a leader vulnerable to pain. Front discovered that leadership carries with it painful responsibility. That responsibility was particularly hard to bear when he was divided within himself, when he was experiencing conflict between his needs and his values, when he had doubts about the people he was leading, and when he also realized that the group was giving him power that exceeded the confidence he had in himself. With this realization, Front confronted a common dilemma in leadership. An effective leader must be of the people in order to identify with the goals of the people. Research suggests that leaders must also be somewhat above the people but not so far above the people as to be threatening to the people (Stogdill, 1974).

However, people who are more effective than other people are usually aware of their superiority, and thus they usually have more confidence in themselves than they have in others. Conversely, people with relatively less confidence in themselves are comforted by the security they feel in the presence of a confident leader. In exchange for the security they feel when the confident leader makes the decisions, they give the confident leader the power to lead them. Reflective leaders may soon discover, however, that the people often have more confidence in their leaders than their leaders have in themselves, and that moreover, out of that excessive confidence, the people will sometimes follow ill-conceived orders in which the leaders themselves have little confidence. Sensitive leaders might then feel they have misused their power.

Front was beset with shame near the end of the story, thinking he had thus misused his power, thinking he was responsible for Wons' injuries at the hands of the Outhans because the group was too foolish to see the weakness in the plan he had carelessly suggested. He blamed himself for not insisting that they abandon the plan. The group members argued otherwise. They judged the plan to be worthwhile, and they believed themselves to be responsible for the consequences of their own judgments.

They saw Front's problem as a failure to have trust in the group. They saw Front as a person who had always the comfort of being able to trust himself, being aware of his own competency, but one who was now having difficulty because, for the first time, he was having to trust others and not just himself. Wons sacrificed his physical security for the group; he risked his life to achieve the group goal. Front had to learn to sacrifice the comfort and security of being able to control his own destiny. As leader, he had to learn to sacrifice the security of being able to do all things himself. The effective leader, in addition to being trusted by the group, must have trust in the group, and Front, not yet trusting of the group, was not yet an effective leader.

As it turned out, unknown to those beneath the Commons, the plan had worked, and Wons' sacrifice had been worthwhile. The group's confidence in Front—and in themselves—had been justified. The Outhans had been frightened away. In real life, leaders must constantly face this dilemma—to trust themselves or to trust the group. Seldom do leaders in real life have the benefit of the immediate and complete confirmation of their choice in this matter that was provided to Front. Moreover, those very characteristics that make for effective leaders tend to give leaders greater trust in themselves than in others, and the almost worshipful trust the people place in their leaders further reinforces the leaders' trust in themselves. Yet leaders cannot do all by themselves, for thereby they exhaust themselves, and also shut themselves off from the resources of the people. Effective leaders must constantly reinforce their trust in the people by daring to trust. The greatest pain competent leaders may face is the agony of standing by while someone else less competent takes the risk for the good of the group. At such times they truly bleed who lead.

*   *   *

Applying the Theory to Yourself

This book is intended as a vicarious experience in leadership. It is intended to entertain as well as to enlighten you about a kind of behavior that I believe is an integral part of the human experience. Each of you is a leader on numerous occasions, if not in name, at least in the participatory sense described in this book. Thus I believe the concepts depicted and explained in this book apply to you. It is my hope you were able to see an aspect of yourself in one or more of the characters described and that you were able to gain insight into your own leadership behavior. I don't believe, however, that vicarious learning can be as effective as learning through actual experience. The leadership-training workshop upon which this book is based is an experiential workshop designed to allow the participants to lead a group in solving a simulated group problem and then to reflect upon and understand the styles of leadership they used during the process. I recommend that, should you have the opportunity to participate in such a workshop, you take advantage of that opportunity.

In the workshop we use another vicarious and indirect way of assessing the participant's leadership style, through a questionnaire similar to the one used by Blake and Mouton. This self report scale, which asks how participants might behave in a series of circumstances, gives the participants some indication as to which of the five leadership styles seems to be their primary style and also an indication of their usual fallback order. Much of the workshop consists of opportunities for the participants to determine, through their actual behavior, whether their pencil and paper assessment accurately reflex their leadership style. Having clarified their styles of leading, the workshop then becomes an opportunity for experimenting with leadership other styles.

The three items you were asked to answer, earlier in this guide, are of the type used in a Blake-Mouton scale. Your answers on this reduced and modified scale, of course will not give a truly reliable estimate of your typical style and fallback order, but your scores may confirm what you've already begun to suspect about your leadership style (see Appendix A).

*   *   *

A Summary of Leadership Principles

Let me see if I can summarize all that has been said about leadership in a set of principles or guidelines. Remember, be forewarned, these principles are value loaded. Nevertheless, if you want to lead effectively you should:

1. First and foremost, define your goal as the leader. You are not likely to get what you want for the group unless you clearly know what you want.

2. Consciously and courageously select and employ those leadership strategies that will most probably enable group members to attain that goal.

3. Continually monitor yourself to be sure that your behavior is not consciously or subconsciously motivated to satisfy personal agendas that do not support the group's goal.

4. Since leaders, like everyone else, may deceive themselves, use feedback from your followers to tell you what you might not know about yourself.

5. Effective leaders are people experts. Continually remind yourself to be aware of the behavior and feelings of your followers. Become especially aware of and skillful in managing group dynamics.

6. Consider the wisdom of cultivating the 9/9 style as your primary leadership style, in which your first inclination when facing a leadership challenge is to trust that your followers are

as competent as you are and just as dedicated to attaining the group goal.

7.   When this turns out not to be so, be flexible enough to quickly fallback to another leadership style that will continue to move the group toward the group goal.

In conclusion, this book is a fictional depiction of several theories of leadership. In addition to its attempt to enlighten through entertainment, frankly it also intends to promote a specific value position on leadership. Leadership, as seen from a humanistic point of view, is the process of enabling others to actualize their potential for humanness. Effective leaders identify with the human race, and they treat others as humans, as ends and not as means. This means that although effective leaders are intensely task oriented, they are primarily involved in tasks that proceed from and benefit the people they are leading and not in tasks in which the people are merely used as tools for accomplishing a goal. I have little doubt that humanistic leadership is the most difficult kind of leadership. However, I believe in the long run it is the most effective kind of leadership for human beings. I hope that through this book you may also come to believe or to reaffirm your belief in humanistic leadership.

In one final attempt at promoting this value position, let's close this manual on leadership by having one last word from Emanuel, Leader of the Ship:

"Because I am of the people, I will follow the people.
Because I follow the people, I will lead the way."

Appendix A

SCORING YOUR LEADERSHIP STYLE QUESTIONNAIRE

Directions: Transfer to the chart below the ranks (1 through 5) you assigned to the five choices on questions I, II, and III. Be sure that you place each rank number by its own letter. For example, if your preferred behavior on Question I was choice d, place a "1" by question I in column 2, before the letter d.

Add up your ranks in all five columns.

Question	1 (9/9)	2 (5/5)	3 (1/9)	4 (9/l)	5 (1/1)
I	___e	___d	___c	___a	___b
II	___c	___b	___d	___a	___e
III	___c	___d	___b	___e	___a
Column Total	___	___	___	___	___

(The total of all five columns must equal 45.)

The numbers in parentheses above each column indicate the leadership style illustrated by the choices in that column. Your lowest column sum indicates your primary leadership style. Your next lowest sum indicates your first "fallback" leadership style, etc.

Now write the Blake-Mouton style that corresponds to your lowest column sum in box 1 below, and then the style that corresponds to you next lowest sum in box two, etc. This is **Your Leadership Style Fallback Order**.

    1   2   3   4   5
  [   ][   ][   ][   ][   ]

The suggested interpretation of the Black-Mouton Leadership Style fallback order is that, when faced with the challenge of leading a group, your first inclination would be to lead in those ways indicated by the style in box number 1. If that style isn't effective, you would fallback to the style indicated in box 2, etc. The readiness with which you might fallback is suggested by the size of the difference of the sums between two styles in your fallback order. Of course, your actual fallback orders is best indicated by your actual behavior in leadership situations, but this exercise, and this novel, should give you the theoretical tools for describing and better understanding your behavior.

Appendix B

HELPING EACH OTHER GROW
D. B. Clark

Feedback *is a tool for the effective sharing of information that can be used for self-development.* Feedback informs us how others perceive us so that we may, if we choose, change our behavior so that others will perceive us differently and we may behave more effectively. Feedback is a useful tool in employee training, enabling an employee to better serve clients and work effectively with colleagues. With cooperating partners, feedback is also an effective tool for improving a relationship.

There is no negative feedback. Although some feedback might not please us, it is information we can use to change ourselves, if we so choose. Therefore, it is either useful or not useful. Some feedback is, of course, very pleasing, suggesting we should remain just the way we are. But, pleasing or unpleasing, useful feedback is always positive.

The challenge is to give feedback, whether pleasing or unpleasing, that is useful. Feedback is more likely to be useful if:

a)   it is requested,

b)   it concerns behavior that was recently observed,

c)   it is given soon after the behavior occurred,

d)   it concerns behavior that can be modified,

e)   and, it is non judgmental.

Non judgmental feedback is neither right nor wrong; it is merely one person's opinion.

Furthermore, feedback is more likely to be experienced as genuine if the expressed opinion is congruent with the feelings experienced by the person giving the feedback. Therefore, the person giving the feedback should share his/her feelings.

Since feedback given following the above guidelines is merely one person's opinion, however genuine and potentially useful, it is understood that the receiver is not obligated to accept it. It is a gift not an imposition. It is not necessary to use the gift. *It is only necessary to say, "Thank you."— and, nothing more.*

Here is a simple, although somewhat mechanical formula, which incorporates these guidelines, that if practiced makes it more likely that your feedback will be useful. When feedback is requested, say:

WHEN YOU DID (or SAID) _____,

(the observed behavior)

I FELT _____, AND I THOUGHT _____.

IT WOULD BETTER FOR ME IF YOU DID (or SAID):

_____.

(the suggested alternative behavior).

Study these examples:

When you said that you would never trust me again, *I felt* hurt, and *I thought* that you were premature in your judgment. *It would be better for me* if you asked me to explain why I did what I did.

When you smiled and squeezed my shoulder, *I felt* relieved, and *I thought* you had forgiven me. *It would be better for me* if next time you smiled sooner.

When you turned your back on the client and rolled your eyes, *I felt* uncomfortable, and *I think* that the client might have felt annoyed with you. *It would have been better for me* and probably for the client as well if you had been more patient in explaining again what you expected the client to do.

When you wore that business suit, *I felt* really impressed, and *I thought,* "Wow, the customer will really trust your judgment now. *It would better for me* and for the company if you dressed that way more often.

When you got red in the face, held your breath, glared at me, and then stalked away, *I felt* frightened, and *I thought* that you might be going off to type my dismissal papers. *It would be better for me* if you had just told me what I did so I don't do it again.

When you kept smiling and repeating in a calm voice what that angry client needed to know, *I felt* grateful, and *I thought,* maybe the client will eventually hear you. *It would be better for me* if you keep demonstrating how you maintain your cool with angry clients.

When you kept insisting that the client was not filling out the form correctly, *I felt* annoyed, and *I thought* you were not listening to what the client was telling you. *It would be better for me* if next time you would paraphrase what the client says to be sure that you are understanding what he is saying.

When that obviously disgruntled client marched in, and *you gave* him your brightest smile *and asked* how you might help him, *I felt* envious, and *I thought* I'd like to be as positive as you. *It would be better for me* if you reminded me to smile more often myself.

Now, use the form on the previous page to detail feedback for someone close to you who might wish to use it to grow. This is just for you to practice giving effective feedback. *Don't share this with that person unless he/she requests feedback,* and not before that person reads a blank copy of this description of feedback to determine whether he or she truly wants feedback.

Appendix C

GETTING THE TASK DONE IN A GROUP:
An Exercise in Group Process

D. B Clark

In democratic or representative forms of government, or in modern industrial or institutional organizations, or even in getting together with a group of friends to plan a party, it is frequently necessary to interact and somehow cooperate with several other individuals at the same time. Being effective in working within such groups of individuals, being able to arrive at decisions, to get tasks accomplished, despite the diversity of opinions, capacities, needs, and desires that characterize individuals in groups is sometimes extremely difficult. Effectiveness in working within a group can be enhanced, however, by acquiring greater knowledge of group process or group dynamics. In other words, you can be more effective in leading groups if you know how people typically behave in groups. To be even more effective, you also need to become more aware of your own typical behavior in groups, what you most often do to facilitate or impede the progress of a group.

This exercise is intended to contribute to your awareness of group process and particularly to your own group process behavior. The exercise assumes you have been appointed by the President to be a member of a select committee, a committee to develop a workable procedure for dealing with a sensitive issue vital to national security. You are a staunch believer and supporter of your government and your country, and you were appointed to this committee because you are an expert in a field that has bearing on this issue. But you are also a stockholder and manager of a company that stands to grain or lose considerable business, depending upon the final procedures developed by this committee.

The committee chairperson turns out to be a nice guy but one who is not overly assertive. So the committee membership has considerable leeway in determining how the committee operates.

Keeping the above factors in mind, decide how you would respond in each of the following situations. Try to select the response that is most like how you actually would respond, given the above conditions. Don't just choose the response you guess to be the "right" one. There is no right response. It all depends upon the situation as described. Indicate your likely response by circling the three-letter code next to your choice.

1. At the beginning of the first meeting a member, who happens to be a representative of a company that rivals yours, begins trying to force his ideas for the final plan on all the other members, discouraging others from talking by belittling their ideas. You would:

Circle One:

LEM   Express your concern that all members should be given the respect of being heard.

BLP   Quickly attempt to counter the apparent gains made by your rival by revealing that your rival has a vested interest in the plan he is suggesting.

DSF   Recommend a plan for gaining better under-standing of this issue consideration.

2.   The chairperson eventually re-establishes order in the meeting. It is decided that the issue is complex and needs further exploration. A short while later, however, another member cleverly pulls together several opinions voiced by others and comes up with a possible final procedure that just happens to parallel your own thinking. You would:

EQP   Strongly endorse that member's suggestions and then call for a vote.

EIF   List a number of other factors about the issue that you know to be pertinent, though not accounted for by the procedure just recommended.

BWM   Remind the group that the agreed-upon operating procedure for this meeting was intensive exploration of the issue.

3.   One of the other members blasts you for your last suggestion. She then launches into a complicated discussion of the issue that, however annoyed you are with her, you realize is truly important and relevant. As she continues to dominate the discussion by her intellect, you suspect some members are becoming resistive because they don't understand her. Others, who do understand, are too intimidated by her to attempt to simplify her ideas so they would be understood by all. You would:

CIF   Suppress your anger at her and attempt to clarify her ideas for the group.

INM   Try to encourage one of the quiet but know-ledgeable members to speak by saying something like, "Bill seems to want to say something."

FLP   Keep out of the discussion and let the resistive members finally shut her up.

4.   The committee members finally get so fed up with her overly intellectual discussion they attempt to shut her up by sneering at her and then narrowing the discussion down to only one aspect of the issue. Even though there could be further aspects of the issue considered, they seem about to agree on how they see the problem, and she seems too hurt to reopen the discussion again. You would:

TIP   Bring up another unrelated topic because the hassling is too much for you.

POM   Point out to the group that by attacking the person rather than her ideas, they are limiting good ideas.

GAF   Continue listing alternate aspects of the issue not yet considered.

5.   Fortunately another member comes up with a plan for quickly and systematically generating a review of all issues related to the problem. Unfortunately his style is so dictatorial, and the group seems so intimidated by him, all they seem to be able to do is passively resist. You would:

LEM   Voice your concern that his manner is interfering with the group's functioning.

CMP   For the good of the group and to get on with his good plan, think of some way to squash the resistance, like implying that he is probably the President's man on the committee.

TFF   Suggest a way his plan could be quickly tested to see if it would actually work.

6.   The chairperson again tries to regain control of the meeting. He asserts his legitimate authority and suggests following *Robert Rules* of *Order.* But you believe this application of "the rules" would be too time consuming. The group apparently

thinks the same way. Recognizing you have greater parliamentary experience than the chairperson, they turn to you to decide what to do. You would:

UDP   Use your knowledge of parliamentary procedure to establish a way of operating that will make the group easier for you to influence.

GTF   Point out to the chairperson that Roberts Rules would be inefficient and suggest for the group's consideration several other possible methods of operating.

BWM   Remind the group that they had agreed to work with this chairperson, and it is the chairperson's prerogative to establish operating procedures.

7.   You like the new respect the committee is now giving you as expert on parliamentary procedures, particularly the way they laugh at the clever way you express procedural pronouncements so as to lighten tension in the group. You notice, however, that one of the quieter members had begun to say things, before she got cut off, that suggests she sees a way to finally summarize all issues pertinent to the problem. You also have an idea of how to summarize the hitherto seemingly unrelated issues, but now a great many people in the group seem insistent on having their say, no matter how repetitious, and you're getting tired of listening to them. You would:

WUP   Attempt making a concise statement of where you believe the committee is in its analysis of the problem.

INM   Make a point of asking the quiet member where she believes the committee is in its deliberations.

DBP   Use your wit to regain the attention of the group and thus relieve some of your own tension.

8.   The quiet member finally gets up her courage and clearly artic-
      ulated the complex nature of the problem facing the group.
      You suspect she is entirely right in her position, but it's not a
      popular position. In fact, if it is interpreted one way, it might
      lead to a final procedure that will not be beneficial to your
      company. The more hostile minority of the committee is now
      lacing into her, implying she has ulterior motives. She is near
      to tears. You would:

      HAP   Restate her analysis in a way more favorable to
             your company and, if she seems to go along with
             your restatement, come to her defense even
             more forcefully.

      TCF   Use your wit and favored position in the com-
             mittee to try to get all members to at least hear
             and understand her analysis, then see if the
             others are at least willing to go along with her
             analysis as a working position.

      POM   Compliment her on her excellent analysis and
             suggest that her attackers could benefit the com-
             mittee more if they questioned her logic and not
             her motives.

9.   Now that all elements of the problem are thoroughly under-
      stood, the committee still must develop the best procedure to
      deal with the problem. Again your old enemy from the rival
      company, in his super-serious manner, seems to be about to
      sway the committee to quickly adopt his self-serving final
      solution to the problem, even though the President had made
      it clear that the committee was to be sure to cover itself by
      considering a wide variety of plans. You world:

      DSF   Recommend a procedure to ensure that many
             possible plans are considered.

BWM   Remind the others of the President's original charge to the committee.

DBP   Use your wit to pull attention away from your overly serious rival to offset his growing influence in the group.

10. The committee chairman decides that the committee should have expert opinion on proven procedures for dealing with the problem. You have some expertise, but you also know one of the least assertive members of the committee is an expert in the field. Unfortunately, he is also an associate of your archrival. Rather timidly, he starts to speak when he is cut off by a very forceful and articulate associate of your own who is great at influencing others but not always too accurate in his information. You would:

INM   Politely interrupt your associate and then make it easier for the timid expert to speak by acknowledging his reputation.

HAP   Let your persuasive associate emphasize those facts and ideas that will sway the committee to eventually accept your preferred plan, and then recognize the timid expert.

EIF   Politely intervene on your associate's talk to recommend that everyone, no matter how knowledgeable, should voice an opinion so as to insure the greatest variety of input.

11. The timid expert finally gets to give his review of the best possible past solutions to the problem. Unfortunately he does seem to stress a solution that would not favor your company, but he wasn't always clear in what he meant. The committee "intellectual" starts to give a much clearer picture of what the

expert meant, but your rival immediately begins to attack her for her "snooty" mannerisms. You would:

BLP   Make sure the committee is made aware of the questionable relationship between the timid expert and your rival, and also point out that his "ambiguous" opinions, as stated, can be interpreted in a manner more favorable to your position.

CIF   Attempt to paraphrase what the timid expert said as clearly and accurately as you are able.

POM   Express your opinion that the committee "intellectual's" mannerisms are irrelevant to the issue, and that in your opinion, her clarity of thinking is benefiting the committee.

12. The committee chairperson thanks the expert for his excellent presentation of past solutions to the problem, but points out that none of these previous solutions was good enough or the President wouldn't have created this committee. He then establishes a procedure that everyone must recommend a plan. Your associate than suggests a clever new solution that would do the job adequately and incidentally would also benefit your company. In his charming, but domineering way, he now seems intent on ramming through his idea. You would:

GAP   Call for the presentation of other ideas to be sure that the best possible solution is forthcoming.

LEM   Point out to your associate that his charming forcefulness seems to be inhibiting others and perhaps discouraging others form expressing worthwhile ideas.

EQP   Strongly second your associate's plan and call for a vote.

13. You presented a plan that, after you stated it, you realized was obviously self-serving and rather dumb. You are thoroughly embarrassed and hurt when many on the committee demonstrate their disgust through their snide remarks. Your associate than restates and even improves upon his former plan. Now, perhaps because they are getting tired, many others are pushing for a quick acceptance of his plan, even though not everyone has yet presented and even though his plan has not been fully studied. You would:

BWM   Remind the committee that following the agreed upon procedure of having everyone present a plan might surface an even better plan.

FLP   Withdraw from the discussion until the others seem to have forgotten your embarrassing performance. After all, you favor your associate's plan anyway.

TFF   Recommend that all aspects of the plan should be studied for feasibility before coming to a vote.

14. In spite of your logical arguments against it, the committee seems to be moving toward the adoption of a plan that would be unfavorable to your company. Somehow, you have got to block its adoption. You realize that, although the plan might work, the reason it seems to be acceptable to the majority is that it is almost like all of the old "tried and true" plans reviewed by the expert. You have just thought of another more radical plan, but you also notice that a quiet committee member, who you know to be very creative if somewhat nonconformist in his approach to things, seems to be disgusted and withdrawing from the whole business. You would:

TIP   Ask the timid expert a question about one of the previously discussed plans, or the "intellectual" to further elaborate on the theory behind the problem, or any other partially related or unrelated topic, just to confuse and delay the process.

CTF   Share your opinion that the committee seems to be settling for a safe but mediocre plan, then introduce your radical plan.

INM   Encourage the creative nonconformist to express what is on his mind.

15. The nonconformist introduces his plan. It turns out to be the fairest and most workable plan yet considered. Except for a minor variation, which would favor your company, it happens to be same radical plan that you were going to put forward. Unfortunately, the committee just doesn't seem to like the nonconformist's manner. Criticism comes at him from all sides. Since you had drawn him out, he now turns to you for help. You estimate that half the committee would probably favor your slight variation on this plan. You realize that, if you also could get the nonconformist to give in to your change in his plan, you could bring it to a vote and win. You would:

WUF   Share your observation that the committee seems more at odds with the nonconformist's manner than with his plan, and ask others to also consider and share any other impediments they experience to the rational consideration of the plan.

POM   Compliment the nonconformist on introducing what you believe to be the best plan so far presented.

CMP   Paraphrase the nonconformist's plan, but with your own variation tacked on, be sure your supporters on the committee recognize the difference, compliment the nonconformist on his brilliance, and then call for a vote.

16. The committee seems to be falling apart. The nonconformist's plan, and your own version are still under consideration, but the plans are not being discussed. Instead, the members seem to be either bickering about irrelevancies or withdrawing into angry silence. The chairperson seems helpless to get the committee moving again. He turns to you, in your role of unofficial parliamentarian, and asks you a question. Suddenly the whole group is silent, and they all await what you have to say. You realize   that, out of their frustration, they are giving you the power to decide for them. You would:

LEM   Voice your concern that the committee seems to be too exhausted and frustrated to function effectively and that out of that frustration it seems they are even willing to let someone else decide for them.

ODP   Get the committee off the hook by strongly urging them to adopt your plan, and then call for a vote.

TCF   Suggest three alternatives, 1) the nonconformist's plan, 2) your version of the plan, or 3) temporary adjournment. Then ask each member to state a preference. If one of the two plans could pass, call for a vote. If neither has a chance, acknowledge that, and then ask for another statement of opinion on adjournment.

SCORING: Notice that in the code preceding each of the choices you could have made on each item, the last letter in the code is always F, M, or P. Count the number of your circled choices that end in F, that end in

M, and that end in P, and record these sums below on the line labeled "Your Score."

	F	M	P
Your Score:	_____	_____	_____

YOUR GROUP DYNAMICS:
Interpreting Your Responses to the Group Process Exercise

This exercise is intended to enable you vicariously to experience the complex process of a committee at work. It is hoped that, as a consequence of fully participating in this exercise, you will gain a greater appreciation of the difficulty involved in group process, a clearer understanding of the dynamics of group process, a familiarity with many of the terms and descriptive behavioral categories used in group process, and an indication of how *you* typically use group process.

There is no right and wrong or good and bad in group process; there is only effectiveness or ineffectiveness in the use of group process. Effective use of group process largely depends upon understanding group process, that is, what motivates people in groups and the techniques and behaviors used in acting upon those motives. Athos and Coffy *(Behavior in Organizations,* 1968) conceptualized group process as the interaction of three systems: the **Required System,** or that which the authorities, bosses, managers, leaders, owners, teachers, etc., want to accomplish through the group and the rules they set up to try to insure they get what they want; the **Personal System,** or what each of the individuals in the group want to accomplish through the group (which might or might not be the same as the required system's wants) and how he or she goes about attaining those wants; and the **Emergent System,** or what actually happens when the required system and the personal systems interact in the group.

How you choose to act in a group at any given moment depends on the roles from which you are acting or the system by which you are consciously a subconsciously choosing to govern your decisions. If, at the moment, you are identifying with the required system, you make decisions to try to achieve the required system's goals. If you are, instead, more concerned with your personal wants, you make decisions leading to the satisfaction of those personal wants.

Another useful conceptual tool for understanding group processing is the **hidden agenda.** The required system dictates the agenda for the group, that which is supposed to be accomplished and how. But each individual in the group might also have a hidden agenda by which he or she is trying overtly or covertly to direct the group.

The two categories of actions that may take place in a problem-solving group are the Task Functions and the Task Behaviors. The two **Task Functions** *are to define the problem and then to solve the problem.* There are three sets of **Task Behaviors** that the group members use to either accomplish or to impede the task functions. These are the **Task Functional Behaviors**, all those rational, logical problem-solving behaviors that are usually necessary to enable the group to understand and solve a problem; the **Maintenance Behaviors**, those behaviors that keep the group numbers motivated, on track, willing to work together, and physically and emotionally capable of operating; and, on the other hand, there are the **Process Problem Behaviors** that, depending upon the system under which one is operating, are behaviors by which a member or sub group may manipulate the other members of the group to accomplish the groups agenda or to consciously or subconsciously promote hidden agendas.

In the exercise "Getting the Task Done in a Group" the President represents the required system. The personal systems (and resulting hidden agendas) are the group members' vested interest in the outcome of the committee's work. At each moment of decision in the committee's work, or each problem or item in the exercise, you were presented with three choices, each of which represents one of the three categories of tasks behaviors, the task functional behaviors, the maintenance behaviors, or the process problems behaviors. Therefore, your choice of how you would typically behave in that situation is perhaps an indication of which of these kinds of task behaviors you are inclined to use when participating in a problem-solving group.

Now, let us identify your typical group task behaviors.

*   *   *

INTERPRETING YOUR SCORES

First, transfer your F, M, and P scores from above. Place them in the F, M, and P boxes below.

		F	M	P
YOUR SCORES				
STUDENT LEADERS	Mean:	7	6.4	2.5
	Range:	4 - 12	2 - 10	0 - 5
FACULTY SENATORS	Mean:	8	5	3
	Range:	4 - 13	0 - 8	0 - 7

This exercise is primarily a teaching device. It is hoped that you will use the exercise to familiarize yourself with the various categories of group process behavior and the ways these behaviors are used to facilitate or impede a group's attempt to accomplish it objectives.

If you were careful and candid in indicating how you would respond to the vicarious group situation, this exercise may also give you insight into how you typically behave as a group member in the real world.

Your F Score is the number of times (out of a possible 16) that, when faced with making decisions, you chose to behave in ways that were apparently intended to move the group effectively toward the stated group objective. A high F score, relative to either of the group norms, suggests you tend to identify with the group objective and would focus your efforts toward accomplishing that objective.

Your M Score is the number of times (out of 16) that you chose to show concern for the feelings of others in the group. A high M score suggests that you are sensitive to others' feelings and would be inclined to show more immediate concern for those feelings than for the group objective. 1t might be that your feelingful concern is primarily intended to enable the group to more effectively return to the group agenda or it might be that your concern is primarily to reduce you own tension (a personal agenda). Only your subsequent behavior in the group would tell.

Your P Score is the number of times (out of 16) that you chose to behave in ways intended to further your own personal objectives. A high P score suggests you would be inclined to behave in ways, in a group, that favor you own personal interest, even when those behaviors might not be respectful of the feelings of others in the group. If your personal objectives are parallel to the group objective, then you might use such behaviors to move toward the group objective. Otherwise, you would be inclined to move toward your personal objectives, in spite of the group.

To gain some notion of what might be a 'high' score in each of these categories of group process behaviors, consider the average scores of the comparison groups given above. The student leaders' group consisted of student organization leaders attending a student organizational leadership workshop. The faculty senators were faculty senate members using this exercise in a work conference to organize their agenda and working relationships for the year. The higher your score is above the average for these groups, the more you can consider your score as 'high' in comparison those leaders.

The preceding analysis informs you about your preferred use of a category of task behaviors. You can learn about the specific task behaviors you are inclined to use by noting the code by your choices in this survey and identifying that task behavior in the previous section in the manual titled "Group Process."

Of course, your typical group behavior will change with the strength of your commitment to a group objective or with the strength of your commitment to your personal agenda. But your scores on this exercise suggest how you would generally behave in a group. It is hoped the exercise will also give you suggestions for experimenting with new ways of behaving that will make you more effective in reaching your objectives, whatever they might be.

Appendix D

COMMUNICATING MORE EFFECTIVELY
WITH SUPERVISEES

There is more than one way for a supervisor to impart information to a supervisee. The same message effectively communicated one way can be totally rejected when communicated another. Obviously, supervisors have to be flexible. To be *effectively* flexible, some kind of general guideline is helpful.

This simple instrument will assess your typical way of imparting information to supervisees and recommend how you might become even more effective.

Respond to the questions within this booklet, compute your score, and then read the interpretive information given on the last page of the booklet.

*   *   *

Directions: Consider the two choices in each of these nine items. Which of the choices is more like the way you would speak to a supervisee? *Circle the letter to the left of your choice.*

1.   a.   "Making an occasional personal phone call is understand-
          able, but it is expected that you will limit such calls."

     x.   "Personal phone calls are to be expected, but it is hoped
          that you will limit such calls."

2.   y.   "With all of these delays, it's understandable that you
          might also be delayed. But if it is at all possible, I would
          like your work on time."

     b.   "I realize that there have been delays, but I still need your
          work on time."

3.   c.   "Regardless of Joe's behavior, I need you to cooperate with
          him to get the job done."

     z.   "I'll do whatever I can to modify Joe's behavior, and I
          hope that you will also be cooperative so that we can get
          the job done."

4.   x.   "Is there anything I can do to help you improve your per-
          formance on the job?"

     a.   "It will be necessary for you to improve your performance
          on the job."

5.   b.   "I want you to cultivate a more positive attitude toward
          your work and your fellow employees."

     y.   "If there's something interfering with your cultivating a
          positive attitude toward your work and fellow employees,
          please let me know what I can do about it."

6.   z.   "You seem hesitant to follow my suggestions. I'm willing to
          consider your opinions before I ask you to act upon this."

     c.   "If you believe that I am in error, I expect you to tell me.
          Otherwise, follow my orders."

7.   a.   "I expect you to speak well of the organization or to make
          your complaints known to me before speaking to outsiders."

x.   "I'm sorry that you are unhappy with the organization. Please give me a chance to answer your complaints before you complain to outsiders."

8.   y.   "I realize that you might not have expected this change from your regular duties. What can I do to help you make this adjustment?"

b.   "I recognize that this is a change from your regular duties, but I expect your cooperation."

9.   c.   "I understand your problem, but I'm sure you understand that it will still be necessary for you to come on time."

z.   "I'm sorry you're having a problem. Is there anything I can do so that you can eventually come on time?"

Determining Your M-R Score

First, compute your Raw Score by counting the number of a's, b's, and c's that you circled (Ignore the x's, y's, and z's).

Your Raw Score _____

Then,

If your raw score =	0 - 1	2	3	4 – 5	6	7	8 - 9
Your M-R Score =	-3	-2	-1	0	+1	+2	+3

COMMUNICATING MUTUAL RESPECT
In Supervisor/Supervisee Interactions

Participatory management theory and just plain common sense suggests that supervisees will be better able to hear the message given by a supervisor and more willing to cooperate if they feel they are respected. But, if the task is to get done, the organization and its representative, the supervisor, must also be respected. In other words, it must be understood that the task is worth doing or that the rules for completing that task are worth following. It is assumed that this essential message will more likely be understood and accepted if it is communicated in an interpersonal atmosphere of "mutual respect."

In organization theory, mutual respect means giving *equal* importance to the requirements of the organization and to the needs and dignity of the employees.*

Any message imparted to the supervisee is of two parts: the cognitive message and the affective message. The *cognitive* message is communicated by the *denotations* of the words employed by the supervisor. The *affective* message is communicated by the *connotation* of the words employed, as well as by the nonverbal behavior of the supervisor. For example:

Cognitive Message: "Come on Time!"
Affective Message: (The affective message varies in relation to the relative importance given to the organization's requirements or to the supervisee's needs and dignity.)

+5   "There is *no excuse* for your *irresponsible behavior.* Either you come on time or you *find another job.*" (The organization's requirements are all-important.)

+3   "*I understand* your problem, but I am sure you understand that it will *still be necessary* for you to come on time." (The organization's requirements are more important than the employee's needs.)

0   *"Let's work out your problem* so that you can come on time." (The
        Organization's and the supervisee's needs are equally important.)

-3   *I am sorry* you are having a problem. Is there *anything I can do* so
        that you can *eventually* come on time? (The supervisee's needs are
        given more importance than the organization's requirements.)

-5   "It *would be nice* if you were to come on time, but *forgive me* if I
        have added to your problem." (The supervisee's needs are all-
        important.)

The relative importance the supervisor gives to the organization's
requirements is connoted by the words italicized in the above examples.
A "0" affective message is ideal, but messages in the range of "-3" to "+3"
might also be effective. The effective supervisor varies the level of affect
to meet the circumstance. A supervisee who is frequently late might
require a +3 message; a troubled but usually punctual supervisee might
deserve a -3 message. Affective messages below -3 and above +3 are usually counter-productive.

The affective message is also communicated nonverbally. The nonverbal behavior of the supervisor will either affirm the cognitive message or
confuse it. Examples of confusing nonverbal behavior are: smiling while
delivering a +3 message or condescending while delivering a -3 message.

Your M-R (mutual respect) score is suggestive of your typical way of
communicating with a supervisee. If your score varies too far from zero or
if you never change your affective message, perhaps you had better experiment with different styles of communicating.

This way of conceptualizing mutual respect was suggested by Peter Diehl.

References

Athos, Anthony G. and Coffey, Robert E. *Behavior in Organizations: A Multidimentional View.* Englewood Cliffs, N.J. Prentice Hall, Inc., 1968.

Blake, Robert R., and Jane S. Mouton. *The Managerial Grid.* Key orientation for achieving production through people. Houston, Texas: Gulf Publishing Co., 1964.

Deutsch, Morton. "The Effects of Cooperation and Competition Upon Group Process In Cartwright, D. and A. Zander, *Group Dynamics, Research and Theory.* Evandon, Illinois: Ron Peterson and Company, 1960 (2nd Ed.)

Hall, Jay. "How to Interpret your Scores from the Conflict Management Survey." Conroe, Texas: *Teleometrics International,* 1973.

Stogdill, Ralph M. *Handbook of Leadership.* New York: The Free Press, 1974.

Breinigsville, PA USA
11 November 2010
249201BV00003B/31/A